Democratic Citizenship and War

This edited volume explores the theoretical and practical implications of war and terror situations for citizenship in democratic states.

Citizenship is a key concept in Western political thought for defining the individual's relations with society. The specific nature of these rights, duties and contributions, as well the relations between them, are determined by the citizenship discourses that prevail in each society.

In wartime, including low-intensity wars, democratic societies face different challenges than the ones facing them during peacetime, in areas such as human rights, the status of minorities, the state's obligations to its citizens, and the meaning of social solidarity. War situations can affect not only the scope of citizenship as an institution, but also the relations between the prevailing discourses of citizenship and between different groups of citizens. Since 9/11 and the declaration of the "war on terror", many democracies have been grappling with issues arising from the interface between citizenship and war. This volume examines the effects of war on various aspects of citizenship practice, including: immigration and naturalization, the welfare state, individual liberties, gender relations, multiculturalism, social solidarity, and state–civil society relations.

This book will be of great interest to students of military studies, political science, IR and security studies in general.

Yoav Peled is Professor of Political Science at Tel Aviv University. **Noah Lewin-Epstein** is Professor of Sociology and Dean of the Faculty of Social Science at Tel-Aviv University. **Guy Mundlak** is a Professor of Law and Labor Studies at Tel Aviv University. **Jean L. Cohen** is Nell and Edward Singer Professor of Political Theory and Contemporary Civilization at Columbia University.

Cass Military Studies

Democratic Citizenship and War

Edited by Yoav Peled,
Noah Lewin-Epstein,
Guy Mundlak and
Jean L. Cohen

Routledge
Taylor & Francis Group

LONDON AND NEW YORK

First published 2011 by Routledge
2 Park Square, Milton Park, Abingdon, Oxon OX14 4RN
52 Vanderbilt Avenue, New York, NY 10017

Routledge is an imprint of the Taylor & Francis Group, an informa business

First issued in paperback in 2012

Typeset in Times by Wearset Ltd, Boldon, Tyne and Wear

British Library Cataloguing in Publication Data
A catalogue record for this book is available from the British Library

Library of Congress Cataloging-in-Publication Data
A catalog record has been requested for this book

ISBN13: 978-0-415-64205-7(pbk)
ISBN13: 978-0-415-55224-0 (hbk)

Contents

Contributors

David Abraham is Professor of Law at the University of Miami Law School, Miami, FL, USA.

Timothy A. Canova is Betty Hutton Williams Professor of International Economic Law at Chapman University School of Law, Orange, CA, USA.

Jean L. Cohen is Nell and Edward Singer Professor of Political Theory and Contemporary Civilization at Columbia University.

Neil J. Diamant is Associate Professor of Asian law and society and chair of the Department of Political Science at Dickinson College, PA, USA.

Yaron Ezrahi is Professor of Political Science at the Hebrew University, Jerusalem.

Ute Frevert is Professor of History and Director of the Center for the History of Emotions at the Max Planck Institute for Human Development, Berlin.

Lev L. Grinberg is Senior Lecturer of Sociology and Anthropology, Ben Gurion University, Israel.

Noah Lewin-Epstein is Professor of Sociology and Dean of the Faculty of Social Science at Tel-Aviv University.

Guy Mundlak is Professor of Law and Chair of the Department of Labor Studies, Tel Aviv University.

Yoav Peled is Professor of Political Science at Tel Aviv University.

Uri Ram is Professor of Sociology and Chair of the Department of Sociology and Anthropology at Ben Gurion University, Israel.

Ornit Shani is a Lecturer at the Department of Asian Studies, University of Haifa.

Alberto Spektorowski is a Senior Lecturer of Political Science, Tel Aviv University.

Gila Stopler is a Lecturer at the Academic Center of Law and Business, Ramat Gan, Israel.

Sharon Weinblum is teaching and research assistant at the Cevipol, Université libre de Bruxelles.

Tung Yin is Professor of Law at Lewis & Clark Law School, Portland, OR, USA.

Introduction

Yoav Peled, Noah Lewin-Epstein, Guy Mundlak and Jean L. Cohen

From the time of ancient Greece until today, Western political thought held citizenship as the key concept for defining individuals' relations with society. The concept encompasses criteria of belonging to the political community, definitions of entitlements to certain rights and commitment to certain duties, as well as standards for evaluating individuals' and groups' contribution to society. The specific nature of these rights, duties and contributions, as well the relations between them, are governed by diverse citizenship discourses that prevail in different societies. A citizenship discourse encompasses the ways, formal and informal, in which citizenship is understood in a particular society and practiced through its various institutions (Shafir and Peled 2002: 4–11).

Three main discourses of citizenship have developed in the western political tradition:

1 The *liberal discourse*, most commonly associated with Western societies, assumes the individual, universal, equal and public nature of citizenship. The liberal discourse is based on the assumption that citizens are "unencumbered selves," that is, essentially uncommitted to any community. The community is seen as the outcome of contractual relations in which the members remain, in principle, isolated one from the other. In the liberal discourse, citizenship is a status entailing a bundle of rights intended to protect one's private sphere from infringement by other members of society and, especially, by the state. The protection of the private sphere brackets public virtue, as the emphasis is placed, instead, on individual values and preferences. Except for a limited bundle of rights that is granted to all citizens, all other rights and duties are the result of a contractual quid pro quo between individuals, and between the individual and the state.

2 In the *republican discourse*, which emerged from the ancient Greek city-states, the rights of citizenship are not guaranteed to everyone equally; neither are they distributed on the basis of any ascriptive criterion. The rights are granted to individuals in accordance with their contribution to the common good of society. In the republican discourse, citizenship is seen as forming a moral community, whose members exercise their citizenship continuously through active participation in the determination, fulfillment and

protection of the common good of society. As Yaron Ezrahi points out in his chapter, participation in the military has always been considered in the republican discourse to be the most important contribution to the common good; that is, as the highest expression of civic virtue.

3   According to the *ethno-national* citizenship discourse, ethnic belonging is supposed to be the primary criterion for membership in the political community. Thus, in a multi-ethnic society (this would apply to practically all contemporary societies), the distribution of rights, duties and privileges is not supposed to be equal, nor to reflect a person's contribution to the common good of society. The sole criterion is the ethnic group in which one is a member.

Historically and conceptually, modern democratic citizenship regimes span the three discourses and combine them to varying degrees. Citizenship regimes change over time and from one place to another. However, there are three features that can be regarded as essential to all of them. First, all citizenship regimes underscore the centrality of membership in a political community, which transcends all other memberships a person might have (for example, in families, clubs, political parties and communities of identity). The centrality of membership in a political community entails some degree of mutual obligation between all members, as manifested by the state (even if this obligation is a thin one, as in the liberal discourse). Second, citizenship regimes adhere to a certain level of equality in the guarantee of rights to all citizens, even if equality is premised on virtuous contribution or ethnicity, as the republican and ethno-national models suggest. Third, democratic citizenship regimes assume the rule of law, which determines the allocation of rights and constricts the power of the executive branch from infringing them.

The minimal commonalities that are shared by all three democratic citizenship regimes face extraordinary challenges in times of war and conflict. Such times strain peace-time norms and routines of citizenship. They induce institutional changes in every aspect of citizenship, including the fulfillment and safeguarding of human rights, patterns of immigration, status of minorities, the state's obligations to its citizens, the expected obligations of citizens to the state, and the meaning of social solidarity. It is precisely these challenges of war, the way they impact different societies, and their effects on citizenship, that are the subject matters of this volume.

During the 1990s, in the short era between the fall of the Soviet Union and the attacks of September 11, 2001, in the United States, discussions of citizenship were focused mostly on its declining "boundedness." That is, on the claim that ties between citizenship, the nation-state and national identity were loosened, as a result of economic globalization and the alleged evolution of a global regime of human rights. Both the protective and the enabling aspects of citizenship, it was argued, were being provided by non-state actors situated in sub- and supra-national collectivities and were increasingly provided to non-citizen residents. With only moderate exaggeration, it could be argued that the overall picture portrayed by these studies (regardless of whether they celebrated or lamented this development) was that citizenship in a nation-state was no longer necessary to guarantee the rights – civil, political and social – traditionally associated with national membership. Concurrently, the civic commitment of citizens to their own national community – solidarity, identity, patriotism, etc. – was also portrayed as being progressively weakened and fragmented, giving rise to communitarian movements and civic education projects that sought to reverse this process (Falk 2000; Hettne 2000; Bosniak 2003; Kofman 2005; Abraham 2006; Basok and Ilcan 2006; Shafir and Brysk 2006; Peled 2007).

Although it may seem paradoxical, the growing sense of insecurity and the ongoing state of war on terror that evolved following 9/11, brought back to the forefront the debates over citizenship and the nation-state. Democratic countries tried to re-assert the role of the nation-state as a shield for its citizens, bringing along, with this reinvigorated objective, the multiple discourses of citizenship – rights, belonging and responsibilities to the common virtue. Although framed in protective terms that seem to be aligned with citizenship, many measures that were adopted by states in the context of the war on terror have actually been criticized for impinging on the rights of citizenship. For example, the Military Commissions Act of 2006 in the US that, among other things, enabled crucial citizenship rights of due process to be denied to US citizens who are declared by the President to be Unlawful Enemy Combatants.

The effects of war on any citizenship regime are overreaching and comprehensive. Short of the total surrender of citizenship rights under what Carl Schmitt famously called "a state of exception," wartimes have had profound effects on all three kinds of citizenship rights, not all of them negative. To illustrate, the civil right of free speech, that includes, necessarily, the right to freely gather information, has been curtailed by censorship and by the denial of free movement to members of the press in various theaters of war, ranging from the Falklands War in 1982, to the two Gulf Wars in 1991 and 2003, to Israel's military operation in Gaza in 2009. The civil rights to freedom, due process of law and private property have also been violated in war situations by the internment or deportation of citizens suspected of being sympathetic to the enemy. Politically, movements protesting the conduct of governments in war have raised questions about the relations between the state and its citizens and the channels through which political demands of the citizenry can be legitimately expressed in times of war. At the same time, political and social rights have often been expanded, during or in the wake of wars, as a result of the far-reaching social mobilization that war required.

The need to preserve democracy and social cohesion in war mandates a serious and systematic discussion of the implications of war for citizenship. The essays in this volume explore some of the theoretical and practical implications of war and terror for citizenship discourses in different parts of the world. The collection of essays is divided into four parts that are based on the different disciplinary and thematic emphases brought by the various authors: a view from political theory, a view from history, a primer on the rights of women and minorities, and the interface between war and economic citizenship.

The first part is devoted to the analysis of citizenship and war from the perspective of political theory. Alberto Spektorowski opens this section with a discussion of Carl Schmitt's contention that a liberal utopia of world peace, universal human rights, open citizenship, and a market economy, spearheaded by hegemonic American imperial power, would lead to total war. Paradoxically, as we now know, this unipolar world order is being enforced through a combination of American military strength, the ideology of human rights and humanitarian intervention, and the new activism of international institutions. As Jean Cohen suggests in the following chapter, the current willingness of the UN Security Council to intervene in cases of grave domestic human rights breaches, and the development of supranational courts to enforce those rights, seemed to indicate that the basic rights of all individuals would be protected, even if their own states failed to do so. However, in many ways, the redefinition of domestic rights' violation as a threat to international peace and security, and the selective imposition of debilitating sanctions on the violators, have become the new vehicle of American hegemony, especially after 9/11. Thus, rather than universal values associated with democratic citizenship, particular and partisan interests have been advanced.

The underlying paradox Spektorowski's chapter points to, is that, in Schmitt's view, the attempt to protect human rights at the expense of national sovereignty, and the attempt of one country to represent universal values, are the only plausible causes of total war. In order to prevent American imperial unilateralism and total war, Schmitt argued, there is a need to strengthen national sovereignty, even at the cost of violating civil rights. Is national sovereignty possible, however, in this interconnected world of the present time? How can national sovereignties stand alone against American power? Schmitt's solution of this riddle was the idea of regional compounds (Bunds). To be precise, Schmitt considered that in order to contrast American liberal hegemony, different powers with their own spheres of influence should rise up. These regional compounds, composed of illiberal homogenous republics, would be the basis of a multipolar world. In order for this multipolar world to be stable, each of these illiberal republics would have to place the idea of mobilized citizenship against the idea of universal human rights.

Jean Cohen's chapter can be read as vindicating Schmitt's concerns, and she draws, albeit critically, on Schmitt's idea of a Bund in proposing a rectification for the problems she identifies. The current discursive frameworks of a "global war on terror" and a "global state of emergency," she argues, pose the apparent necessity of a tradeoff between human rights and human security, domestically and internationally. Moreover, it seems that, under the "responsibility to protect" doctrine, the global protectors of "human security" now tend to undermine rights, constitutionalism and democracy, strengthening arbitrary domestic and global executive power at the expense of parliaments, courts, and the rule of law. In her view, the current form of emergency and security discourse has turned the international institution meant to protect global security and human rights, the UN Security Council, into a body that threatens constitutionalism everywhere.

The remedy proposed by Cohen is the further constitutionalization of the UN, undermining the special status granted to the five permanent members of the Security Council, and forging a comprehensive Bund-type organization for all member states.

In the concluding chapter of the political theory section, Sharon Weinblum challenges the common idea that a state's security politics are the outcome of a security–liberty balance (or a tradeoff between human rights and human security, in Cohen's terms). Her analysis draws on constructivist and cognitive studies of public policy. It shows that in many cases citizenship laws, enacted with the justification of security interests, are in fact the outcome of a struggle between conflicting belief systems about the proper conception of the ideal regime. Thus, her chapter demonstrates that, in Israel, security-oriented citizenship laws actually reflect the imposition of a majoritarian vision of the polity over competing visions. Drawing on this particular case, Weinblum avers that deconstructing security politics as such would enable us to overcome the static security–liberty paradigm, and make fruitful comparisons between various types of security politics.

The second part of the volume is devoted to historical studies of citizenship and war in the United States, Germany, Great Britain, China and Israel. In the first chapter Tung Yin and David Abraham argue that the combined effects of globalization and of 9/11 have caused the issues of immigration and citizenship in the US to become Schmittian affairs, where the worthy "us" is confronted by the enemy "other." Contrary to the prediction of the 1990s, which downplayed the role of states and traditional state-based citizenship, they claim that the growing power of exclusion, and especially of deportation, enhanced the significance of national citizenship. As the US government seeks to undermine constitutional protections in three ways – making it irrelevant who you are, where you are, or whose custody you are in – the benefits of the legal status of "citizen" for the defense of rights, especially of minority rights, have become more pronounced.

In the next chapter Ute Frevert looks at the Schmittian friend–foe dynamics of inclusion and exclusion in three countries at war – Germany and Britain during World War I, and the United States during World War II. In all three cases, she argues, the states did not draw the line at designating and fighting the external foes. They also needed internal enemies, "bad" citizens against whom the "good" citizens could prove their true worthiness. Wartime provides ample opportunity to prove civil allegiance and patriotism, and therefore, during war, states raise the bar and actually assess who is a good citizen and who is not. In this way war gives rise to heightened suspicions and doubts over citizenship and its assumptions of universality and equality among the citizens.

Neil Diamant's chapter on China draws attention to the ambivalent effects of war on practices of citizenship. The Chinese case, he shows, is a striking exception to the rule that military service during wartime plays an important role in promoting citizenship, particularly when understood in terms of respect and appreciation, rather than formal rights. Unlike many other countries, China failed to significantly raise the status of its military veterans. The reason, according to Diamant, is that the *type* of war shapes how citizens respond to veterans' post-war claims for citizenship status. Unlike the "total" wars experienced by Europe and the United States, which involved mass mobilization of the citizenry, the limited and border wars that defined China's twentieth-century wartime experience did not generate elites who were committed to supporting veterans' demands for higher status. This analysis has important implications for the wars currently being fought by Western powers, which resemble China's border wars more than they resemble the mass-mobilization type of war, like World War II.

In the final chapter of this part, Yaron Ezrahi analyzes the declining respect for Israel's military forces in Israeli society, which he attributes to two primary factors: the increasing brutalization of the IDF's conduct towards the Palestinians and the substitution, since 1967, of the traditional image of the Jew as a victim for the earlier, republican ideal of the citizen-soldier. This change, Ezrahi argues, is closely related to the decline of the republican discourse of citizenship and the resultant head-on confrontation between the liberal and ethno-national discourses in Israel's political culture.

The third part, dealing with the rights of women and ethnic minorities, opens with Ornit Shani's chapter on the Muslims in India. Shani raises the questions of why and how a prolonged narrative of Muslim threat to the integrity of the nation has been sustained within the Indian polity, despite the fact that, on the whole, Muslims in India did not endorse secessionist politics, or mobilize politically along religious lines. She proposes that the "Muslim Problem" played a role in the processes of state building in India by enabling the new state to contain significant threats to its integrity, particularly from persistent and deep caste and class conflicts. Hence, the notion of a "Muslim Problem" evolved as a result of the dynamic interplay between four discourses of citizenship: liberal, republican, ethno-national, and a non-statist, social discourse of citizenship.

Gila Stopler's chapter deals with the rights of Jewish women in Israel. Stopler argues that, contrary to common perception, women's inequality in Israeli law does not stem only from the fact that personal status matters are under the exclusive jurisdiction of religious law. Two additional, closely related reasons for the inferior status of Jewish women's rights are Israel's insistence on defining itself as a Jewish state, in spite of the bi-national composition of its citizenry, and the ongoing conflict between Israel and its Arab neighbors. Both of these factors contribute to the demographic threat felt by Jews in Israel in the face of the Palestinians' much higher fertility rates, leading to a strong natalist conception of Jewish women's citizenship.

Uri Ram's chapter turns our attention to Israel's Palestinian citizens. In 2007 a number of Israeli-Palestinian NGOs issued what came to be known as the "vision documents," outlining their visions of the future relations between Jews and Palestinians in Israel. In these documents the Palestinian citizens speak collectively for the first time in the language of *recognition* – demanding collective national rights – rather than the in language of *distribution* – demanding a more equitable allocation of resources. Ram analyzes these documents and offers a critical commentary on their nationalistic assumptions and their lack of a civic vision for a post-nationalist state.

The fourth and final part of the volume deals with social and economic citizenship. Timothy Canova argues that the Washington Consensus, of unregulated markets and privatized authority, has fostered an "asymmetrical," rights-based model of citizenship, which is contrasted with the "reciprocal" view of citizenship, in which fundamental rights and freedoms are reciprocal to civic obligations. The latter model had been instrumental in mobilizing the resources of American society in the era of World War II, the Marshall Plan, and the G.I. Bill of Rights. The former, neo-liberal model, Canova argues, has undermined the war-making and peace-keeping capabilities of liberal democracies.

The final chapter of the volume, by Lev Grinberg, discusses the mobilization of civil society against the violence directed by the state toward its declared enemies. Grinberg compares the reaction of Israeli public opinion to the First Lebanon War (1982–1985) and the First Intifada (1987–1993) with its reaction to the Second Intifada (2000–2004) and Second Lebanon War (2006). Whereas the earlier conflicts led to mass mobilization of Israeli citizens against the use of violence and to the establishment of several civil society organizations and human rights movements, and finally to Israeli recognition of the PLO and peace talks in 1993, the later conflicts produced the opposite effects: suspension of political negotiations, demobilization of civil society, human rights deterioration, and the conclusion that the military must be better prepared for future wars. What accounts for the change, Grinberg argues, is the (neo-)liberalization of Israeli society in the 1990s.

On the face of it, war is just another exigency imposed on, or decided upon, by a community of people. It is no different than a budget crisis or an unforeseen hurricane. It has nothing to do with the fundamental questions of citizenship. However, as the essays in this volume demonstrate, war deeply impacts our perceptions of citizenship: it accentuates fundamental dilemmas in the construction of a citizenship regime and depicts the tradeoffs within the determination of who is included within the citizenship body, and what citizenship implies and requires. The liberal discourse of equality comes under pressure because its bundle of rights is compromised for the sake of security interests. The republican discourse recruits and drafts the community to protect itself from those who wish to undermine it. The ethno-national discourse seeks to clearly demarcate the boundaries between insiders and outsiders to ensure internal cohesion.

Citizenship aids in carving borders between states, and between groups of people, and raises the potential for confrontation. Traditionally wars were fought over borders, and the battle for inclusion and exclusion overlapped with the territorial battle. The current decline of the Westphalian order did not eliminate the function of war, but enabled wars across remote and multiple borders, which are aimed at changing rules of power and economic dis/advantage. Minority groups in dispersed locations mount opposition to hegemonic orders. Disputes over borders no longer exhaust the causes and strategies of war. Internal affairs are similarly linked to ethnic tensions, and demographic disputes within the state are also linked to the changing world order. Universal utopias of worldwide peace on the one hand, and strong national boundaries that overlap with citizenship regimes, on the other, no longer seem to be practical working assumptions. Current struggles for democratic voice and inclusion take place at different levels of the global and the local.

The use of violent force in such struggles is what distinguishes wars and states of conflict from deliberative democratic affairs. Democratic responses to such uses of violence, through the amendment of the norms associated with citizenship, are legitimized by the various discourses of citizenship. A critical observation of these democratic responses illustrates that they too rely on power to react to, but also to proactively prevent, causes of war. The essays in this volume depict what motivates such changes, as well as the gains and losses to democratic citizenship. The attempt to secure communities from the perils of war, a highly important objective in itself, is often used to justify laws that compromise human rights, embrace and solidify hegemonic values in a new world order, allot prizes for allegiance and sanctions for dissent and doubt, redistribute resources to those who most comfortably nest within the common perception of loyal insiders, tag and restrict those who are deemed a threat. The essays depict that solidifying citizenship actually requires the constitution of an "Other" – non- or second-class citizens, marked by attributes of gender, ethnicity, class, and so on. The cleavage between the groups is constructed by privileging some and concomitantly denying resources and power to others. The identity of insiders and their sense of solidarity benefits from the denial of identity to others.

Are these tradeoffs limited to wartime? It seems they are not. They are embedded within the practice of citizenship itself. As noted, wartime and a state of conflict strain the institutional structures of society and in this way aid us in penetrating the cherished dimensions of citizenship. Only a few decades ago, citizenship and the rights associated with it were practically taken for granted in most Western democracies. In times of peace and prosperity, and with the rise of the welfare state and then various rights movements around the world, it even seemed possible and desirable to loosen the reins of citizenship, accommodate the many, and endorse an inclusive percept of membership. Yet the chapters included in this volume reveal the fragility of citizenship. When tension endangers the gains of some, be they gains of identity, economic resources or personal security, the institutions of citizenship closely huddle the citizens to vindicate the threat. Wartime is therefore an opportunity to be reminded of what brought the citizens together to begin with, as well as a useful time to disassociate those who never fitted well within the core of the citizen body. Hence, the dynamics portrayed in this volume should not be read as telling a story of exceptional times. Instead, they are to be read as a reminder of the ongoing strength and weaknesses of citizenship.

This volume originated in an international workshop titled "Democratic Citizenship and War" that took place at Tel Aviv University in December 2007. We would like to thank all the participants in that workshop, especially those whose papers were not included in this volume, for making the workshop the stimulating intellectual event that it was. The workshop was made possible by a grant from the Marc Rich Foundation, administered through the Sackler Institute of

Advanced Studies at Tel Aviv University. Additional funding was provided by the Minerva Center for Human Rights and the Stuart and Judy Colton Chair for Law and Security, both at the Buchman Faculty of Law, and by the Gershon Gordon Faculty of Social Science, at Tel Aviv University. We are grateful to these institutions for their support.

References

Abraham, David, 2006. "The Boundaries and Bonds of Citizenship: Recognition and Redistribution in the US, Germany, and Israel," in *The Politics and History of Migration*, ed. Anthony Grafton, Princeton: Princeton University Press.

Basok, Tanya and Susan Ilcan, 2006. "In the Name of Human Rights: Global Organizations and Participating Citizens," *Citizenship Studies*, 10(3), 309–327.

Bosniak, Linda, 2003. "Citizenship," in *Oxford Handbook of Legal Studies*, ed. Peter Cane and Mark Tushnet, Oxford: Oxford University Press, pp. 183–201.

Falk, Richard, 2000. "The Decline of Citizenship in an Era of Globalization," *Citizenship Studies*, 4(1), 5–17.

Hettne, Bjorn, 2000. "The Fate of Citizenship in Post-Westphalia," *Citizenship Studies*, 4(1), 35–46.

Kofman, Eleonore, 2005. "Citizenship, Migration and the Reassertion of National Identity," *Citizenship Studies* 9(5), 453–467.

Peled, Yoav, 2007. "Towards a Post-Citizenship Society? A Report from the Front," *Citizenship Studies*, 11(1), 95–104.

Shafir, Gershon and Alyson Brysk, 2006. "The Globalization of Rights: From Citizenship to Human Rights," *Citizenship Studies*, 10(3), 275–287.

Shafir, Gershon and Yoav Peled, *Being Israeli: The Dynamics of Multiple Citizenship*, Cambridge: Cambridge University Press.

Part I

Citizenship and war

The view from political theory

1   Carl Schmitt

Republican citizenship, repression of liberal rights and multi-polarity

Alberto Spektorowski

It is hardly surprising that Carl Schmitt, the author of *The Concept of the Political*, is remembered for his theories on the state of exception and authoritarian rule, and for his unforgettable advocacy of the Nazi takeover and political regime. However, despite his advocacy of the Nazi regime, Schmitt's reputation as a political theorist did not decline after World War II. Moreover, his post-war critiques of liberalism and of American hegemony inspired not only a post-modern New Right but also several intellectuals on the Left. Most particularly, Schmitt's later writings on the end of colonialism and the dangers of globalization offered an original insight into the theoretical relationships between a multipolar world, liberal rights, and the concept of republican citizenship.

This chapter focuses on Carl Schmitt's contention that a liberal utopia of world peace, human rights, open citizenship, and a market economy, spearheaded by a hegemonic American imperial power, would lead to total war. Paradoxically, as we now know, this unilateral world order is being enforced through a combination of American military strength, the ideology of human rights and humanitarian intervention, and the new activism of international courts. As Jean Cohen suggests in Chapter 2, the new willingness of the Security Council (SC) to intervene in cases of grave domestic human rights breaches, and the development of supranational courts to enforce those rights, seemed to indicate that the basic rights of all individuals would be protected, even if their own states failed to do so. (Cohen, 2008) In more ways than one, the redefinition of domestic rights violations as a threat to international peace and security, and the selective imposition of debilitating sanctions, has become the new vehicle of American imperialism, especially after 9/11. The underlying paradox this chapter points to is that, in Schmitt's view, this attempt to protect human rights at the expense of national sovereignty, and the attempt of one country to represent universal values, is the only plausible cause of total war. In order to prevent American imperial unilateralism and total war, Schmitt argued, there is a need to strengthen national sovereignty, even at the cost of violating of civil rights. However, is national sovereignty possible in this interconnected world of the present time? How can national sovereignties stand alone against American imperialism? Schmitt's solution was the idea of regional compounds. To be precise, Schmitt considered that in order to challenge American liberal hegemony, different powers with their own spheres of influence should rise up. These regional compounds, composed of illiberal homogeneous republics, would be the basis of a multipolar world. In order for this multipolar world to be stable, each of these illiberal republics would have to place the idea of mobilized citizenship against the idea of universal human rights.

Thus Schmitt appears as the advocate of a new world order in which cohesive republicanism at the national level serves as a basis for plurality at the international level. In this sense Schmitt follows and expands on the concerns of other authors, beginning with Thomas Hobbes, regarding the question of sovereignty and war. These concerns stem from a number of assumptions: First, that no civil society can be built without a supreme authority; second, that given the existence of sovereign states, it is impossible to think of a centralizing power in the international sphere, since states would always oppose it; third, that precisely because of the second assumption, international war is seemingly inevitable. The question, however, is what type of war? Indeed, in the face of justified pessimism about the possibility of international peace, there is still a need to review which instruments could reduce the chances for war among nations. In the eighteenth century, Immanuel Kant made the revolutionary argument that peace is possible even in the absence of an international authority, if states were to adopt republican constitutions which would serve as the basis for a constitution of nations under a cosmopolitan law. Although Carl Schmitt's republican collective identity draws on Kantian republicanism, it is still utterly different from Kant's: it does not respect cosmopolitan law and individual rights. If the Kantian liberal republic might be portrayed as inviting perpetual peace, Schmitt's illiberal republic, the basis of the regional compounds, can fight moderate wars. Paradoxically, while the search for perpetual peace may bring total war, Schmitt's option, by not trying to eradicate war altogether, may actually prevent total war. According to Schmitt, republican identity implies a clear distinction between different types of "enemies": On the one hand, a legitimate *external* enemy, with whom relations of power and competition are set up following international law, within a "division of the world," and an illegitimate *internal* enemy, who is the subversive rebel. The latter is the bandit or the revolutionary, responsible for civil war, who has to be eliminated at all costs in order to preserve law and order. As noted, the paradox is that internal repression and a mobilized national citizenry within regional ensembles or *Grossräume*, and the ensuing organization of a multipolar world, provide the underpinnings for a tense relationship between respectable enemies, but will prevent the total war which is bound to result from a liberal imperialist utopia.

Why is this important and what does it imply for the questions of citizenship and human rights? Following Schmitt's logic, we have to conclude, for example, that violations of human rights are preferable to humanitarian or imperialist intervention. Saddam Hussein's authoritarian rule in Iraq, or a de-facto military regime in Argentina, are preferable to an Anglo-American imperialist war against these sovereign countries. A mobilized citizenry prepared for war in either Iran, Cuba, Venezuela, or Palestine, is preferable to being subdued by liberal colonialism. Finally, a division of the world into regional powers, or geographic spheres of power (*Grossraum*), displaying different conceptions of the good, morality and culture, helps to preserve a moderate status quo (Lilla, 1997). In sum, peace cannot be achieved by promoting democracy or human rights, but by preserving a conflicting "status quo" of different regional compounds, composed of sovereign entities whose citizenry is mobilized for war, and where individual rights are repressed. Indeed a world divided between a variety of regional compounds, or spheres of influence, composed of non-liberal, "authoritarian" or semi-totalitarian societies, may guarantee a politically manageable international tension which might prevent major confrontations.

Most especially, Schmitt's later writings on the end of colonialism and the dangers of globalization offered an original theoretical insight into this relationship. In sum, peace is not achieved by promoting democracy, or human rights, but by preserving a conflictual "status quo" of different regional compounds, composed of sovereign entities whose citizenry is mobilized for war.

A critique of the liberal world

Schmitt's critique of universal liberalism is probably what most intellectuals of the post-modern Right and Left share with him. What unites Schmitt's defenders is a belief concerning his steady preference for democracy over liberalism. Most interpreters are inclined to accept Giovanni Sartori's remark in this context, that liberalism can be defined as whatever Schmitt was not. Schmitt equates liberalism with technology. As John McCormick notes, Schmitt stresses that liberal governance-based constitutional and institutional guarantees of limited government are shaped by a neutralizing technical force. In other words, politics, which represents the ever-present possibility of conflict, is actually neutralized by technology (McCormick, 1997: 4). Moreover, we may argue that Schmitt's criticism of liberalism in such influential Weimar works as *The Concept of the Political* (1927) or *The Crisis of Parliamentary Democracy* (1923), are extensions of a more general critique of modernity which appears for example in *Political Romanticism* (1919) or *Roman Catholicism and Political Form* (1923).

In *Political Romanticism* Schmitt is concerned with the idea of cultural debility. According to Schmitt, both romanticism and liberalism led to passive indecisiveness – the purported cause of Germany's ignominious defeat in World War I. (Holmes, 1995) In this sense, the German middle class, infected by excessive liberalism, forgot who to retaliate against when attacked, so they became skeptical, relativistic, and apolitical, unable to distinguish between friend and foe. In other words, liberals place too much confidence in three impersonal mechanisms: the rule of law, the free market, and the inevitable triumph of truth in open discussions. "Liberal democracy" is defined by Schmitt, in his *Parliamentarianism and Mass Democracy* (1929) as just another form of liberalism intended not for self-identified communities but for the entire human race. This comment underscores a troublesome feature of open universal nations in

Schmitt's eyes. This type of nation usually brings intellectuals to power who are pushing their own highest universal values, a problem that Schmitt dealt with in 1959 in a perceptive essay, *On the Tyranny of Values*. Universalized out of their cultural and historical context, traditional liberal values are no longer seen as the particular achievement of a particular people. Rather, they are viewed as absolute norms and inviolable principles derived from the kind of rationality accessible only by intellectuals, experts and professionals, whose objectification in "the rule of law" can override any allegedly "fascist" choice. Unlike Ernst Kelsen, Schmitt always saw "the legal order" in concrete terms, grounded in the traditions and customs of the society that enacted it, rather than in terms of liberal legality predicated on ever growing legislative mandates (what Schmitt called "motorized legislation").

Schmitt's specific appropriation of what was a largely French legal discourse on institutionalism reveals much about how he understood the challenges and opportunities of this historical moment. Pursuing this connection also reveals an important institutional dimension to Schmitt's Weimar-era writings on the state. Schmitt informs us that it is a French jurist, the great public law professor Maurice Hauriou (1856–1929), who rediscovers this supposedly "German" form of legal thinking for the twentieth century. Hauriou's work on institutions was, Schmitt claims, the "first systematic attempt of a restoration of concrete-order thinking since the dominance of juristic positivism." In the complex twentieth-century political environment, Hauriou showed how institutions – even government institutions – have to be understood as independent forms in their own right, with their own legal structures and their own systems of authority. In this context Hauriou was moved to redefine the institution of the state as that entity capable of preserving and ordering the many different established institutions within any given society (Bates, 2006).

After he became acquainted with Maurice Hauriou's work, in the late 1920s, Schmitt began to emphasize the pre-legal institutional framework that he characterized as "concrete order." Among other things, as we shall see, this is one of the main reasons why he was eventually expelled from the Nazi Party in 1936. To put it in more precise terms, Schmitt attempted to explain the existence of legal science and the state by the fact that, although the idea of law (*die Rechtsidee*) which forms the basis of any political power, is universal, and empirical, reality reveals a plurality of conflicting political powers.The main task of legal science is to analyze the problematic nexus between the idea of law and a plural empirical reality and to assess the *sense* of the state, which is intermediate between the idea and an order-less political reality (Zarmanian, 2006).

Schmitt marks the difference between the idea of liberal pluralism, which in his mind threatens the sovereignty of the state, and the very idea of politics, a different type of pluralism. Anglo-American liberal pluralism as an underlying universal monism relies on the power of civil society, represented by autonomous units, and on limitations imposed on the power of the state. However, as Schmitt notes, this type of pluralism falls under the dominion of economic interests and depoliticizes conflicts. The only way to wield control over a depoliticized community, is through an ideological mobilized community led by an authoritarian state. An external enemy, or a state of tension with foreign agents, contributes to that aim.

More importantly, Schmitt advocates international pluralism, meaning autonomous unities that refuse to be subsumed under the legal or economic supremacy of a particular instance (say the United States) when it is performing the role of the bearer of an omnipotent and universal moral principle. Schmitt's plural international community is sustained by state sovereignty. The state as a unity which reduces differences in civil society serves, however, as a higher marker of pluralism, the pluralism of an international order.

Liberal pluralism, in this sense, is a misrepresentation. The liberal state seeks the unity of the different associations composing it, but it is a fake unity, as liberal unity is represented by the ultimate "monism" of "humanity." Liberal pluralism thus annihilates the space of the political. The problem is that since the political world is plural, whenever a "world state" looms, attempting to embrace in itself all of humanity, foreclosing both conflict and civil war, then what remains is neither politics nor state, but the worst type of violence. This is an important and conclusive concept. What would remain is that humanity becomes an ideological instrument of imperialist expansion, and the outcome would be the sparking of major criminal wars (Schmitt, 1976: 53–54).

Fighting in the name of humanity leads to the delegitimation of the enemy, to "crusaders' wars." Thus "just wars" waged by liberals become genocidal. In contrast to the idea of struggling in the name of humanity, there is "conflict between enemies." The concept of the enemy in Schmitt's theory implies respect for the opponent. The friend–enemy distinction is the essence of the political.

As Schmitt notes, "every religious, moral, economic, ethnic or other antithesis transforms into a political one if it is sufficiently strong to group human beings according to friend and enemy..." (1976: 37). For Schmitt the political distinguishes correctly between the real friend and the real enemy, and the real friend–enemy grouping is existentially so strong and decisive that it supersedes and reorders all the other social conflicts. Nonpolitical conflict becomes political, pushes aside and subordinates ... religious or purely economic criteria and motives. As Giovanni Sartori correctly stresses, for Schmitt the question of emphasis, the degree of intensity in the conflict, becomes determinant for defining the political. However, the interesting thing is that despite the "friend–enemy" formula, which implies the intensification of the conflict that might lead to war, Schmitt is reluctant to dishonor the absolute enemy. Is this so? As we shall see next, while the internal enemy (the terrorist grappling against national unity) is disrespected the external enemy is and should be treated with respect.

In order to understand what is at stake for Schmitt, and how this analysis affects his idea of an alternative pluralism, one must be cognizant of the historical-political background to his writing. His polemic against the expropriation of the word "humanity" is part and parcel of his critique of the post-World War I order, a critique that intensified during the 1930s and after World War II. His specific definitions of sovereignty and politics are not aimed at liberalism in general but specifically the Anglo-American world led by the United States. Already in his "Volkerrechtliche Formen des modernen Imperialismus," a text published in 1932 which is still relevant today, Schmitt examined the new form of imperialism represented by the United States.

The targets of his critique were the war-guilt clause in the Versailles Treaty, the rehabilitation of the "just war" doctrine, the Kellogg–Briand Pact of 1928, and the presuppositions behind the creation of both the League of Nations and the United Nations. To be precise, Schmitt argued that the "war-guilt" clause at Versailles turned a war of competing national interests into a just war against an unjust enemy. It is not difficult to see how revisionist, nationalist, and eventually fascist interests were served by his analysis. To argue against the international community at that time was clearly perceived as illiberal. Although the Left in the 1930s was illiberal, too, an anti-internationalist and anti-universal sentiment could only survive on the Right, or be exploded by the Right. For several observers, thus, Schmitt's conversion to Nazism was a logical process. However, paradoxically, the reason for his shift of attention from "state" politics to the international realm after 1936 was partly due to his marginalization by the Nazi regime. He had to divert his attention to "safer" subjects, such as the international realm. Nonetheless, it is in the international realm that Schmitt found the archetype of a trans-epochal and general theory of a legal order, based on the concept "state of exception" developed in his earlier work.

It is in this phase, however, that Schmitt discovered the element that allowed him to bring his previous reflections on the legal and the political to a comprehensive and trans-epochal theory. This element was space (Zarmanian, 2006: 63). The collapse of medieval unity left the forces of plurality uncontrolled and gave way to the epoch of the wars of religion. In his *Land und See* Schmitt points out that this epoch presented no spatial awareness: powers waged wars in Europe in order to have a right over lands outside Europe, and they conducted wars on lands outside Europe in order to win the wars of religion in Europe. At the same time, the great maritime powers of the age waged war on the sea, often through pirates, to control land outside Europe, and terrestrial powers tried to gain supremacy over the oceans by waging war on land.

This state of exception, of war of all against all, was brought to an end by a sovereign decision: the victors in the Thirty Years War established, in the treaties of Westphalia (1648) and Utrecht (1713), a new *nomos* through the selection of subjects concerned with various spaces. The cornerstone of the new *nomos* was the state as an institution claiming a monopoly on violence and law within a territory with closed borders. Through the establishment of the state, a clear distinction was drawn between internal and external war. Whereas the former was suppressed through a sovereign decision, the latter against external enemies is fought by the whole mobilized nation. On the one hand, European sovereigns protected their citizens from external violence; on the other hand, they protected external powers from violence launched by their citizens. Recognition of statehood was, then, not only a source of rights (the right to wage war), but also a source of duties–and the certification of a trust (Zarmanian, 2006: 63).

Der Nomos der Erde, **the Grossraum and the new world order**

The most sober examination of the effect of de-concretization on international politics which occurred with the collapse of the *jus publicum Europeaum* during World War I and its aftermath, was undertaken by Schmitt in a post-World War II work, *Der Nomos der Erde* of 1950. In this work, Schmitt analyzed the conception of "European," territorially based international law versus US (or Anglo-Saxon) universalism. Ironically, however, Schmitt lamented the passing of territorial and statist European international law, which he viewed as no longer sustainable, given the fact of US global military superiority, rivaled only by Soviet power. Thus, in the works that center on the idea of "nomos der Erde," when Schmitt looks to the future he seeks a new, alternative conception of balance, equilibrium, or division in the world, which would prevent the triumph of US liberal universalism; that, for the time being, was only opposed by Sovietism, which Schmitt regarded as spiritually empty. He expressed a hope that "destruction" would bring forth some new beginning, and he counseled against "despair." According to Robert Howse however, true to the consistently realist, anti-idealist aspiration of his thought, Schmitt could not articulate such a nomos, given the overwhelming technological and military facts of the post-war era, and the extent to which they looked without favor on any territorially based Eurocentric concept of global order (Howse, 2006: 93–103).

For Schmitt, that self-assured self-transcendence of the United States and the Soviet Union may have been possible during the Middle Ages, an era of absolute standards. However, now with the growing agnosticism of the post-medieval age, attempts to determine just causes became more arbitrary (Schmitt, 1950, 2003). The loss of transcendence meant the loss of sufficient reason with regard to the determination of the legal and political order within a state, so the decisiveness of modernity has affected the international scene as well.

What kind of order could replace the *Jus publicum Europaeum*? These questions were at the center of Schmitt's preoccupation in the 1950s and 1960s when he thought of the possibility of a new "nomos of the Earth." He indeed analyzed how the dualism created by the Cold War and the polarization between capitalism and communism could evolve, and imagined several possible scenarios. One scenario is a post-American world order under a new equilibrium guaranteed by the United Nations. The other scenario, which is much more interesting, is the establishment of a new global order based on the existence of several autonomous regional blocs. This would provide the conditions for an equilibrium of forces among various large spaces, instituting among them a new system of international law. The difference from the old *Jus Publicum Europaeum* according to Chantal Mouffe is that this last world order relying on autonomous regional blocs is truly global and not Eurocentric (Mouffe, 2005: 249; Schmitt, 1952).

Carl Schmitt had expressed these ideas on a regionalist, differentialist world already in his first internationalist works which were based on the concept of

Grossraum (Zarmanian, 2006: 61). His theory of the "*Grossraum*" is the first attempt to reconcile universe and "pluriverse" by suggesting that the state form should be replaced by grand territorial units. The interesting thing was his claim that minor political units which cannot defend themselves should give up autonomous war but maintain their political distinctiveness, and live under the hegemony of a leading political unit. In such a political frame only the hegemonic power would have a right to make war, both within the *Grossraum* (to protect its members from each other) and outside it (to protect the *Grossraum* from alien powers). As can be immediately grasped, this solution, influenced by the Nazi doctrine, had the potential to lead to despotism, even though Schmitt explicitly designed his theory of the *Grossraum* as a legal construct guaranteeing plurality.

In *Der Nomos der Erde*, however, Schmitt specifically pointed out how an authoritarian *Grossraum* could be contained. He reintroduced the medieval concept of empire and imperial *potestas*, for example, which recognized the nature of contention in a plurality of princes or kings. The new order is created through an act of contention which is universal. That entails the act of containing plurality in a unity creating order through the establishment of an equilibrium between universe and "pluriverse," between unity and plurality. According to Schmitt this equilibrium within the Empire should not to be identified with a mere balance of power. It is an equilibrium stemming from a collective self-awareness and a dynamic character.

Up to this point it is quite clear why Schmitt's critique of universal ideas and description of the historical process that geared them, was largely accepted by the post-modern Left. Schmitt's quarrel with America's post-1917 role inspired the Left. As Lyotard noted, "Why would the affirmation of a universal normative instance have universal value if a singular instance makes the declaration? How can one tell ... whether the wars conducted by the singular instance in the name of universal instance are wars of liberation or wars of conquest?" (Lyotard in Rasch, 2000: 14).

Schmitt would claim that these are his own questions, because they go to the heart of the nature and possibility of conflict. The crusade war in the name of high values undermines the political which is based in a permanent conflict.[?] Chantal Mouffe adapts this concept for our times. "Bush's use of moral categories of good and evil to designate his enemies and his messianic kind of discourse about the American duty to bring freedom and democracy to the world is the kind of discourse that Schmitt clearly despised" (Mouffe, 2005: 246). In more ways than one, George W. Bush's war on terror could be sensibly included in A. Kojève's idea of a war for recognition, which contrasts precisely with Schmitt's recognition based on the "friend/enemy" formula. Indeed with the conceptual triumph of the regime of rights, in principle, the recognition of each individual's humanity can be achieved adequately through work and citizenship in a just *Rechtstaat*. We should remember that in his *Outline of a Phenomenology of Right*, Kojève articulates the notion of universal recognition as tending toward a legal order beyond the (nation-)state, through explicitly accepting and then "reversing" the Schmittean concept of friend/enemy. However, as noted,

Kojève's version, which might fit Bush's concept of war for a pro-American democratic world order, differs from Carl Schmitt's multilateral and multi-normative world order. The new legal order beyond the nation-state is complemented and supported by the managerial revolution. As Piccone and Ulmen suggest, the managerial-liberal thought confronts the twentieth and now the twenty-first century through obsolete, historically-specific categories presented as universal catgories (Piccone and Ulmen, 2002: 3). No country is more representative of both the new legal order and the managerial revolution presented as a universal category than the United States. The question is whether Europe is different; Should Europe should be portrayed as an agent promoting a distinct path of modernity and of legality?

For legal theorists, Schmitt contributed to clarifying the different frames of understanding legal theory between Europe and America. As Martti Koskenniemi has observed, a commitment to a certain vision of international law is commonly presented as a European trait, which divides Europe from the United States. "European" international law premises perpetual peace based on rules that protect state sovereignty and sustain a world divided into territorial states. It is at odds with the American preparedness to wage "total war" in the name of some purportedly universal ideal, such as "human rights" or "democracy" (Koskenniemi, 2004, p. 504).

As William Rasch noted, the European civil wars of the sixteenth and seventeenth centuries signaled in Schmitt's view a transfer of power from one universal doctrine to another. The English war against Spain was a world war between northern and southern Europe, between Calvinist Protestantism and Jesuit Catholicism. More importantly, perhaps, it was a confrontation between two worldviews: one continental and land-based and the other a global vision, based on control of the seas. This is the basis of the Anglo-American economic imperialism conducted under the banner of humanity (Rasch, 2000: 17).

Liberal and republican citizenship

Terror, we are informed by the Left, is related to Bush's politics, which pretend to represent universal values. An alternative, multipolar, world might be constituted by regional blocs whose organic entities are based, internally, upon Schmitt's concept of sovereignty. However, in order to have a multipolar world composed of different regional compounds, each regional compound should be composed of organic republics, stripped of liberal institutions protective of human rights. The idea is that any domestic struggle for universal human rights protected by a liberal constitution plays in the hands of the liberal empire. A similar view can be used in all issues related to the protection of economic rights and private property. Liberal institutions guarantee human rights and economic rights of the bourgeoisie. A "democratic" republic of mobilized citizens should disarticulate liberal institutions that serve imperialist powers, and should strive to homogenize and pacify the state. We see thus that the notion of sovereignty is still the key player that holds together both the top-down homogeneity of the state and the heterogeneity of a structured plurality of states that guarantee the space of legitimate politics (Rasch, 2000: 17). This self-organizing pluralism depends however, not just on a logic of autonomy and differentiation but also on a specific reading of European history that reconstructs an idyllic interlude between two competing universalist doctrines. The important point here is that we are in a very clear trade-off. War means struggle for universal values; peace entails sovereign identities which might violate human rights in their struggle against anarchists.

The results of Schmitt's republicanism are synthesized by Étienne Balibar. It seems that Carl Schmitt and his modern followers who have been deemed "pro-sovereignty" do not refer to the distinction between friend and foe in an indiscriminate manner. They essentially want to distinguish between a legitimate collective enemy, or adversary, who is also an equal (a *hostis* in the Latin sense), with whom relations of forces and competition are set up following international law within a "division of the world," and an illegitimate interior enemy, who can be the subversive rebel, the bandit or the revolutionary, responsible for civil war, who has to be eliminated at all costs in order to preserve law and order. In the end what has to be avoided is the specter of the "war," where interests and ideologies become mixed, as the history of the twentieth century testifies (Balibar, 2001).

The question is, what does the idea of a homogeneous state mean? Who and how is the collective "we" defined? Are we talking about an organic entity of an open republicanism, which could be authoritarian but still open to foreigners? The idea of "we the people" represents also for Schmitt the act of constitution. We are defined in the act of articulating the declaration. We can assume that Schmitt partly differs from both the organicist and the liberal theories developed in the pre-war period and in the Weimar years. These theories had tried to overcome the problem of conflict among the various powers claiming legitimacy. Indeed organicist theories of legality were promoted by the German Right. For them the German *Volk* represented a unique organism (Galli, 1996). This was the result of natural laws (race or "natural" geography) or, in its historicist and romanticist version, the laws of historical development. Accordingly the laws of the state were legitimate, not because of its power, but because the state is driven by the laws of necessity. Liberal theories tried to derive an idea of justice from the Kantian concept of liberty and the categorical imperatives of practical reason, which are universal and common to all humanity. According to Schmitt, both approaches – as different as they were in their objectives, methods, and contents – failed to account for the legitimacy of the state and its law. Their flaw was that they tried to find a univocal formulation, where the idea of law aimed to achieve a perfect order. Schmitt remarked that this does not happen in empirical reality, which reveals no shared notion of justice or lawfulness.

The question thus is what is Schmitt's alternative. Expressed in terminology borrowed from Kant, Schmitt argues for a domestic, democratic despotism based on the indivisibility of sovereignty in order to construct an international republican order. In his work *The Crisis of Parliamentary Democracy* Schmitt claims:

Every actual democracy rests on the principle that not only are equals equal, but unequals will be treated equally. Democracy requires therefore first homogeneity and second – if the need arises – elimination or eradication of heterogeneity.... the idea that every adult person simply as a person should be politically equal to every person, this is a liberal nor a democratic idea.

(Schmitt, 1998: 9)

According to Paul Gottfried the association of democracy with cohesion and unity was a feature of pre-modern republicanism; but it is far from clear that the term democracy in the twentieth century applies predominantly to communities. Though not false, Schmitt's definition of democracy thus is at least somewhat forced and made to serve as an authoritarian traditionalist pole to liberal constitutionalism. In this sense it fitted the unstable constitutional predicament of the Weimar Republic and European public life after World War I. According to Schmitt, "the central concept of democracy is the people (Volk), not mankind [Menschheit].... There can be – if democracy takes a political form – only popular democracy, but not a democracy of mankind [Es gibt eine Volksdemokratie und keine Menscheitsdemokratie]" (Schmitt, 1988: 9). Democratic homogeneity, according to Schmitt, presupposes a common historical memory, common roots, and a common vision of the future, all of which can subsist only in a polity where the people speak with one voice. The existence of a people thus "must remain above all formulations and normative beliefs.... The most natural way of the direct expression of the people's will is by approvals or disapprovals of the gathered crowd, i.e., the acclamation" (Schmitt, 1928).

In general terms we might accept that Schmitt sought a concrete foundation for law, able to withstand unstable social and economic conditions. He had no intention of politicizing law, but rather sought to ground it in the life-world of a particular people (Schmitt, 1974: 36). As he often reiterated, all law makes sense only at a particular time and in a particular place. Clearly, if concrete orders such as tradition, family, community, and faith are regarded as the building blocks of fascism, then most societies have been "fascist" since time immemorial.

No legitimate legal order can be abstracted from these "concrete orders" without law deteriorating into the abstract and instrumental tool of any party, as it did with the Nazi Party in Germany and with the Communist Party in the Soviet Union.

Despite his Catholic background and his rejection of racial Nazi legitimacy, it seems that Scheuermann's liberal interpretation which detects Schmitt's (alleged) insistence on social/racial homogeneity as the most stable foundation for the legal order, is at least a view that should be considered. The authoritarian republicanism promoted by Schmitt looks like the idealizing of some sort of ethnic/homogenization of politics (Scheuerman, 1999: 122–123).

The state, thus, should be a homogenizing state. However, Schmitt was aware that despite his defense of the nation-state the modernization process undermines borders. Whether we like it or not the world will be sub-divided into autonomous and social systems, economics, religion, science and education and morality. Moreover what Schmitt could not have perceived during his era is the constant process of multiculturalism in Western societies. New ideas on post-national citizenship would become helpful for immigrant communities, while national or regional identities which have been repressed by the republican unitary state have reemerged.

However, what seems to be more striking here, is an emerging picture where only strong national identities are a guarantee against universal capitalism. Regional compounds such as the Andean countries, Venezuela, Ecuador, Bolivia, Nicaragua, and Honduras under Chavez's political leadership are models to follow. In each of these countries liberal rights are violated and a mobilized citizenry is manipulated under a populist confrontational leadership. However, paradoxically this type of anti imperialistic regional compound, which can be organized as regional federations, would guarantee a balance of power in the international sphere, and the ensuing consequence would be the preservation of world peace. No interventions in the name of market capitalism, or human or civic rights would be accepted.

Federalism, *Grossraum*, and Schmittean concept of republican citizenship

The idea of a regional compound as the basis for a multipolar world is advocated by intellectuals of both the Right and the Left, especially those ideologues who oppose American liberal homogenization with the idea of unity and diversity as expressed in regional compounds or ethno-federalist organizations.

Schmitt's concept of federalism is the idea most likely to provide some responses to the dynamics of unity and differentialism that have impacted both Right and Left critics of liberalism. The problem, however, is that except for sections on federalism in *Verfassungslehre*, and some remarks in *Der Hüter der Verfassung*, there is no abundance of references to federalism in Schmitt's works (Bandieri, 2002: 48). According to Ulmen, Schmitt's concept of federalism is incomplete and differs from the Proudhonian integral federalism which is endorsed by the leftist journal (Ulmen, 1992; Piccone and Ulmen, 2002). We suggest however, that Schmitt's concept of federalism or confederalism is not far from Proudhon's integral federalism, and plays an important role in the meaning of an organic citizenship in a republican democracy which is part of large compound republics united in a confederative or federative union. According to Schmitt, control of a territory by the state may occur in two ways: either with a territorial articulation of power among the parts dependent on the whole – the center – which monopolizes control; or with one where everything, including the center, depend on the parts, and central control is distributed between the whole and the parts. The first is a unitary, while the second is a federal model. To be specific, the focus of his analysis is the role of federalism in the Weimar Constitution. While the first three parts of *Verfassungslehre* discuss the antithesis between liberalism and democracy, the fourth, "The Constitutional Theory of the Federation," concludes the volume with a discussion of the antithesis between "democracy and federalism.". Whatever the shortcomings of this analysis, it provides an important jumping-off point for a debate on the problems and prospects of federalism.

The core of Schmitt's argument is found in the section on "The Legal and Political Antinomies of Federation." He considered three antinomies; the most important for our debate is the third. The first antinomy is that while the goal of federation is to safeguard the political independence of each member state, membership in a federation requires that each member state resigns its right of self-preservation to the federation. The solution is that the whole idea of self-preservation has a meaning when we are confronted with a real enemy, which actually does not exist because within a federation of homogeneous entities war is an excluded possibility. The second antinomy is that while every member of the federation seeks to assure its self-determination, every federation intervenes in order to protect each member's self-determination. The solution of this antinomy is that self-preservation can only be endangered or negated by an essentially alien interference, and since federal intervention in the affairs of member states does not constitute alien interference (because the federal constitution is part of the constitution of every member state) there is no existential threat to autonomy. The third and most general antinomy is the most decisive because it concerns not only the nature of federation but of sovereignty. The essence of federation, according to Schmitt, lies in a dualism of political existence: in a bond of federally constituted collective existence and political unity and in the continuing existence of a plurality of individual political entities. Such a configuration can be expected to lead to many conflicts which must be resolved. The moment this duality – this tension between particularism and unitarism – is resolved on either side, the federation ceases to exist. The solution to the third antinomy should thus be stressed because it is the substantive characteristic of federation. Since the federation is first and foremost an attempt not only to organize common defense and to find a common ground of coexistence but to guarantee the existence of autonomous political entities, the question of homogeneity is crucial. Indeed a Federation is legally and politically possible only where there is "homogeneity" (Schmitt, 1928).

In this sense the solution to the third antinomy is the solution to all antinomies, i.e., the homogeneity of all member states.

Following Montesquieu, therefore, Schmitt maintains that opposing types of state principles and political convictions cannot coexist in a federal framework. However, for Schmitt the type of state whose citizens can hold common convictions is a non-liberal republic, which will be part of an authoritarian confederation. The question thus is: in which way is this type of confederation pluralistic, either in an ethnic or political point of view?

Paradoxically while the coexistence of democracy with federalism would lead to a unitary state like the United States, "a distinctive type of state–a federal state without a federal foundation," a true federation cannot precisely be democratic. In a true federation – a confederation as well as a federal state – a multiplicity of political entities coexist with the "federation." What Schmitt probably had in mind is a concept of a multi-ethnic confederalist "empire" or a Nazi dominated zone of influence or *Grossraum* which is authoritarian at the top and ethnorepublican at the local level. Although there is tension between ethnic groups, this is a constructive tension. For several authors the possibility of the uprising of a new pluralistic *nomos* in which conflicts would be kept in check, namely a federalism of the Lothingian Germanic variety (as elaborated by Proudhon) is reappearing. This a comprehensive vision of the world that would replace the federal state of the Hamiltonian variety, which Schmitt considered an equivocal juridical construction.

In other words, while the Hamiltonian type of federalism stimulates liberal rights and intervenes in order to protect them amidst the components of the federation, in the alternative type of Schmittean confederation, the components can repress individual rights and promote an activist citizenship while determining as well who is in or out in its republican unity. The unity of this confederal diversity is ensured by common ethnic background of all the indigenous groups, for example, of the ethnic groups of Europe. Schmitt thus saw the possibility of a new global *jus publicum* composed of "a balance of several *Grossräume* which set among themselves a new law of peoples, at a new level and with new dimensions."

From a Schmittean perspective of order, then, we might have world cultural pluralism, internal cohesion at the federal level, repression of "foreign outsiders," political opponents; however, world peace will be maintained between regional compounds.

Conclusion

Schmitt citizenship: New Left and New Right

Is Schmitt an asset of the New Left? Is it of the New Right? Of both? We might now identify three aspects of Schmitt that have proven influential for both the New Right and Left: (1) the separation of democracy and liberalism in the attack upon representative parliamentary government; (2) the assertion of the political against the neutralizations of bureaucracy and technology; and finally, the most complicated of all, (3) an emphasis upon the limits of the political friends and enemies, sovereignty and the exception, which defines the question of belonging to the polity. In this article we dealt critically with this last point, while adding Schmitt's ideas on *Grossraum* and multilateralism.

In the past, Max Adler, Franz Neumman, Otto Kirchheimer and even Jürgen Habermas have in different ways made sense of Carl Schmitt. For example Max Adler's idea of the solidaristic coercive order, that fuses social and political democracy, might be seen as reception of Schmitt's ideas. Otto Kirchheimer's claims that democracy and capitalism cannot coexist because in following capitalism, the judiciary gives private property (legality) absolute primacy over publicly agreed principles (legitimacy) are elements that can be seen as Schmittean. Even Habermas's recuperation of Schmitt's issues in his liberal-republican claim that modern judicial systems have detached themselves chronically from the discursive sources of political legitimacy might be seen as making correct use of Schmitt in a critical perspective (Thornhill, 2000).

Today more than ever, the Left is enticed by Carl Schmitt. Indeed, the transition from Herbert Marcuse to Carl Schmitt, via Michel Foucault's ideas on power and domination, was welcomed by the New Left, who perceived in Schmitt's anti-liberalism and concept of power a welcome substitute for Marxist economic and historical theories. Cuba is welcomed by Schmitteans of the Left and Right despite its repression of human rights, in so far as it stands for national unity against American imperialism.

Ernesto Laclau, Chantal Mouffe or the intellectuals of the journal *Telos* such as Paul Piccone and Gary Ulmen among others on the Left, have clearly been influenced by Schmitt. In addition, there is no question that Carl Schmitt is useful to the intellectual French and European New Right. Probably one of the chief advocates coming from the Left is Chantal Mouffe. Mouffe praises Carl Schmitt's criticism of the institutions of liberal democracy and in her personal debate with deliberative democrats on the one hand and aggregative democrats on the other, Mouffe gets close to Schmitt's concept of "national democracy." The aggregative type of democracy sees democracy as interest aggregation, while the deliberative model is guided by moral normative considerations and the search for a common good. Both approaches are rational and overlook, according to Mouffe, the political importance of passion in politics.

Nationalism cannot be understood by aggregative models, but by passion. The national *demos* and the passion that accompanies it is the basis for Mouffe defense of Schmitt's concept of the political.

Reluctant to accept the idea of legal pluralism and group rights, Mouffe defends the agonistic principles which demand agreement about principles while accepting dissent about interpretations. In this way she reformulates Schmitt's, friend – enemy formula into a friend – adversary formula. Paradoxically Mouffe's radical pluralism attempts to save liberalism from Schmitt's criticism. In other words by shifting the balance from the liberal rule of law to popular democracy and equality, Mouffe believes that the democratic project could be saved from radical Right populism. Indeed, similar to Geroges Sorel in France and Henrik de Mann in Belgium among others, who strove to save socialism through revolutionary syndicalism or national corporatism, and opened the gate to fascism, it seems that Mouffe like other post-Marxian leftists contributes to the politics of identities that best suits the project of the New Right in Europe. Carl Schmitt is a vital theoretical factor in this endeavor.

The European New Right led by Alain de Benoist captures the spirit of Schmitt's intersecting points between nation-state and federalism better than Chantal Mouffe and the New Left. They understand that Carl Schmitt's multi-polar world is the best scenario for the reconstruction of an exclusionist European ethno-nationalism. The European New Right thus claims to fuse the radical anti-liberal facets of the Left and the Right into a new vibrant "Third Way." The new approach based on differentialist ideology encourages both natives and foreigners to essentialize their cultural roots, each one of them in their "own nomos." From that point on the New Right envisions a multipolar world, composed of several regional compounds, each composed of non-liberal republics.

In opposition to the idea of the end of history, "... characterized by the global triumph of market rationality" claimed de Benoist "... a new 'Nomos of the Earth' is emerging. The twenty-first century will be characterized by the development of a multipolar world of emerging civilizations: European, North American, South American, Arabic-Muslim, ... etc. These civilizations will not supplant the ancient local, tribal, provincial or national roots, but will be constituted ... by them."(Benoist and Champetier, 2000) Implicit in this claim is that both Europe and the developing world countries should rescue their own authentic "tribes" and philosophy of life. It is not only right and constructive that Evo Morales and Chavez in Bolivia and Venezuela attempt to revive and empower indigenous cultures, that is true also for Europe. The Basques, Catalans, Scottish, Flemish and the northern Italians are the ethnic identities conforming a new federal Europe, which differs from the liberal union.

Only under an authentic European plurality, composed of its ethnic nations, but closed to immigration, which completely differs from the liberal European union, will Europe recover its central protagonist role in world politics. Why is this so,? Because according to Benoist "while the European Union, built as a mirror of the United States, lacks authenticity and creates a market favorable to the United States, a non-liberal ethno-regional Europe diverges and contrasts with that of the United States" (Benoist, 1993–1994: 201). In his critique of the liberal union de Benoist claims that "...the paradoxical result of the liberal union is that the creation of that single market [liberal European Union] of 320 million inhabitants with their strong purchasing power will favor first of all not the Europeans, but their competitors" (*Éléments*, 1980: 1–3). By pointing to the contrasting features between a liberal European Union and a new type of ethno-federalism, the New Right attempts to re-constitute the concept of Europe as a real political power. A true European sovereignty "can be attained only with the regionalization of large continental ensembles" (Benoist, 1996: 136).

In other words, following Carl Schmitt's ideas on *Grossraum* and regionalization of power, the New Right attempts to recreate the dream of an ethno-regional European empire composed of ethnic republics free of liberal rights and immigrants. On the one hand, as noted, a new post-colonial Europe should represent its ethnic peoples emancipated of the imposition of liberal rights. For the New Right thus Basques, Catalans, Flemish, North Italians, are the new ethnic nations, that sooner or later would prefer national unity and the defense of national culture to liberal rights. However, as noted these nations won't stand alone. They become according to the New Right the components of a new anti-imperialist confederation. Similar to Europe, other world cultures should reorganize themselves under an anti-imperialist myth, as Bolivia, Venezuela and Ecuador are doing under Hugo Chavez's leadership. The striking fact is that by addressing ethnic regionalization, the New Right fulfills the two fundamental goals of racism and anti-imperialism.

Indeed, on the one hand by invoking regionalism and a new "European nativism," under a post-nationalist pluralism, the New Right promotes a new sophisticated way of excluding cultural minorities. On the other hand, by invoking a common struggle against American globalization, the New Right supports the developing world struggle against American imperialism. In that sense a racist Europe, free of immigrants, shares with the developing world a common struggle against what Carl Schmitt most criticized, American moral imperialism imposed through the politics of human rights, free markets, and post- national citizenship

In sum, the spirit of Schmittian confederation seems to be better exposed by the Right, or by a synthesis of Right and Left, which in more than one sense is a reflection of the old fascist synthesis, something that Benoist understands quite well. Instead of citizenship in times of war, this can be defined as the absence of citizenship in order to preserve peace.

References

Bates, D. 2006. "Political Theology and the Nazi State: Carl Schmitt Concept of the Institution," *Modern Intellectual History*, 3(3), 415–442 at p. 424.

Balibar, E. 2001. "Citizenship without a preexisting community." Lecture delivered at Bard College on March 19, 2001.

Bandieri, L. M. 2002. "Carl Schmitt and federalism," *TELOS,* Winter, 11, 48.

Benoist, A. 1996. Three Interviews with Alain de Benoist, *TELOS* 98–99 (1993–94).

Benoist, A. 1996. "Confronting Globalization," *TELOS*, 2(108).

Benoist, A. de and Champetier, C. 2000. "The French New Right In The Year 2000." Introduction. 115 (Spring 1999): 117–144

Cohen, J. 2008. "A Global State of Emergency or the Further Constitutionalization of International Law: A Pluralist Approach," *Constellations,* 15(4), 456.

Éléments. 1980. Editorial, "L'Europe de 1992: Un mauvais conte de fées," 65.

Galli, C. 1996. *Genealogia della Politica. C. Schmitt e la Crisi del Pensiero Politico Moderno,* Bologna: Il Mulino.

Holmes, S. 1995. *The Anatomy of Antiliberalism*, ch. 2, "Schmitt the Debility of Liberalism," Cambridge, MA: Harvard University Press, p. 45.

Howse, R. 2006. "Europe and the New World Order: Lessons from Alexandre Kojeve's Engagement with Schmitt's 'Nomos der Erde'," *Leiden Journal of International Law*, 19, 93–103

Koskenniemi, M. (2004) "International Law as Political Theology: How To Read *Nomos der Erde*'," *Constellations.* Vol. 11, No. 4.

Lilla, M. 1997."The Enemy of Liberalism," *The New York Review of Books,* 44(8), May 15.

McCormick, J. 1997. *Carl Schmitt's Critique of Liberalism. Against Politics as Technology*, Cambridge: Cambridge University Press, p. 4

Mouffe, C. 2005. "Schmitt's Vision of a Multipolar World Order," *The South Atlantic Quarterly,* 104(2), Spring, 245–251.

Piccone, P. and Ulmen, G., 2002. "Uses and Abuses of Carl Schmitt," *TELOS*, 122, Winter.

Rasch, W. 2000. "Conflict as a Vocation. Carl Schmitt and the Possibility of Politics," *Theory Culture and Society*, 176(6), 1–32 at p. 2.

Scheuerman, W.E. 1999. *Carl Schmitt: The End of Law*, New York: Rowman & Little-field

Schmitt, C. 1928. *Verfassungslehre*, Munich und Leipzig: Duncker & Humblot

Schmitt, C. 1952. "Die Einheit der Welt," *Merkur* 6, 1–11

Schmitt, C. 1974. "Uber die Bedeutung des Wortes Nomos," in *Der Nomos der Erde im Volkerrecht des Jus Publicum Europaeum*, Berlin: Duncker & Humblot.

Schmitt, C. 1976[1927]. *The concept of the political*. Chicago: University of Chicago Press.

Schmitt, C. 1986[1919]. *Political Romanticism*, trans. Guy Oakes, Cambridge, MA: MIT Press.

Schmitt, C. 1988a[1923]. *The Crisis of Parliamentary Democracy*, trans. Ellen Kennedy, Cambridge, MA: MIT Press.

Schmitt, C. 1988b[1928]. *Verfassungslehre*. Munich and Leipzig; Duncker and Humblot.

Schmitt, C. 1988c. "Volkerrechtliche Formen des modernen Imperialismus," in *Positionen und Begriffe im Kampf mit Weimar- Genf- Versailles 1923–1939*, Berlin: Duncker and Humblot.

Schmitt, C. 1996a[1923]. *Roman Catholicism and Political Form*, introd. G.L. Ulmen, Westport, CT: Greenwood.

Schmitt, C. 1996b[1979]. *The Tyranny of Values*, trans. Simona Draghici, Washington, DC: Plutarch Press.

Schmitt, C., 1998[1923]. *The Crisis of Parliamentary Democracy*, trans Ellen Kennedy, Cambridge, MA: MIT Press.

Schmitt, C. 2003[1952]. *The Nomos of the Earth in the International Law of the Jus Publicum Europeaum*, trans G.L. Ulmen, New York: Press

Schmitt, C. and Maschke, G. 1995. *Staat, Grossraum, Nomos*, Berlin: Duncker & Humblot.

Thornhill, C. 2000. "C. Schmitt after the deluge: a review of the recent literature," *History of European Ideas*, 26, 225–264.

Ulmen, G. 1992. "Schmitt and federalism: Introduction to *The Constitutional Theory of the Federation*," *TELOS*, Spring, Issue 91.

Zarmanian, T. 2006. "Carl Schmitt and the Problem of Legal Order: From Domestic to International," *Leiden Journal of International Law*, 19, 41–67 at p. 46.

2 Security Council activism in the age of the war on terror*

Implications for human rights, democracy and constitutionalism

Jean L. Cohen

Introduction

The current discursive frameworks of a "global war on terror" and a "global state of emergency" pose the apparent necessity of a tradeoff between human rights and human security, domestically and internationally. Moreover, it seems that the global protectors of "human security," under the "responsibility to protect" (R2P) doctrine, now tend to undermine rights, constitutionalism and democracy, strengthening arbitrary domestic and global executive power at the expense of parliaments, courts, and the rule of law (IDRC 2001; UN 2004). Indeed, the current form of emergency and security discourse has altered the meaning of the R2P in ways that threaten constitutionalism everywhere. There is nothing new about constitutionalism and rights coming under stress in the context of war or crisis. Now, however, the threat comes not only from domestic executives (or militaries), not only from the unilateral actions of the world's "sole superpower," but also from the international institution meant to protect global security and human rights: the UN Security Council (SC).

The new security paradigm: the Security Council starts legislating

September 11 provided the occasion for a new discourse of a global state of emergency and the need for a permanent war on terror. On September 28, 2001, the SC adopted Resolution 1373, invoking Chapter VII powers but departing radically from its previous practice and language – imposing general obligations on states to prevent and combat terrorism (Rosand 2003: 333n5; Marschik 2005). States are ordered to take actions designed to prevent support for terrorists, to suppress the financing of terrorist acts, to freeze funds and other assets of any persons or entities suspected of terrorist activity or of supporting it, to strengthen border security and prevent the movement of terrorists, in part by tracking migrants and refugees, and to become parties to the UN's anti-terrorism conventions and protocols. Most remarkably, states are required to change their domestic laws to criminalize terrorism (and its financing) as a separate offense in national codes with harsher punishments than those attached to ordinary crimes.

Each nation is called upon to upgrade its legislation and executive machinery to "fight terrorism." Thus Resolution 1373 creates uniform obligations for all 191 member states of the UN, going well beyond earlier counterterrorism conventions and protocols (sponsored by the General Assembly), binding only on those who have become parties to them (Rosand 2003: 334). The resolution established a subsidiary organ – the Counter-Terrorism Committee (CTC), a plenary committee of the Council – to monitor state compliance with the resolution (Szaz 2002: 902). All this in the absence of any definition of terrorism (this is left to the states to define) and coupled with a disavowal of responsibility to monitor the human rights violations that these requirements might entail (Scheppele 2006: 17; Rosand 2003: 340).

There were important predecessors to this. Resolution 1267, passed by the Council in 1999, initially addressed support by the Taliban regime in Afghanistan for suspected terrorists. It was expanded into a complex sanction regime adopting global measures against anyone anywhere associated with the Taliban, Osama bin Laden or Al Qaeda (Rosand 2004: 758; Marschik 2005: 471n64). The 1267 Committee was established as a subsidiary organ to monitor state compliance with Council-imposed targeted sanctions and to maintain a consolidated list of individuals and entities alleged to have the above-mentioned associations. The list is updated and managed by the 1267 Committee. This was the first Chapter VII regime of "smart" sanctions based on the assumption that targeting individuals is an improvement over past UN general sanction regimes that harmed innocents.

Subsequently, Resolution 1540, adopted in April 2004, sought to block non-state actors from acquiring WMDs. It required states to adopt laws prohibiting the acquisition or transfer of WMDs to non-state actors, and to take effective enforcement measures and institute domestic controls to prevent their proliferation. This resolution also established a monitoring committee.

However, Resolution 1373 posed the most direct threat to basic due process and property rights of those listed (Hoffman 2008; Marschik 2005). Any state may propose a name for the CTC list; members have 48 hours to object. The CTC operates on the basis of consensus. There are no evidentiary guidelines and very few requirements for the submitting state. A person can be placed on the list and subjected to sanctions, without being given the opportunity to demonstrate that the listing is unjustified or even to know the reasons and evidence that led to their name being listed. As for delisting, this may be initiated by the state of a suspect's nationality or residence, but the procedure is onerous (Chesterman 2004–2008: 16–19).

No court is in a position to evaluate the evidential basis on which a person or entity is placed on the list, because access to information on which that decision was based is not available. There is no procedure for a formal appeal or review mechanism (Chesterman 2004–2008: 16–19).[1] In response to the World Summit Outcome Document, which called on the Council to ensure fair and clear procedures for listing and delisting, Resolution 1730 (2006) strengthened procedural safeguards to protect individual rights by establishing a focal point to receive delisting requests (UN 2005). However, any Council member can still veto the removal of a name, without having to give reasons.

Given the absence of legal remedies, the threat posed by this resolution to the rights to due process, to a hearing, to property and to freedom of movement is real. As Julia Hoffman correctly notes, the lack of access to and review of information at all stages of the process is striking (Hoffman 2008). Moreover, the danger that the listing process will be used for political purposes by states to quell their internal opposition by framing participants as terrorists is real. Resolution 1566, passed at the request of Russia after the Breslan school massacre, set up a task force to study expanding the list of terrorist individuals and entities beyond those associated with al Qaeda and the Taliban. In short, blacklisting individuals enables domestic executives to enlist the international community on the state's side of a local conflict by invoking the SC resolutions that have constructed the global anti-terrorist campaign (Scheppele 2006: 56–57).

The Council has thus arrogated to itself a judicial function in listing individuals as terrorists – by implication as global outlaws – although in doing so under Chapter VII it avoids formally making a determination of criminal activity, which would warrant due process regulations and careful evaluation of evidence. As one analyst puts it, blacklisting is a strange type of punishment, since Council decrees lay down no prohibited activity against which the named individuals' actions or omissions are to be measured (Cameron 2003: 179; 2006).

Moreover, Resolution 1373 portends an emerging Council practice involving an even more radical threat to constitutionalism on the domestic and international levels. Whereas in the 1990s the problem was the apparent arbitrariness in labeling domestic conflicts, humanitarian crises, and rights violations, threats to *international* peace and security, here we encounter a different problem. There is no great stretch in construing transnational terrorism as a threat to international peace and security. However, there is indeed a very great stretch when the SC arrogates to itself the competence to identify not particular, but general, permanent yet amorphous threats to the existing order, and responds by legislating for the international community as a whole, thereby informally amending the UN Charter, usurping constituent authority, and radically changing the way international law is made and its function. Why?

In the pre-9/11 epoch, the prevailing model of SC intervention was the enforcement/security model. In that model, despite its flaws and openness to abuse, the powers the Council invoked were executive in character, and they were exercised in response to particular conflicts and emergencies. By their nature, sanctions were restricted by a limited purpose and timeframe, whether or not specific temporal limits were stipulated (Szasz 2002: 902). Once the purpose was achieved, the mandate ended.[2] The relevant decisions of the Council were thus executive and political. They had the shape of commands relating to a specific situation, just what the Council was designed for, even though the nature of the situation altered from the external to the internal.

In relation to that model, resolutions 1373 and 1540 are highly innovative in six respects:

1   They are not related to a specific threat or dispute, even though they were
     inspired by 9/11, but rather to a vague, generally construed threat.
2   They lack any explicit or implicit time limitation.
3   The binding obligations they impose on all states are permanent.
4   Significant portions of them address generic issues and establish binding
     general rules of international law, instead of having the status of specific
     decrees or commands addressed to a specific context. If legislation is the
     enactment of abstract norms that are directly binding on all member states
     and which regulate their rights and obligations on general issues with long-
     term effects, the SC has started legislating (Szasz 2002; Talmon 2005:
     175–193). The difference between that and legally binding executive
     decisions ("measures," in the language of the Charter), that enforce the
     peace in a specific political crisis, is clear (Marschik 2005: 461).
5   The SC arrogated to itself the competence to enact abstract norms, directly
     binding on member states of the UN which are to be immediately effective
     and which undermine existing domestic constitutional provisions or norms
     that conflict with these rules, thereby changing domestic constitutions. If we
     include 1267, the Council has thrice imposed resolutions involving substan-
     tively intrusive legal regimes that bypass the usual vehicle of community
     interest, the multilateral treaty.
6   The Council now resorts to its own subsidiary organs rather than to standing
     institutions in other relevant treaty regimes to ensure legislative success and
     compliance (Alvarez 2003; 2006: 199–217).

One analyst has portrayed these developments as amounting to a new mode of
exercising power by the SC (led by the US) that he called "global hegemonic
international law." Hegemony operates through non-reciprocal patron–client
relations involving pledges of loyalty in exchange for security or economic benefits, replacing pacts between equals grounded in reciprocity and substituting for
formal equality of states (Alvarez 2003: 199). Given the veto and the advantages
of permanent membership on the Council, if the Permanent Members (P5) are in
agreement, all it takes to secure binding action is to successfully pressure or
entice four of the remaining ten non-permanent members.[3] This hegemonic form
of lawmaking is legal under existing Charter rules: "Neither P-1 nor the other
permanent members of the Council are violating the law by taking advantage of
the privileges they have been granted" (Alvarez 2003: 216). The point is that
hegemony can be exercised within multilateral institutions and via international
law: it need not take the form of unilateralism or lawbreaking. The exercise of
hegemonic power can be collective, legal, institutional and juris-generative,
hence the appellation "global hegemonic law" (Alvarez 2003: 199).
    Kim Scheppele has shown that, unlike earlier democratic and rights-
enhancing multilateralism, this version of global governance undermines the
domestic separation of powers in favor of domestic executives and greatly
strengthens the executive power of the P5, singly and collectively, in the UN and
the world at large (Scheppele 2006). She documents convincingly the ways in

which the security regime put in place by the Council spurs and reinforces the creation of new, vague and politically defined crimes, surveillance programs, moves toward preventive detention and aggressive interrogation by security-minded domestic forces – national executives, militaries, police and security agencies. Their power is thereby expanded at the expense of domestic parliaments and courts while civil liberties are eviscerated. Transnational links among national executives, militaries, police and security agencies have been extended while their relation to and control by domestic parliaments and courts have been attenuated; hardly good news for constitutionalism (Scheppele 2006: 4–5). Many heads of states and governments are able to invoke obligatory Council resolutions to push through rights-violating domestic laws, thereby expanding their own power, justified as compliance with international law. Those states that seek to resist the SC's command to criminalize terrorism as a separate offense, arguing that their criminal law is equipped to handle it, are subject to pressure by the CTC, erected to monitor national compliance. Weak states are forced to comply, executives seeking to become stronger willingly play along; others, committed to constitutionalism, rights and the separation of powers, are pressured to conform (Scheppele 2006: 8–11, 20–21).

Scheppele's point, like Alvarez's, is that the Council does all this legally. Emergency governance is not lawless; it proceeds through a plethora of rules, decrees, regulations, legal administrative measures, and international and domestic legislation (Scheppele 2006: 50). It is not the absence of law, but the development of a new form of global security law and the legal pressures placed on domestic governments to comply with it, that is the problem. But it is one thing to show that the Council's emergency governance involves rule-making, and legislation that is technically legal, it is quite another to maintain that this is a legitimate exercise of its powers. The bodies created by the Charter are indeed ascribed the competence to interpret their own powers to carry out their functions. The presumption of legality for SC action and expansive interpretations of its powers has been the norm since the 1990s. However, the Council's authority to take binding decisions under the Charter does not amount to a constitutional right for it to legislate for the world (Alvarez 2006: 194; De Wet 2004: 137).

One could try to invoke the concept of implied powers, and the principle of effectiveness, to justify recent Council resolutions as the necessary exceptional response to the emergency situation created by transnational terrorism. In other words, the Council could be acting like a commissarial dictator, suspending some Charter rules and norms, assuming plenary powers, abrogating the albeit rudimentary separation of powers and existing constitutional guarantees of due process and other human rights of suspects in the war on terror, so as to act effectively in the face of threats to the basic order and to restore it once the threats are dealt with (Schmitt 1928a, 1928b). After all, on the treaty reading of the UN Charter, the SC is an emergency executive, established to identify and respond to crises, i.e. to declare the exception and to protect international peace and security. On the constitutional interpretation of the Charter, the SC was established to protect the legal order created by the Charter and public international law. But this justification for deviating from existing norms would have to fit in the framework of the exceptional and temporary nature of police enforcement measures. It is not evident that legislative powers are required for efficacy or deducible from the concept of implied powers (Marschik 2005: 463–464).

Indeed in the public debates over Resolution 1540, many states expressed concern that it could become a precedent and constitute "subsequent practice" establishing general legislative powers of the Council. Members of the non-aligned movement explicitly rejected a legislative role for the Council, arguing that this is not a function envisaged in the Charter and that the Council is structurally inappropriate to legislate for the UN, because it is not a representative body (Marschik 2005: 476–480). Others insisted that, in principle, legislative obligations such as those foreseen in the draft resolution should be established through multilateral treaties in whose elaboration all states can participate.

At issue is the encroachment on the allocation of powers established by the UN Charter. By arrogating to itself the competence to legislate in this way, the Council has taken a step away from a commissarial dictator, for it is using the discourses of a war on terror, and emergency, not in order to protect an existing constitutional order but to institute a new one. Legislation is distinct from suspending certain rights and issuing binding decrees targeted to a specific situation, and it is not the function of a commissarial dictatorship. Moreover, in so doing, the Council is changing the material constitution of the Charter, engaging in an informal amendment, using the lower track of lawmaking and bypassing the higher track in the formal amendment rule (conflating the two tracks).

What even critics fail to see, however, is that by so legislating for the world, the SC may be exercising its legal power to make binding decisions, but it is nonetheless doing something doubly illegitimate: usurping the constituent authority belonging to the international community of states and materially changing the constitutional treaty through informal amendments, both in precedent-setting ways. In the process it is radically undermining the principle of sovereign equality, creating not only a new substantive legal regime but also a new form of hierarchical global lawmaking and governance. To invoke Habermas's concepts, it uses law as a medium to introduce a new form of global governance, undermining law as an institution meant to control and limit the exercise of public power by legal and constitutional norms.

The usurpation of global constituent power and its condition of possibility

Under customary international law, all states have the equal right to participate in international lawmaking based on consent, including making binding bi- or multilateral treaties.[4] They are the co-authors, not only the subjects of international law. The UN Charter is a constitutional treaty, open to two different modes of interpretation. It is possible to find a legal basis for a dynamic interpretation of the Charter in the notion of "object and purpose" in the Vienna

Convention on the Law of Treaties, but on the treaty model, the teleological interpretation of their competences by the organs of the UN would still be relatively restricted (Rama-Montaldo 2005: 504–513). The constitutional interpretation is more permissive. Yet from the perspective of the Charter as a formal constitutional document, any major change to the organizational allocation of competences, to the functions ascribed to the organs or to the organization as a whole, would have to proceed through formal amendment, via the amendment rule in the Charter (Fassbender 1998: 98–159). The assumption of legislative functions by the SC transgresses both of these readings. Given objections to a legislative role for the Council voiced by UN member states unconvinced that such powers are needed for security in the war on terror, the treaty model doesn't work, but neither does the constitutional interpretation. For by assuming the competence to legislate, the Council is not only transforming its function from enforcement and policing, it is also changing the material constitution and amending the Charter by stealth. The assumption of legislative power and its actual legislation thus have a double status: general laws are being made by an executive body and constitutional change – an exercise of constituent power – is being perpetrated by that same body insofar as it ascribes to itself the competence and capacity to legislate for the world, thereby introducing a radically new way of global lawmaking.

Article 109, stating the procedures by which the Charter may be altered, stipulates a two-thirds vote of the General Assembly including *all* the permanent members of the Security Council, thereby extending the veto of the P5 to the amendment procedure (UN Charter, Articles 108, 109). Fundamental change to the Charter and to the functions ascribed to UN organs should take place via this process. The veto presumably was meant to serve as a negative check, to block alterations unwanted by the P5. However, in the current context it has an enabling function. Once the SC starts legislating, radically redefining its powers and function, the veto means that there is no constitutional check to such actions. Whatever informal constitutional changes the P5 manage to push through the Council cannot be undone via the amendment process, because any permanent member can veto the corrective. The P5's veto power blocks not only needed reforms that the P5 don't want, it also blocks a constitutional response to amendments by stealth. This is a usurpation of the constituent authority of the member states – the sole entities with the authority to collectively formally change the material constitution of the Charter either via the amendment rule or via the creation of a new constitutional treaty. There is no court authorized to decide the competence of UN organs, to police the rudimentary separation of powers, or to maintain the formal two track structure of lawmaking erected by the Charter – i.e. the distinction between ordinary rule-making and constitutional change established by the amendment rule. Nor is there an effective legal or institutional remedy that could be used to undo informal amendments pushed through by the P5 in the SC.

Obviously, the condition of possibility of this radical shift was there since 1945. The P5 have always been in a structurally different position from the rest of the member states in the UN. *It is the unprecedented use being made of their structural position today that creates a new legitimation problematic.* The issue is not simply a matter of inequality – of the P5 having greater power or privileges, like weighted votes or extra say in rule-making or certain immunities. Nor is it simply a matter of anachronism, correctible, say, by including other twenty-first-century great powers within the privileged circle of permanent members. The problem is the constitutional and structural difference of the mode of relationship of some members to the organization thanks to the amendment rule. Everyone knows that the veto in the Council exempts the P5 from having the rules they make being applied to themselves. Everyone knows that there can be no enforcement of Charter principles against a permanent member or against someone they protect. Everyone also knows that the veto in the amendment rule puts the P5 in the position to block changes to their status and discretion.

Thus, for the P5, the Charter is a treaty and the UN a traditional international treaty organization. They remain external to the constitutional dimension of the UNO. They participate in an organization which for them is no more than a confederation, and to whose rules, on the classical treaty model, they are subject, conditional on their consent. For them, the principal/agent relationship still obtains: while they participate in a treaty organization which is a third party actor, they retain a sort of Westphalian sovereignty, singly and collectively, *vis-à-vis* that organization. For them, both the formal and the informal amendment rule is the classical amendment rule of a confederation, based on the principle of unanimity.

None of this is so for the other members of the UN. For them, the organization created via the Charter is not a confederation, or a classical treaty organization; it is what Carl Schmitt called a *Bund* – a structure in-between a federal state and a confederation of states, a "global governance institution" in today's parlance (Schmitt 1928b, ch. 29). The non-P5 member states are fully subject to the rules and decisions of UN organs with or without their individual consent. They are also subject to an amendment rule that is not based on unanimity but on a qualified majority. Analytically such an amendment rule is typical of a Bund, wherein a qualified majority of member states can amend the constitutional treaty of the organization, through a process in which each state has one vote. In such a structure, all the member states are within the organization, under its constitutional law and equally subject to it even though they retain their sovereignty in the sense that their legal systems are autonomous, as is the legal structure of the Bund.

Thus what the formal amendment rule of the Charter constructs is a hybrid structure in which some of the member states belong to a confederation, while others belong to a "Bund": their relation to the constitutional treaty and to the rules made by UN organs is radically different. Moreover, despite its assertion of the principle of sovereign equality, the UN Charter has formalized a hierarchy between the two types of members. The P5 are not bound by the same constitutional rules which bind the others, and they are often in the position to dictate these rules. The problem is not that member states of the organization retain their sovereignty, or that the organization is constitutionally pluralist in the sense that it constitutes an autonomous legal order yet is composed of member states whose own constitutional legal orders are also autonomous. Rather, the problem is that the formal amendment rule and the veto power in the Council construct a hierarchy within the overall hybrid nature of the organization, placing the permanent members in a position outside of the constitutional order created by the treaty. The permanent members are able to participate in making rules and decisions that others must comply with but from which they are exempt, and to bypass the amendment rule and make material constitutional changes, usurping the constituent power of member states, to which there is no legal or institutional remedy thanks to that very amendment rule. The P5 can thus exercise constituent power and revise the Charter by stealth, with the veneer of legality, if they get the requisite number of votes.

The legitimation problem

Permanent membership and the veto right of the P5 in the Council were initially accepted by member states, for the sake of exceptional peace enforcement. It was clear that these privileges contradicted the principle of sovereign equality articulated in Article 1 of the Charter. However, once the Council assumes a general legislative role, the threat to the principle of sovereign equality within and outside the UN system and to the basic structure of public international law becomes far more radical. The new legislative role transfers the inequality in peace enforcement to a much wider sphere (Marschik 2005: 486). First, it means that member states lose their right to equally participate in making international law, and to consent or make reservations or persistently object to it as they can in the multilateral treaty-making process. Article 103 of the Charter stipulates the supremacy of Charter obligations over any other international agreement. Since states must obey Council decisions, they do not have the option of opting out that exists under customary international law nor do they have any role in making it as is the case in treaty law. Second, as a recent commentator on Resolutions 1373 and 1540 succinctly put it:

> The P5 effectively control the Council. Should the recent trend of targeting individuals by means of sanctions be taken up in legislation, the inequality could extend to the creation of rights and obligations of the States' nationals. The practice of equipping the primary norms with special monitoring mechanisms ... could ... extend the inequality further from norm creation to the monitoring phase and into enforcement.
>
> (Marschik 2005: 486; see also Koskenniemi 1995: 338–348)

The recent legislation by the Council indeed has the effect of undermining the sovereignty of most states other than the P5, insofar as their ability to participate in international lawmaking and to make their own domestic law autonomously, are concerned (Scheppele 2006: 1–30, 59–72). On the other hand: "Executives in terrorist-target strong countries as well as those in terror-implicated weak states are all increasing their powers in the anti-terrorism campaign, even as more powerful states use transnational institutions to further dominate weaker ones" (Scheppele 2006: 11). It is, after all, executives that are behind the expansion of Council powers. These changes in the UN Charter structure and in the general system of public international law do not bode well for the rule of law. If this *de facto* UN reform is not successfully challenged by a counter-project, then the securitizing, normalizing, regulatory techniques of administering and governing populations rehearsed in "humanitarian occupations" will be generalized to other states, carried out either by reinforced domestic executives and/or global policing agencies that run roughshod over rights, constitutional limits, and counter-powers (Fox 2008).

This is the level on which the charge of *illegitimacy* is pertinent: the amendment rule is bypassed via informal amendment that institutes radical changes to the international legal order and the Charter itself (by turning the Council into a legislative body) which cannot be undone by a constitutional court or via formal amendment. All this is indeed juris-generative: new law and a new form of lawmaking have emerged. Unfortunately, the new legal order that this quiet revolution seems to be ushering in is one in which a hegemonic form of global right can violate both human rights and the sovereign equality of states with apparent impunity.

The problem we face is not whether a global state of emergency can be responded to with ordinary legal methods, but whether the newly active SC can be legally limited, its legislative initiatives scaled back, the threats it poses to constitutionalism and human rights reversed, and a new dualistic sovereignty regime based on the rule of law and the principles of sovereign equality and human rights reinstituted within the UN Charter system. I am not convinced that transnational terrorism poses the kind of existential threat to the world order that could justify instituting a general state of emergency rule or the self-ascription of plenary powers on the part of the SC to legislate and institute a new form of global law. I am convinced that a viable counter-project should encompass what others have already referred to as the further constitutionalization of public international law (Habermas 2006). However, much depends on how we understand this.

The further constitutionalization of public international law is a feasible, albeit difficult to obtain, utopia. If we accept that the need for global governance is real in certain areas, and that global governance institutions are here to stay, then bringing them under the rule of law is indispensable for their legitimacy. The UN as a global governance institution faces a triple legitimacy deficit today. On the substantive level, SC rulings that violate basic human rights undermine the legitimacy of the Council as the protector of the values of the Charter and the international community. On the procedural level, the expansion of its powers to include quasi-judicial and especially legislative functions, in addition to a new unanticipated scope of executive enforcement, raises serious questions about the rudimentary separation of powers and deficient system of checks and balances within the Charter structure. On the meta-procedural level, the usurpation of the constituent authority of member states through informal amendment, to transform the Council into a hegemonic global lawmaker, whose obligatory rulings eviscerate the cardinal principle of sovereign equality in the making of public international law, undermines the credibility of the Council as an impartial agent of the international community. Since there are no internal legal correctives to such uncontrolled exercises of power, it also throws into doubt the constitutional reading of the Charter.

What should be done?

The need to rectify these legitimation deficits is now pressing. Two dilemmas have to be confronted in such a project: (1) How to further constitutionalize this domain of international law, thereby creating a new form of global law that, given a world of sovereign states with vastly different characteristics, is nonetheless not imperial. (2) The necessity of binding sovereign states to a law that is autonomous with respect to their own constitutions, whose validity is not based on state consent in the classical contractual way, and which concerns in part how states treat their own populations, in addition to regulating the *jus belli*. I argue that the solution to both dilemmas lies in a dualist conception of international/ world society and a pluralist understanding of constitutionalism. International society is still a segmentally differentiated system of sovereign states, but it is increasingly imbricated in a functionally differentiated world society composed of globalizing legal orders, states, networks and individuals (Cohen 2004). The constitutionalization of the public international law regulating the global political system has to be understood as the institutionalization of a new dualistic sovereignty regime, in which states retain their legal and political autonomy and constituent authority but within which the supra-national legal order of a revised UN Charter is also construed as autonomous *and* constrained by constitutionalism. This would entail bringing the P5 inside the Charter, and interpreting the transformed global constitutional order in the theoretical framework of constitutional pluralism. It would also entail re-institutionalizing the principles of sovereign equality and human rights to apply to global governance institutions and not only to states.

We don't have to start *ex nihilo*. The UN Charter was created through an intergovernmental process between states, and signed as a treaty. Like any typical intergovernmental organization, the bodies established by the treaty have no general legislative competence, only those delegated powers necessary to carry out their enumerated functions; their rules and decisions bind states only in certain agreed-upon domains; the domestic legal orders of the member states remain autonomous and non-derivative. Even the dispute settlement system, located in the International Court of Justice, is state-based, voluntary, and lacks an enforcement mechanism: neither individuals nor international organizations have standing and member states can withdraw from the system. In principle, states could also exit the UN at will. These are the classic features of an international treaty organization, which has the international society of sovereign states as its referent.

However, there are important features of the Charter that escape the treaty model and make sense only on a constitutional reading. The UN Charter created a "third party actor," meant to endure indefinitely, and it defined the structure of the organization setting out the powers and functions of its organs, the rights and duties of its members (Fassbender 1998: 63–159; Sloan 1989).

It serves as a *constitutional* treaty in both the material and formal sense of the word. As a material constitution, the Charter involves a set of substantive norms (sovereign equality, human rights, peaceful settlement of disputes, domestic jurisdiction, self-determination, etc.) as well as procedural and institutional norms that establish organs and delimit their powers, including primary and secondary rules. As a formal constitution, the Charter is a solemn written document that may be changed only under the observation of special prescriptions. In an unprecedented step for international organizations at the time, the founding member states decided not only to create an institution with the power to decide the legality of the use of force; they also opted for majoritarianism in the amendment rule and in ordinary decision making processes, qualified in the ways already described (Fassbender 1998: 63–159). The supermajority required for amending the constitution establishes its formal character, its relative rigidity, and its superior rank vis-à-vis the rules its organs make. This was a radical break with the standard unanimity principle for treaty organizations (Fassbender 1998: 11). Moreover, the Charter established an autonomous legal order that it asserted to be supreme in the event of a conflict with other treaty obligations of the members.[5] This legal order delimits the terms of membership, and the organization has acquired many new members since it was created. It has as its referent the international community of states it helped transform and construct into an integrated legal community with community interests, purposes and values (Fassbender 1998: 50–59, 91; Grimm 2005). On the constitutional reading it is this legal community that the organs of the UN are supposed to represent. By implication, the constituent units are legally subordinated to their new creation: its rules apply to them irrespective of their continuing consent. This is the meaning of an autonomous legal order of constitutional quality.

To be sure, the constitutional dimension of the UN Charter is at best rudimentary: there is no court with compulsory jurisdiction to police the formal constitution or enforce the material one; there isn't an adequate separation of powers or system of internal checks and balances; there are no real protections for basic rights; no global court of human rights; no compulsory dispute settlement system; no mechanisms to ensure accountability; etc. *Thus the constitutional reading has to be seen as aspirational.*

The greatest impediment to the constitutional reading, however, is not its rudimentary character; it is the weakness of the Charter with respect to a third dimension of the meaning of constitution, the normative one, without which the other two would be uninteresting. Constitution in the normative sense entails constitutionalism: meaning, at the very least, that the powers and governing bodies established in the constitutional legal order are regulated and limited by it. The point of the constitutionalization of public power is to place it under law and subject it to legal limits. Constitutionalism also means that certain substantive values, including human rights, the rule of law, the exercise of public power for public purposes and the community's wellbeing, inform and orient a particular institutional order (Weiler 2005: 184–187).[6] It is on this normative level that the constitutional nature of the Charter falls short, for the permanent members of the SC are in but not really under the legal order of the Charter: they are absolute in the old fashioned sense.

It should be obvious what the further constitutionalization of this constitutional treaty must entail. The central contradiction of the UN Charter – that it creates the possibility of an institutionalized collective hegemony of the great powers yet is designed to pursue goals that are in the collective interest of the international community – has to be resolved in a constitutionalist direction. There is no going back to a traditional treaty organization for the UN Charter system (Fassbender 1998: 111). Instead, constitutionalization would have to entail bringing the P5 into the Bund structure that exists for the other members. Accordingly, the veto in the amendment rule would have to be abolished and some form of double voting system established that takes power into account. This is the most obvious way to create a constitutional remedy to constitutional usurpation and to preserve the two track rulemaking process established by the formal constitutional structure and yet bring the P5 into the system. Security is about power and a realistic collective security system cannot ignore the distribution of power in the world, or the difficulties of transition from the existing institutionalization: hence the necessity for double voting tracks that acknowledge this. But the principle of sovereign equality must also be acknowledged and effective. Thus there would have to be two tracks of voting in the amendment process, one in which each state has one vote, the other weighted according to considerations of power, and organized in such a way that each track has a chance to check the results of the other. The dramatic new legislative role of the Council should be scaled back, as this is not an appropriate organ for global lawmaking.

Constitutionalization in this sense would abolish the hybrid nature of the UN but it would preserve the dualism of the UN Charter as a constitutional treaty, albeit shifting the relations between its component parts. A new sovereignty regime would be created within the Charter system in which member states would retain their legal autonomy and constituent authority but the supranational legal order of that system would also be construed as an autonomous, constitutional order that constrains its members. In other words, further constitutionalization would mean that the system would be transformed into a Bund. But, crucially, this constitutionalization must be understood in the theoretical framework of constitutional pluralism – the heart of the Bund concept and the appropriate analogue of the concept of a dualistic sovereignty regime in a globalizing world.

As already indicated, I borrow the concept of a Bund from Carl Schmitt's *Verfassungslehre* (Schmitt 2008[1928b]: 383–395). Accordingly, the distinctive feature of a Bund is that it constitutes a permanent union freely agreed to by member states, albeit changing their status by bringing them within a new and autonomous legal community. Ideal-typically the Bund is a political form involving a mode of integration different from both a treaty organization (confederation) and a federal state. A *Bundesvertrag* is a constitutional treaty that creates a unique type of dualist order. It constructs an autonomous, constitutional legal and institutional order for the organized supra-national community of states whose conflicts must now be resolved through law. The supra-national community attains a political existence insofar as it acquires the *jus belli*, although its member states may retain it, *vis-à-vis* the outside. The legal order of a Bund is autonomous, supreme in its specified functional domains, endowed with the competence to use its powers enumerated in the constitutional treaty. Member states are bound by its decisions whether or not they ratify them individually. Moreover, the Bund may even intervene in member states to enforce its law with regard to its specific functions and in this respect the internal order of the member states is no longer impermeable. As a political unity the Bund must be represented: it must have an assembly of all member states, and executive organs for administrative and enforcement work (Schmitt 2008 [1928b]: 284–285, 389).

Nevertheless, member states retain their autonomous legal and political existence – they remain sovereign in their own eyes. It is the nature of a Bund that it seeks to preserve and respect their political and legal autonomy. The states' political existence does not derive from, nor does the validity of their legal systems inhere in the *Bundesvertrag*; the latter is not in a hierarchical relation to the former. The member states' powers are not enumerated or functionally delimited, although certain prerogatives can be withdrawn from their domestic jurisdiction.

If one reasons from the standpoint of a constitutional pluralist approach, the amendment rule of a Bund should reflect its position between a treaty organization and a federal state.[7] Whereas for the former, the amending powers, the states, are outside the treaty and, classically, amending the treaty requires unanimity, in the case of a federal state, the "states" are within the constitution and can be treated as organs of the federal union. Thus a typical federal constitutional amendment rule could involve the use of a federal senate but for its ratification it would rely on individual voters of the federal state. For a Bund, as for a confederation, the amendment rule would maintain the states as the sources of constitutional change, but the idea of bringing them within the constitutional treaty would mean that a majority of these formally equal states (one state one vote) would be able to bind the minority. This is a way of bringing all the states into the constitution while ensuring that they remain the authors of it. A Bund thus would have only a single source of legitimacy: its constitutional authorities remain the member states, although adhering to its own constitutional principles and rules and respecting basic rights also enhances its legitimacy. A good example of a Bund amendment rule is the ratification portion of the US Constitution's Article 5, the ultimate hurdle in the amendment process in the US. It is a federal state, yet the US has the amendment rule of a Bund. Paradoxically, the EU is a Bund that has the amendment rule of a confederation. Both the processes of informal amendment in the US and many of the struggles around the European constitutional treaty can be related to these paradoxical and inconsistent arrangements.

It is important to emphasize that sovereignty is neither divided nor shared in a Bund structure, an oxymoronic idea insofar as sovereignty entails the supremacy of a legal order and the autonomy/self-determination of a political community regarding its political form. Instead, in a Bund the ultimate decision about the locus of final authority, or which legal order's claims to supremacy is valid (and will prevail), is deferred.

Schmitt thought of a Bund as a mode of political organization suitable for a restricted group of states, not as a global structure in which all states would be members. He deemed it inherently unstable due to its internally contradictory character. Schmitt identified three contradictions in the Bund structure. First, a Bund's constitutional treaty aims to preserve the autonomy of member states, yet it transforms their constitutional status insofar as they are subject to its autonomous legal order, thus diminishing their political autonomy, especially regarding the *jus belli*. Second, there is a tension between the impermeability of a sovereign legal order and the tendency of a Bund to intervene to enforce its own legal order. Third, there is a tension between the autonomous political entities in the same organization, none of which can annihilate or subordinate the other through a comprehensive legal hierarchy (Schmitt 2008 [1928b]: 388). Accordingly, Schmitt was convinced that for a Bund to exist at all there has to be substantive homogeneity of the population along some important salient lines (religion, nationality, class or civilization), as well as structural homogeneity of the political principle of organization of each member state (monarchical, republican or liberal-democratic). Yet even this would allow only temporary deferral of the final decision as to where sovereignty lies. Recall that for Schmitt sovereignty is not a legal but an existential concept involving the ability to make the ultimate political decisions (Schmitt 1985). Given his monistic conception of sovereignty, and his friend/enemy concept of the political, a decision-less constitutional structure such as that of a Bund is ultimately doomed. Conflict is inevitable and when it occurs over something that matters enough to both sides, power, not law, will decide where sovereignty lies and the Bund structure will collapse.

I have argued elsewhere against the existential conception of sovereignty as well as the friend/enemy conception of the political that underlies this negative assessment (Cohen 2008). Nevertheless, Schmitt raises important issues, although his analysis confusingly conflates legal-normative and realist power considerations. Understood as a normative project, the tensions inherent in a Bund structure (a constitutional treaty organization) can be productive. They need not lead to destructive instability or culminate in conflicts that force a "decision" about the locus of sovereignty. From this perspective a reform project of the UN Charter system that envisions its further constitutionalization should aim at establishing a Bund-like structure – the most appropriate form of global political community that is the analogue to the global legal community. Constitutionalization in this sense would constitute a new special form of polity rather than simply regulating that which already exists. There is no need for the kind of homogeneity Schmitt insists upon, but only for an overlapping consensus on the basic purposes, functions, values and procedures articulated in the constitutional treaty establishing the Bund. There is also no reason why it cannot be global in scope, despite the cultural and institutional diversity of member states. As already indicated, constitutional pluralism is the appropriate analogue of the concept of sovereign equality in a globalizing world order, and of a new sovereignty regime. It means that within a constitutional treaty organization, both the supra-national legal order and the constitutional orders of the member states are autonomous, and neither is comprehensive in jurisdiction, although the former must be functionally delimited. They can coexist so long as each respects the self-determination of all the political communities as well as the basic principles of the overarching Bund. If one adds the feature that while the UN reformed into a Bund would continue to have the monopoly of the legitimacy to determine the use of force internationally, member states would continue to retain the right to self-defense as well as the actual forces, then it is clear that we are speaking of a dualist structure and a new sovereignty regime.

Accordingly, it is perfectly conceivable that a state can give up the *jus belli* (except for self-defense), accept that all states are bound by certain enforceable human rights norms, and even open up its territory to jurisdiction by a functionally delimited supranational legal order, and still be sovereign. From the internal perspective, the state is sovereign so long as there is an autonomous self-determined political relationship between the government and the citizenry, and so long as its legal order is supreme. The sovereign domestic constitutional legal order can delegate competences and even accept the primacy of rules made in the appropriately designated manner by a supranational organization in certain domains, since it is the capacity of the sovereign domestic legal order to make such delegations and to accept such decisions. From its internal perspective, the domestic legal order remains supreme and retains interpretative autonomy over jurisdiction and over issues of compatibility of external decisions with its internal constitutional legal order. But internal autonomy need not be tightly coupled to exclusivity of jurisdiction. It is certainly possible to conceive of autonomy and sovereignty without comprehensive territorial exclusivity (Walker 2003: 23). The development of functionally delimited supranational jurisdictional claims in the global political system organized into a Bund can thus supplement and overlap without abolishing the autonomy of segmentally differentiated territorial sovereign states (Walker 2003: 18–32).

Yet within such a structure, the constituent authority would remain with the member states acting in an assembly by majorities binding minorities, thus within the constitution. A suitable amendment rule would provide for a constitutional response to informal amendments from within or outside the organization. This would mean that the constitutional treaty of the global political system (reformed UN Charter) organized into a Bund-like structure changes the status of the parties and the nature of their relationships. But even though the constituent authority of member states is given legal form in the amendment rule, and is exercised within the Bund, their sovereign equality and autonomy remains intact and the former remains functionally delimited (Walker 2003: 18–32).

The stance of constitutional pluralism reveals that each autonomous legal order sees itself as supreme in terms of validity: each has its own *Grundnorm* in the sense that the basic constitutional norms and legal sources are not derived from any higher legal system. From the internal legal/normative perspective of the constitutional order of each member state, the reason why the rules of the Bund are binding and supreme is ultimately that the member state's constitutional order has accepted its rulemaking capacity and supremacy in certain functionally delimited domains or for certain purposes. From the perspective of the constitutional treaty, or Bund, its rules are supreme in its relevant functional and purposive domain, because it is an autonomous legal order whose supremacy is explicitly acknowledged. The internal perspective is perforce monist. From the external, theoretical, reflexive perspective, however, these are interrelated yet distinct constitutional orders in a dynamic non-hierarchical relationship with one another, which must devise ways to avoid destructive conflicts.

This is why constitutional monism has to be avoided on the level of meta-language (Walker 2003). Constitutional pluralism is empirically, pragmatically and normatively far more compelling regarding the idea of further constitution-alization of the global political system. It is, to be sure, an external perspective – of the political or legal theorist – but I believe it can also inform that of the internal legal practitioner. The stance of constitutional pluralism is linked to the unavoidable political problematic of legitimacy and mutual recognition regarding the construction of legal orders. The basic idea is to acknowledge that autonomous legal orders can exist in the global political system – of sovereign states and of the global political system itself – and that the latter's claims to autonomy, supremacy and constitutional quality can exist alongside the continuing claims of states. The relation between these orders must be seen as heterarchical and horizontal, rather than as hierarchical and vertical. This empirical and epistemological claim is accompanied by a normative and political one: as against monist sovereigntism and monist globalist cosmopolitanism, neither of which are compelling descriptions of the world today or models of feasible reform, constitutional pluralism involves the normative idea that what is required to handle competing claims to authority coming from national and supranational constitutional sites *is an ethic of political responsibility* premised on mutual recognition and respect (Walker 2002: 337–338).

Constitutional pluralism thus entails the normative commitment of taking seriously both sovereignty and monism in the internal perspective of an autonomous legal order and pluralism on the meta-level (Walker 2003: 18). Autonomous legal systems, by their nature, each assume the role of higher law. Constitutional pluralism entails acknowledging these competitive claims to independent political and legal ultimate authority. This can indeed lead to collisions and conflict when a major disagreement arises over substantive or jurisdictional issues: the question of who decides has different answers in the domestic and global context. There is no court that can invoke an impartial, higher jurisdiction or validity to settle the matter. One cannot claim, as cosmopolitan monists are wont to do, that if a constitutional treaty has constitutional quality, the condition of validity of the constitutions of the member states derives from it. The reverse sovereigntist position is also untenable for a constitutional treaty organization, because the language of delegation, consent, or principal/agent does not fit so many of its features. But collisions can also lead to reflexivity and cooperation: tension need not end in fragmentation of either legal system. The unity of a legal system requires that each new legal decision is coherent with previous legal decisions. It is possible to have coherent legal orders in a context of competing determinations of the law (and competing claims to ultimate authority) so long as all the participants share a commitment to the project of maintaining and improving a coherent global legal and political order and adjust their claims accordingly (Maduro 2003: 527–528).

What is required is political and juridical judgment – the willingness to make the effort to avoid ultimate conflicts by anticipating them and trying to cooperatively resolve them (Weiler 2005: 184–190, advocating "constitutional tolerance"). A non-hierarchical conception of the relationship between norms and courts and political actors at each level, and informal cooperation could prevail given the appropriate level of reflexivity on the part of the relevant actors (Walker 2003: 18). But reflexivity requires communication, an internal attitude toward global law and willingness to justify legal interpretations in universal rather than parochial terms. (For the concept of the "internal atti- tude" see Hart 1994: 55–66; Maduro 2003: 530.) Such "constitutional toler- ance" is a political normative stance, predicated on a shared project of constructing a legitimate and fair supranational legal and political order of which states are members (and of the desirability of the project of a global rule of law) (Weiler, 2005: 184–190). Given legitimacy, devising mechanisms to facilitate adjustments to respective claims over jurisdiction and authority to avoid collision is certainly not impossible.

Indeed, the status of claims to legal autonomy and supremacy is inseparable from the political question of legitimacy. Political theory cannot come up with mechanisms for "ordering pluralism" from the internal validity perspective, but it can reflect on the conditions of political legitimacy that all legal systems ultimately depend on for their efficacy (Delmas-Marty 2006). There are differ- ent versions of the constitutional pluralist approach, but they all involve taking a reflexive theoretical and normative political stance that relates the legal ques- tion of internal validity to the political question of external legitimacy. (For a description of the various approaches and a critique see Cruz 2007: 18–26.) Reflexivity is crucial in the kind of dynamic system that a Bund would entail. The key point for the global political system is that disputes need not lead to disintegration so long as political legitimacy is maintained and prudence is practiced by supra-national institutions and by member states. Instead of seeing constitutional pluralism as a problem, it should be seen as an ingenious solution to the dualism and complexity of the world order (Maduro 2005a: 50–52, 55–58).

Finally, there is the obvious question: why adopt the stance of constitutional pluralism and propose the Bund structure in the first place? There is a norm-ative and a strategic answer to this question. As already indicated, the Bund is based on the equal sovereignty of member states, and constitutional pluralism with its inherent dynamism is the conceptual analogue to the idea of (chang-ing) sovereignty regimes. While I cannot go into detail here, I argue that we should understand sovereignty as a negative concept involving supremacy of a domestic legal order and autonomy in the political sense of self-determination (non-imposition by foreigners) by a polity of its political regime and constitu-tional order. Accordingly, sovereignty protects the special relationship between a citizenry and its government and the possibility of basing this relationship on principles of constitutionalism and democracy. The principle of sovereign equality accords this to all states. The Bund structure provides for collective action, problem solving, and rulemaking on the global level, but it protects and is based on the legal and political autonomy (sovereignty) of member states. On the global level functional equivalents for democracy are possible (account-ability, avenues of influence for civil society, non-decisional parliaments, com-munication about best practices, subsidiarity, etc.) but they could never amount to the kind of representative democracy and effective electoral participation possible on the level of the modern state or even a regional polity (Dahl 1999; Pettit 2006: 301–324).

We must learn from the difficulties posed by the democratic deficit on the intermediary level of the EU and see that there is a strong normative argument for the constitutional pluralist position. While a federal structure with a working parliament could conceivably resolve the democratic deficit on the European level, this is very unlikely on the level of the globe. (For a different view see Falk and Strauss 2001: 212–220). Low-intensity constitutionalism, however, is possible on the global level (Maduro 2005b: 340–348.) Thus for those wedded to republican political principles and democratic aspirations, the constitutional pluralist approach is the best way to protect and expand domestic democratic achievements.

There is also a strategic answer in our current context. The constitutional pluralist approach opens up the possibility that domestic or regional high courts could, *faute de mieux*, indirectly review decisions by the organs of a constitutional treaty organization that undermine the basic constitutional struc-ture of the organization by usurping the constituent authority of the member states, or that conflict with their domestic constitutional principles by violating the basic rights they guarantee.

Conclusion

The SC now engages in global governance tasks that go beyond its traditional purposes and functions including humanitarian interventions, the erection of highly transformative interim administrations of occupied territories, the imposi-tion of sanctions directly targeting individuals (some of which violate their basic rights), and the issuing of binding resolutions that require domestic legislation by member states. In the process, it is eviscerating constitutionalism on all levels of the international political system, and undermining the foundational Charter principles of sovereign equality and human rights. As a response to the danger that a new form of global rulemaking con-dominium might emerge, I have argued for low-intensity constitutionalization that would keep to the dualist structure specific to UN as a constitutional treaty organization but bring it within the rule of law and ensure that its rules and decisions are rights-respecting.

Constitutionalization involving the step to a Bund structure would also help constitute an international political community as the appropriate analogue of the legal community in the global political system. Insofar as it revitalizes the principle of sovereign equality internal to the UN *qua* global governance institution, the latter would attain a degree of democratic legitimacy regarding the right to rule in its designated domains because all states would have a voice, under accepted decision rules, within the inclusive organization. A minimal democratic legitimacy would thus emerge even if full congruence between the subjects and authors of the law (typical of representative national democracies), in the case of those individual rights which become hard international law, would not be provided (Cohen 2008). On the other hand, participation of all member states in Charter revision to establish the rules for deciding which rights should acquire that status, and for regulating interventions, occupations, and responses to terrorism would be an important step in the right direction. This may be as good as it can get for the foreseeable future.

My purpose in this chapter was to argue that a new dualistic sovereignty regime, that constructs a normatively appropriate interconnection between human rights and political autonomy, and which is understood in the theoretical framework of constitutional pluralism, still has a chance against tendencies towards con-dominium or empire. I see the discourse of the constitutionalization of international law as part of a counter-project to global hegemonic international law. Since reform of the veto is so difficult, limits to Council misbehavior must first come from other constitutionalist orders, assuming the political will and legal ingenuity is available. At present and in the foreseeable future, the only constitutional sources of legal limits on the SC absent a formal amendment of the amendment rule that abolishes the veto are those in existing constitutionalist polities that see themselves, and are seen as, autonomous. By revealing that legitimacy will be lost when rights, constitutionalism and the rule of law are undermined, the constitutional pluralist approach, used intelligently, could have a recursive effect, in the long run contributing to the development of the political will to scale back Council usurpation and even to amend the Charter amendment rule, introducing more effective separation of power and checks and balance mechanisms and a more integrated international political community. This is one way to break the vicious circle of discretionary self-aggrandizing global and domestic executive powers mutually reinforcing one another at the expense of constitutionalism, rights and political autonomy everywhere.

Notes

* This paper was first prepared by the author as part of the distinguished lecture series given at the Collège de France, May 2008. An earlier version was published in *Constellations* 15: 4 (2008).
1 SC Resolution 1735 (2006) stipulates that the Secretariat inform states of residence or nationality within two weeks of listing. These states are asked to inform the listed person or entity.
2 This is not true for humanitarian interventions that end in "humanitarian occupations." While these are targeted to specific crises in specific states, all too often the mandates of the occupiers or "peace enforcers" are open-ended. The administrations are highly legislative and transformative. See Fox 2008; Cohen 2006/2007.
3 The US usually gets what it wants but not always, as the failure to get SC authorization for invading Iraq most clearly revealed.
4 They can also opt out of customary international law by being a persistent objector. See Byers 1999.
5 Article 103 of the UN Charter, the "supremacy clause," states that "in the event of a conflict between the obligations of the members of the United Nations under the present charter and their obligations under any other international treaty agreement, their obligations under the present Charter shall prevail."
6 For some radical democratic theorists, a normative conception of a constitution requires full democratic legitimacy (equal representation of all affected) in the process of creating and adopting the constitutional text. It also must establish procedural norms for law-making that enable democratic politics along with protection of basic rights. See Burnkhorst 2005: 88. I believe we have to settle for a less demanding concept of legitimacy for the global political system at this time.
7 Carl Schmitt never clarified the amendment rule for a Bund. I am very indebted to Andrew Arato for pointing this out and for clarifying the issues in this paragraph and others throughout the text.

References

Alvarez, José E., 2003. "Hegemonic International Law Revisited," *American Journal of International Law* 97, p. 873.

Alvarez, José E., 2006. *International Organizations as Law Makers*, New York: Oxford University Press.

Burnkhorst, Hauke, 2005. "A Polity without a State? European Constitutionalism between Evolution and Revolution," *International Journal of Constitutional Law* 3: 88–106.

Byers, Michael, 1999. *Custom, Power and the Power of Rules: International Relations and Customary International Law*, Cambridge: Cambridge University Press.

Cameron, Iain, 2003. "U.N. Targeted Sanctions, Legal Safeguards and the European Convention on Human Rights," 72 *New Jersey Journal of International Law*, 159.

Chesterman, Simon, 2004–2008. "The U.N. Security Council and the Rule of Law," *Final Report and Recommendations from the Austrian Initiative*.

Cohen, Jean L., 2004. "Whose Sovereignty? Empire versus International Law," *Ethics & International Affairs* 18: 3, 1–24.

Cohen, Jean L., 2006/2007. "The Role of International Law in Post-Conflict Constitution-Making: Towards a Jus Post-Bellum," *NY Law School Law Review* 51: 3, 498–532.

Cohen, Jean L., 2008. "Rethinking Human Rights, Democracy and Sovereignty in the Epoch of Globalization," *Political Theory* 36: 4, 578–606.

Cruz, Julio Baquero, 2007. "The Legacy of the Maastricht-Urteil and the Pluralist Movement," *European Working Papers RSCAS*, 13: 18–26.

Dahl, Robert A., 1999. "Can International Organizations be Democratic? A Skeptic's View," in Ian Shapiro and Casiano Hacker-Cordon eds., *Democracy's Edges*, Cambridge: Cambridge University Press.

De Wet, Erika, 2004. *The Chapter VII Powers of the United Nations Security Council*, Oxford: Hart.

Delmas-Marty, Mireille, 2006. *Le Pluralisme Ordonne*, Paris: Editions du Seuil.

Falk, Richard and Andrew Strauss, 2001. "Toward a Global Parliament," *Foreign Affairs* 80: 212–220.

Fassbender, Bardo, 1998. *U.N. Security Council Reform and the Right of Veto: A Constitutional Perspective*, Boston: Kluwer Law International.

Fox, Gregory H., 2008. *Humanitarian Occupation*, Cambridge: Cambridge University Press.

Grimm, Dieter, 2005. "Integration by Constitution," *International Journal of Constitutional Law* 3: 193–208.

Habermas, Jurgen, 2006. "Does the Constitutionalization of International Law Still Have a Chance?" in *The Divided West*, Cambridge: Cambridge University Press.

Hart, Herbert Lionel Adolphus, 1994[1961]. *The Concept of Law*, Oxford: Clarendon Press.

Hoffman, Julia, 2008. "Terrorism Blacklisting: Putting European Human Rights Guarantees to the Test," *Constellations* 15: 4.

IDRC, 2001. *The Responsibility to Protect: Report of the International Commission on Intervention and State Sovereignty* (Ottawa).

Koskenniemi, Martti, 1995. "The Police in the Temple – Order, Justice and the U.N.: A Dialectical View," *European Journal of International Law* 6.

Maduro, Miguel Poiares, 2003. "Contrapunctual Law: Europe's Constitutional Pluralism in Action," in Walker, ed., *Sovereignty in Transition*, p. 525.

Maduro, Miguel Poiares, 2005a. "Sovereignty in Europe: The European Court of Justice and the Creation of a European Political Community," in Mary L. Volcansek and John F. Stack, eds., *Courts Crossing Borders: Blurring the Lines of Sovereignty*, Durham, NC: Carolina Academic Press.

Maduro, Miguel Poiares, 2005b. "The Importance of Being Called a Constitution," *International Journal of Constitutional Law* 2: 3, p. 336.

Marschik, Axel, 2005. "Legislative Powers of the Security Council," in Ronald St. John Macdonald and Douglas M. Johnston, eds, *Towards World Constitutionalism: Issues in the Legal Ordering of the World Community*, Leiden: Brill, pp. 431–492.

Pettit, Philip, 2006. "Democracy, National and International," *The Monist* 89: 301–324.

Rama-Montaldo, Manuel, 2005. "Contribution of the General Assembly to the Constitutional Development and Interpretation of the united Nations Charter," in Macdonald and Johnston, eds., *Towards World Constitutionalism*.

Rosand, Eric, 2003. "Security Council Resolution 1373, The Counter-Terrorism Committee, and the Fight against Terrorism," *American Journal of Constitutional Law* 97: 2.

Rosand, Eric, 2004. "The Security Council's Efforts to Monitor the Implementation of Al Qaeda-Taliban Sanctions," *American Journal of Constitutional Law* 98: 4, 747.

Scheppele, Kim Lane, 2006. "International State of Emergency: Challenges to Constitutionalism after September 11," paper presented to the Yale Legal Theory Workshop.

Schmitt, Carl, 1928a. *Die Diktatur*, München/ Leipzig: Duncker & Humblot.

Schmitt, Carl, 1928b. *Verfassungslehrer*, München/Leipzig: Duncker & Humblot (English tr. 2008: *Carl Schmitt, Constitutional Theory* (Durham and London: Duke University Press).

Schmitt, Carl, 1985. *Political Theology: Four Chapters on the Concept of Sovereignty*, Cambridge, MA: MIT Press.

Schmitt, Carl, 2008 [1928b]. *Constitutional Theory*, trans. and ed. Jeffrey Seitzer, Durham, NC: Duke University Press.

Sloan, Blaine, 1989. "The United Nations Charter as a Constitution," *Pace Yearbook of International Law* 1: 61–126.

Szaz, Paul, 2002. "The Security Council Starts Legislating," *American Journal of International Law* 96.

Talmon, Stefan, 2005. "The Security Council as World Legislature," *American Journal of International Law* 99, 175–193.

UN, 2004. "A More Secure World: Our Shared Responsibility," Report of the Secretary General's High Level Panel on Threats, Challenges and Change (New York) *www.un.org/secureworld.*

UN, 2005. "2005 World Summit Outcome, General Assembly Resolution," September 16, Document A/RES/60/1, www.un.org/summit2005/documents.html.

Walker, Neil, 2002. "The Idea of Constitutional Pluralism," *Modern Law Review* 65.

Walker, Neil, 2003. "Late Sovereignty in the European Union," in Neil Walker, ed., *Sovereignty in Transition*, p. 23.

Weiler, J.H.H., 2005. "On the Power of the Word: Europe's Constitutional Iconography," *International Journal of Constitutional Law* 3: 2/3, 173–190.

3 Beyond the security vs. liberty paradigm

An analysis of "security" politics in Israel

Sharon Weinblum

Introduction

When faced with a state of emergency or with a security crisis, political actors tend to take measures curtailing basic rights and liberties, which they justify by the need to find an appropriate balance between liberty and security of the citizens (Waldron 2003), an argument which is in most cases endorsed by the judiciary branch (Norton and Collins 2004). Interestingly, the security vs. liberty paradigm has also entered the academic sphere where scholars, especially constitutionalists, tend to interpret and analyze security decisions in those terms (Ackerman 2004; Cole 2004; Ignatieff 2004). As a consequence, security politics, especially anti-terrorist policies have often been studied as compromises between liberties and securities of the citizens.[1]

Despite the relative consensus on the security vs. liberty framework of interpretation, especially since September 11, 2001 (Waldron 2003), the paradigm poses some heuristic difficulties when it comes to grasping the *processes* that take place when a state takes security measures. Indeed, despite the use of the term "security" by realist scholars of the International Relations discipline neither "security" and "threat" nor "liberty" can be seen as defined once and for all. Drawing on critical studies of security (Waever 1995; Buzan *et al.* 1998; Huysmans 1998) and the cognitive approach of public policies (Sabatier 1987; Muller 2000; Muller and Surel 1998; Sabatier and Schlager 2000), this chapter aims at overcoming the heuristic flaws of the security vs. liberty interpretation by offering a more dynamic approach of security politics. More specifically, it aims to demonstrate that the choice for specific security tools is to be understood in relation to conflicting belief systems where the central cores relate to the regime that political actors favor and idealize. In other words, it shows that security policies are much more than a compromise between security and basic rights: they are a reflection of these conflicting belief systems as well as a locus of reconstruction and imposition of the latter.

The chapter focuses on citizenship laws that have been passed by the Israeli parliament, the Knesset, in the name of security and which have led to the curtailment of basic rights. A qualitative discourse analysis is carried on, which seeks to deconstruct the argumentation of the Knesset Members (MKs) in favor and against the laws in order to identify the conflicting *belief systems* that under-lie the positioning on the laws. The cases under study are several debates over two security amendments that produced major consequences in terms of rights and liberties: the Citizenship and Entry into Israel Law (temporary order, 2003) and the amendment 9 of article 11 of the Law on Citizenship (2008). The choice of these specific laws is both explained by their content – security and basic rights of the citizens – and by the fact that they opened intense debates over their justifications and legitimacy in the political arena. The sources used for the ana-lysis of the debates are on the one hand, the bills that were presented to the Knesset, where either the government or the MKs must present the laws' ration-ales, and on the other, the debates which took place in the Knesset during the first, second and third readings of the laws.

The focus on the legislative assembly and on legislative texts only, although quite restrictive, is justified by the particular position of the political arena in the framing and imposition of interpretation frameworks in society. All the same, using parliamentary debates as the principal sources of analysis could seem limited. However, it appears to be a "strong institutional locus for researching political positioning among the political elite over time" (Huysmans and Buon-fino 2008: 766) and to grasp the belief systems in struggle.

On the structural level, the chapter falls into two parts. After a brief presenta-tion of the theoretical approaches which have led to the analysis, a second and main part of the chapter is devoted to the analysis of the debates over the laws on citizenship.

Security laws as a reflection of regime struggle: theoretical background and hypotheses

The "liberty-security balance" (Waldron 2003) paradigm or the notion of a "lesser evil" (Ignatieff 2004) are often used in order to understand the develop-ments linked to the state of emergency. This comprehension of the state of emer-gency is all but new and can actually be traced back in most of the classic liberal philosophers' thought. Hence, Locke theorized the notion of *prerogative* where the executive receives the temporary power to curtail basic rights in order to secure safety, and Montesquieu noted that "there are cases where a veil has to be drawn, over liberty, as one hides the statues of the gods." This framework of interpretation is also present in many constitutional documents, which usually admit that some rights can be diminished when it is necessary for security reasons[2] and hence we also find traces of this paradigm in political discourses.

However, interpretation in terms of the liberty–security balance is problem-atic, not so much from a moral point of view,[3] but rather on a heuristic level, if we want to understand the processes leading to the definition of security policies and how their promoters achieve their imposition in the political arena. First, it seems problematic from an empirical perspective. Indeed, as will be seen, the concern for a balance between security and liberty is not referred to or mobilized by the entire spectrum of political actors when security or emergency policies are under discussion. Furthermore, the liberty–security paradigm is problematic from a theoretical perspective as it promotes a very static vision of both security and liberty, which seems flawed in many respects. Therefore, the article offers a new type of questioning and analysis based on three different theoretical approaches, which offer a much more dynamic comprehension of the processes under study.

The first major approach that inspires the following analysis is the constructivist and critical study of security, mostly theorized by Waever and Buzan. In their contributions, the authors have renewed the approach on security by showing that, far from being an objective ontological given, security must rather be comprehended as a constructed and evolving reality (Waever 1995; Buzan *et al.* 1998). More precisely, security and threat should be understood as constructions framed by the elites' speech act or the labeling of certain issues, actors and phenomena as security problems. As a result, instead of the static notion of security, Waever has suggested using the notion of "securitization," which suggests the idea of a process. This approach has been very much amended and criticized since then while the notion of the speech act has been fruitfully mobilized to analyze several types of developments including the processes of securitization of ethnic or religious groups (Jackson 2007) and of immigration (Huysmans 2000; Duez 2008).

The second type of studies which helps us get a new understanding of security politics is the constructivist approach of public policies, which has demonstrated that pre-existing social constructions influence the policy agenda and the selection of policy tools. In their analysis of "target populations," Schneider and Ingram have for instance shown that the rationales used by political actors to justify the agenda "differ depending upon the social constructions of target populations" (Schneider and Ingram 1993: 339). When analyzing the United States' decisions in foreign and security policies, Campbell also established that the State's security policies depended directly upon pre-existing social constructions, namely in this case, the way the State defined its own identity (Campbell 1992). This thesis was later reasserted in the case of the Israeli elite in the framework of foreign policies (Peleg 2004).

Finally, scholars analyzing changes in public policies through a cognitive approach have confirmed the importance of social constructions in the formation of such policies. In his studies, Sabatier has for instance shown that public policies must not be seen as mere responses to identified social problems but as the outcome of a struggle between several *advocacy coalitions* trying to impose their *belief systems* (Sabatier 1987). Decomposing three levels in these belief systems; the central core referring to very general beliefs; the policy core including "crucial perceptions and normative beliefs applying to a public policy sector" and secondary aspects that apply to specific parts of this sector (Sabatier and Schlager 2000: 227–228), he has hypothesized that secondary elements can change due to a learning process while the central cores change only if a major exogenous development occurs. Besides, the cognitive approach of public policies has also highlighted that "the subject of public policies is not only to 'solve problems' but also to construct frameworks of interpretations"[4] (Muller 2000: 194). Thus, like the constructivists, these scholars have not only shown that the pre-existing social constructions or framework of interpretations influence public policies but also that policies influence and reframe these constructions.

All these studies thus stress, on the one hand, that representations have a major weight in the demand formulation of political actors whose belief systems evolve over time, thus engendering particular policies and tools. In this way they help us make a link between policies and pre-existing normative perceptions or belief systems. Drawing on the conclusion of these researches and basing my argument specifically on the cognitive approach theory, the central thesis of this chapter is that the laws, which are passed in the name of security, must not be seen as tools chosen to respond to a clearly identified threat in a trade-off between security and liberty. Rather, I argue that they should be envisaged as the outcome of a struggle between belief systems in conflict in the political arena. To draw on Sabatier, these belief systems would be constituted of secondary elements: the specific tools proposed by the legislator; of a policy core: the general visions of how to safeguard security; and of a central core: the regime perceived as ideal. In other words, the position on security politics would depend upon vision of security that would only make sense in relation to what the actors regard as the ideal regime. To come back to classical political philosophy, we could thus deconstruct Hobbes' *Leviathan* as a policy core elaborated in order to protect a central core: men's physical security. All the same, Locke's model of the *prerogative* is more than a balance between liberty and security: it is a tool to safeguard the natural right that Locke envisages as the most fundamental, namely safety (Neocleous 2007).

In this chapter, I do not aim to explain the changes in specific policy tools. Consequently, I do not focus on the debates regarding secondary elements. I do not seek to explain the configuration's developments in terms of belief systems present in the Knesset. Rather, the aim is to understand the passing of "security" laws by identifying the belief systems in struggle in the parliament and to draw conclusions on the consequence of a certain belief system's imposition for the polity.

Security and laws on citizenship: a struggle between conflicting belief systems

The amendments under scrutiny have modified two laws on citizenship: the Law on Citizenship (1952) and the Law on Entry into Israel (1952). The first one provides that citizenship can be granted to a person on the basis of several elements: (1) the Law of Return (1950) which allows all Jews and their descendants to immigrate to Israel; (2) residence; (3) birth; and (4) naturalization, which includes marriage under article 7.[5] The second law gives the authority to the Minister of Interior to grant visa, temporary and permanent residence permits to a foreign person other than a Jew who came under the Law of Return.

From the beginning, the laws included a security dimension. Article 2 of the Law of Return provides that citizenship on the basis of the Law of Return can be denied if the person requesting citizenship is engaged in an activity directed against the Jewish people or is likely to endanger public health or the security of the State. Moreover, article 11 (a), section 3 of the Law on Citizenship provides that if a naturalized citizen "has committed a breach of trust towards the State of Israel, a District Court may, upon the application of the Minister of the Interior, revoke such person's naturalization." In 1968, an amendment suppressed the mention of naturalization so that article 11 applies to any Israeli citizen. In 1980, an amendment was also introduced to the law according to which

> a citizen who enters in an illegal state according to section 2 (a) of the Law on prevention of infiltration (1954) or is granted the citizenship of such a state,[6] will be regarded as having renounced Israeli citizenship and will lose his citizenship from that day on.

The clause applies also to the children of the person if they do not reside in Israel.

However, the securitization of the laws on citizenship especially increased after the second Intifada, with the introduction of the Citizenship and Entry into Israel Law (temporary law, 2003) and the amendment 9 of the article 11 of the Citizenship Law (2008) on which the next sections focus. The first debates under study are those over the initial passing of the Citizenship and Entry into Israel Law (temporary law, 2003), which can be seen as a turning point in terms of securitization of citizenship. Then, the debates for the reenactment of this law from 2004 on are analyzed. Finally, the debates over the amendment number 9 of the Law on Citizenship, 2008 are studied.

The Citizenship and Entry into Israel law (temporary regulation 2003): universal democracy vs. defensive democracy

In March 2002, the government voted a decision preventing the granting of citizenship and residence permits in Israel to Palestinians. After the Supreme Court demanded to legislate on the issue, the government turned its decision into a bill and proposed it to the Knesset. The bill provided that:

> During the period in which this Law shall be in effect, notwithstanding the provisions of any law, including section 7 of the Nationality Law, the Minister of the Interior shall not grant a resident of the region [Judea and Samaria and the Gaza Strip] nationality pursuant to the Nationality Law and shall not give a resident of the region a permit to reside in Israel pursuant to the Entry into Israel Law, and the regional commander shall not give such resident a permit to stay in Israel pursuant to the defense legislation in the region.

After several debates in the Internal Affairs committee and in the plenum, the law was voted in July 2003 with 55 voices for, 23 against and no abstention (third reading of the law).

An analysis of the rationales and of the arguments presented in the Knesset in the first, second and third readings leads us to identify three major actors positioned in two groups: the initiator of the law (the government) supported by the group in favor of the law (the religious parties and the coalition parties) on the one hand, and the group opposing the law on the other (composed of the Labor party, the Meretz and Arab parties).

According to the bill presented by the government, the first rationale of the law was to respond to the exceptional security context: the perpetration of bomb attacks by Palestinians who had been granted either citizenship or permanent residence permits after having married an Israeli citizen. The security context was referred to in the bill as "the present conflict between Israelis and Palestinians" and as the "terror attacks," which were taking place on the territory and hurt the State of Israel and its citizens (Citizenship and Entry into Israel bill). This security context was presented as an exceptional situation and the law was presented as part of a state of exception. Hence, in the bill, the government demanded that the law was passed as an emergency regulation, which would be in force for one year, after which the Knesset could reenact the law only if the security situation needed it. When presenting the law, the government's representatives insisted very much on the exceptional character of the situation, which justified extraordinary steps regarding human rights. Thus, in his speech, the Minister of Interior started with these words:

> I want to tell you that this is not a law which I am happy with. I agree that this kind of measures should not be introduced in the legislation because for me, a society should allow family unification. However, the situation does not give us the choice and this law is emerging because we have no choice.
>
> (Minister Poraz, first reading of the law)

In this context, the notion of "defensive democracy" was invoked by the government to describe the need for a democracy in times of emergency, to exceptionally use non-democratic means in order to guarantee security of the State and of its citizens.[7]

Against the government's rationales, the law's opponents first focused on the security rationale itself. Although most of the MKs of this group referred to the terrorist attacks Israel was confronted by and thus agreed on the insecurity context Israeli citizens were living in, they challenged the validity of the security justification. For instance, one MK stated that "the government has ideological considerations that aim at scaring the Israeli public for demographic and birth control, by using the security argument again and again" (MK Makhoul, first reading of the law). Others emphasized the excessiveness with which the security argument was used by the government to justify rights curtailment. MK Galon from Meretz for instance stated that "It is true that the State of Israel must defend itself for its well-being and its security, but until what point is it possible to go in the name of security?" (first reading of the law). The second major point of contention related to the divergent vision of basic rights the law's opponents and its promoters presented. Here and against the emergency argument, the opponents challenged the very idea of infringing basic rights in the name of security. The law's opponents put the emphasis on the need to respect the right to family unification and to privacy, which were all basic rights seen as non-alterable in a state aiming at being a democracy. Another part of the MKs under-lined the "racist" dimension of the law. The argument was that the implementation of the law would apply first and foremost to Arab citizens who were more likely to marry a Palestinian resident than any other Israeli citizen. In this perspective, the law's opponents asserted that the law engendered a collect-ive punishment against the Palestinians who were all discriminated against in their right to marry freely, while the threat the State was facing came from spe-cific individuals rather than from the whole population.

Against these arguments, the supporters of the law articulated four counter-arguments. First, regarding the security context, the government and its sup-porters responded with a dramatized vision of the situation. While the bill had originally referred to the quite neutral conception of the "conflict opposing the Palestinians to the Israelis" and to the emergency situation, during the second and third readings, the promoters of the law mobilized the notion of "state of war" more than 30 times (second and third readings of the law). Second, against the argument that basic rights were not alterable whatever the situation, the par-tisans of the law raised two counter-arguments. Most of them confronted the right to marriage and to privacy of the Palestinians and the Arab citizens to another basic right: the Israeli citizens' right to life presented as the most essen-tial right that the State is entitled to protect. At the same time, both the govern-ment and the MKs referred to "defensive democracy" or to the need for a "democracy to protect itself" by exceptionally curtailing basic rights. On this issue, they emphasized the "difficult questions concerning the balance between human rights, the rights of the individual and the foundations of democracy on the one hand and the security needs on the other" (MK Stern, second reading of the law). In response to the opponents concerning the racist dimension of the law, the law's supporters answered that any Israeli person who would want to marry a Palestinian resident would be affected by the law, be they Arab or Jewish. Finally, against the critique concerning collective punishment, they stressed the impossibility of putting in place a case-by-case procedure in such matters as prevention against terrorist infiltration.

From the analysis of these debates, it is possible to identify two major visions of the threat, basic rights and regimes overlapping the two major positions over the law (in favor of the law and against it). Regarding the perception of the security context, if the two parts have referred to the threats the State was confronted by, we have seen that the supporters of the law have mobilized the notion of either "conflict between Palestinians and Israelis" or of a "state of war," hence stressing the opposition between the Israeli citizens and the "enemy foreigner," while the opponents have stressed an exceptional terrorist threat, hence contradicting the

Table 3.1 Debate structure in 2003

	Supporters	Opponents
Main argument	Need to face terror attacks	Security argument is only a pretext
Other justifications	Find a balance between liberty and security	Racist, anti-democratic Collective punishment
Vision of security context	War–conflict	Terrorism
Vision of the threat	Palestinian residents–potential terrorists	Terrorist individuals
Vision of human rights	Need to find a balance between right to life and other rights	Inalienable
Belief system	Defensive democracy	Universal democracy

vision of a clear identifiable threat. Thus, while the proponents of the law have presented the origin of the threat as emanating from "the Palestinians" as a cohesive social group, the opponents objected to this vision of the threat, which they labeled "racist". Second, the vision of basic rights put forward by the groups has differed greatly as well. While the proponents of the law underlined the need to find a balance between liberties of some (citizens and non-citizens) and security of the majority, the opponent group presented the rights of both citizens and non-citizens as inalienable. Underlying these visions and the positions of the MKs on the law, two different belief systems based on two regime central cores can be distinguished amongst which the first one imposed itself in the debates:

1   The *defensive democracy* belief system: promoted by the initiator of the law and a part of its supporters, this model is very similar to Locke's prerogative where, in times of emergency, the government is allowed to curtail temporarily the rights and liberties in order to preserve the majority's security. In this perspective, the State's *raison d'être* or the central core, is to preserve the majority's right to life.
2   The *universal democracy* belief system: promoted by a minority of MK, according to this model, the existence of the State is necessary to defend and protect all basic rights and distribute them equitably.

Debates over the prolongation of the law (2004–2007): the introduction of the defensive ethnocracy belief system

When the Citizenship and Entry into Israel temporary law arrived at the end of its term, the Knesset was asked to reenact the law, first in 2004 and then in 2005 and 2007. In 2004, the law was prolonged as a decree, voted by the Knesset after one reading. In 2005 and 2007, it has been passed after a regular procedure, due to the introduction of "humanitarian" amendments[8] taken mostly under the pressure of the Supreme Court[9] and of a new section expanding the scope of the law to citizens from Syria, Lebanon, Iraq, Iran and Gaza and to "anyone living in an area, in which operations that constitute a threat to the State of Israel are being carried out." The debates over the prolongation of the law on Citizenship and Entry into Israel are not studied separately because of the changes introduced by the law, which are considered as secondary elements. Rather, they are analyzed in a distinct section due to the drastic rupture that occurred on the semantic level.

As in 2003, two major positions can be identified in the discussions: that of the initiator and of the supporters of the law (mainly composed of the coalition partners and of the religious parties) and that of the law's opponents (composed of the Meretz and the Arab parties and of the Labor Party in 2004). However, contrary to the simple conflict between two belief systems opposing those claiming that the "state of war" justified basic right curtailments in order to guarantee security (the defensive democracy model) to those stating that universal democracy values needed to be protected even in times of insecurity, a third kind of belief system emerged in 2004 under the pressure of the law's opponents who introduced the issue of demography in the Knesset.

The issue which had already been raised in 2003 by MK Makhoul progressively gained attention in the debates and reached a peak in 2005 when all the opponents speaking in the plenum mentioned in their speech that the security argument "is false and is contradicted by the words of honorable persons such as the Prime Minister [...] who says that it is a demographic law" (MK Makhoul, second reading of the law). Basing themselves on declarations heard outside of the parliament, the opponents challenged the security rationale and highlighted the demographic orientation of the law. MK Galon for example stated "I hear the national security services and the ministers of the government and the MKs, and all are saying: we are scared of the demographic danger" (MK Galon, second reading of the law, 2005). One of the law's opponents went even further by asserting that the real fundamental question to be asked regarding the law was in fact whether the State first wanted to define itself as democratic or as a Jewish state (MK Oron, second reading 2005).

While the demographic issue had been vastly overlooked by the law's supporters in 2003 who did not respond to Makhoul's critique, this time, the debate focused largely on the issue and the original question "to what extent physical security justifies right's curtailment," which dominated in 2003 progressively shifted to "to what extent the preservation of a Jewish state justifies right's curtailment of the non-Jews?". In response to the question, the supporters of the law crystallized in three groups. A first important group composed of members of the coalitions categorically contested the demographic aim and stressed the defensive democracy argument, the exceptional state of emergency and the specific security objective of the law. A second group also composed from the government parties mobilized the defensive democracy model, while at the same time assuming the identity and demographic dimensions of the law. One Shinui MK for example stated that:

> It is true that preventing Palestinians who married to Israeli citizens to reside in Israel hurts democratic principles of rights equality, but we are a Jewish state by definition, as it has been defined at the independence. And with all due respect and sympathy, there exists a basic right to every son of the Jewish majority, to conserve and protect the State identity, namely its national, cultural identity, its public structure and its security. The decision is right even if it goes – and this is the case – against human rights.
>
> (MK Golan, second reading 2005)

In the same perspective, another MK combined both the defensive democracy model and the defense of the identity argument: starting by the statement that "the right to marriage is a very important right. But what if it stands against the right to security?", the same MK ended with the claim that "the right to family unification is an important right [...] but what the Arabs are asking is that the Jewish people renounce their right to self-definition, and this is really the issue of the debate" (MK Kahlon, plenary debates, 2004). Finally, a third minority group essentially composed of religious MKs overlooked the defensive democracy model and justified the legitimacy of the law by the fact that there exists "a right to fundamental defense, to demographic defense. We need to safeguard the Jewish majority in Eretz-Israel and all the answers are guided by this fact" (MK Zeev, plenary debates, 2004). For the last two groups, the security argument was thus seen from a new perspective. It was not only conceived as the possibility for Israeli citizens to preserve physical integrity and life but also or specifically as the capacity of the State to preserve the Jewish identity of the majority and of the State. In this perspective, the threat which was first described as emanating from the Palestinian residents because of their national links with terrorist movements was reconstructed as that coming from the mere presence on the territory of any non-Jewish person due to its otherness.

From this analysis, it is again possible to identify and link the vision of the security context, the perceived threat and the basic rights perception to the position on the law (see Table 3.2). This time however, three different types of belief systems have been in conflict:

1   The *defensive democracy* belief system: promoted by the initiators of the law and its supporters, the central core of this belief system is the protection of the majority's right to physical security. The policies to safeguard it are based on the Lockean prerogative model where basic rights can be curtailed in time of emergency.
2   The defensive Jewish democracy or *defensive ethnocracy*:[10] promoted by a section of the law's proponents (Likud and religious parties), in this model, the State is seen as necessary first and foremost to guarantee the preservation of the ethnic community and the identity of the State. It does so by preventing the *other* from establishing itself on the territory.
3   The *universal democracy*: promoted by a minority of MKs, in this model the State is necessary to defend basic rights and universal values. It does so by preserving the equal distributions of the rights.

Between these three belief systems, the defensive democracy belief system imposed itself once again. The supporters of the defensive democracy and the defensive ethnocracy models were however able to find a common position over the law. Both models indeed justified the limitation of the right to family unification of the Arab citizens and Palestinian residents. Besides, some of the ethnocracy defenders were also able to mobilize the defensive democracy arguments, a more legitimate and more widely shared vision of the regime, in order to justify their position on the law.

Amendment to the Law on Citizenship (2008): defensive democracy as conditional democracy

In July 2008, a new law was passed, which amended article 11 of the Law on Citizenship. The addition of this amendment followed several private bills presented to the Knesset after the first cases of citizenship cancellation and the

Table 3.2 Debate structure in 2004–2007

	Supporters 1	Supporters 2	Opponents
Major argument	Response to protect the citizens' security	Tool to protect the state's identity	Demographic objective
Other arguments	Rights and liberties can be dangerous tools	Rights and liberties can be dangerous tools	Racist Collective punishment
Vision of security	State of war	War	Terrorism
Threat perception	Potential terrorists	Demographic threat of the non-Jews	Terrorist individuals
Human rights vision	Need to find a balance between right to life and other rights	Basic right to defend the state's identity	Inalienable
Belief system	Defensive democracy	Defensive ethnocracy	Universal democracy

"Bishara affair."[11] Amongst those bills, many aimed at altering the procedures under which the Minister of Interior could use his authority. Others also required an alteration of the conditions under which citizenship could be granted and canceled. Guilad Erdan's bill, which received the support of the government and was finally voted in July 2008, entailed both aspects. On the one hand, the bill submitted proposed to alter the power of the Minister of Interior, who would pass his authority to cancel citizenship to administrative courts (except for the cancellation concerning a person who has been naturalized on the basis of false information). On the other hand, the bill provided a definition of "breach of trust," which after several discussion in the Internal Affairs committee were defined as "acts of terrorism, including support and aid to terrorist activities and belonging to a terrorist movement; acquisition of citizenship or permanent residence of a country considered at war with Israel [including Gaza]."[12] After numerous discussions in the plenary and in the Internal Affairs commission, the bill was voted with 26 votes in favor against 5 (third reading of the law).

An analysis of the debates leads to the identification of two major positions toward the law: that of the initiator of the law, supported by the Likud, the coalition parties, the religious and extreme right parties on the one hand; that of the left wing party Meretz and of the Arab parties. A dialectic debate between initiator-opponents and supporters of the law is again visible.

In Erdan's proposition, three major arguments were raised to justify the bill. The major rationale presented to support the law was the security context. The bill indeed mentioned that its objective was to create an efficient tool to "combat the enemies of Israel and the terrorist movements" (proposition 1708/17). Erdan's bill suggested that the existing law, which had been used no more than twice, was not efficient in this regard and therefore it proposed to "regularize the issue of the citizenship revocation for acts of breach of trust." Thus, while previous propositions had earlier suggested limiting cancellation of citizenship or denying it totally on the ground that it was in opposition to international charters,[13] Erdan's bill reasserted both the efficiency and the legitimacy of citizenship's cancellation. Referring to the concept of defensive democracy, Erdan first stressed that because the status of citizen provided rights and liberties that could be used against the State by "terrorists and their supporters," it should be better controlled. The bill concluded that in certain cases, canceling citizenship could constitute an efficient tool to "combat the enemy of Israel and terrorist movements." Finally, the bill mentioned that "a citizen cannot be citizen of a state that it aims at destroying."

In response to Erdan's rationales, the opponents of the bill invoked three major counter-arguments already partially raised during the debates on the Citizenship and Entry into Israel law. The first and most often mobilized argument concerned the curtailment of rights and liberties. The argument based itself on the existence of international conventions forbidding statelessness on the one hand, and on the implication of the cancellation of citizenship "a basic right from which every right follows" (MK Khenin, second reading of the law). A second argument tackled the illegitimacy of conceiving citizenship revocation as a penal sanction. Several MKs mentioned that regarding the important panel of "very tough punishments such as life sentences, it is not necessary to add cancellation of citizenship" (MK Beilin, second reading of the law) to the legislation. Finally, against Erdan's argument that the bill would regularize an existing tool, several MKs raised the illegitimacy "to normalize an abnormal prescription" (MK Khenin, first reading of the law).

To these critiques, the proponents of the law responded with several arguments, which in comparison to the debates on the law on Citizenship and Entry into Israel insisted much less on the security context. While the security context was a major element in Erdan's bill to justify the revocation of "such a basic right as the right to citizenship" (MK Erdan, first reading of the law), the supporters of the law evoked the terror context only twice and never mentioned the state of war which was invoked in the previous debates. Drawing on other arguments used by Erdan, the majority of the law's supporters mobilized three main counter-arguments. The first one related to the defensive democracy argument. Answering to MK Khenin, one promoter of the law for instance asserted that "every right knows limits and curtailment. There is no absolute right" (MK Eytan, first reading of the law). Responding to those challenging the creation of a new kind of penal sanction, several supporters of the law endorsed the idea that the revocation of citizenship was indeed an efficient sanction as no other one existed in the penal code against those who "assassinate their mother" (MK Eytan, second and third readings of the law). They also presented this sanction as a legitimate punishment for those suspected of wanting to "kill the State," hence unworthy of enjoying citizenship and the rights engendered by this status. Against these persons, the proponents of the law suggested that "a state is very enlightened if it tells them: if you act against the State you pretend that you belong to, you do not deserve to be its citizen" (MK Rivlin, first reading of the law).

Here again, it is possible to identify two belief systems with their own threat perception and conception of basic rights and with their specific central cores (see Table 3.3) and to link them with the positions on the law. While for the supporter of the law, the security context was not very much mobilized, the perceived threat was clearly labeled as that coming from "disloyal citizens." On the other hand, the law's opponents did not refer to the security context at all. Regarding basic rights, the same kind of antagonism as was present during the previous debates between the balance model promoters and those defending the inalienability of basic rights was again present during the discussion. However, the defensive democracy proponents added to the model of the balance, the notion of merit or conditionality, which was not present thus-far. The two major belief systems in conflict between the two groups can thus be summarized as follows:

1   The *defensive democracy* belief system: promoted by the supporters of the law, in this model the State's first objective is to protect the majority's right to physical security. The policies to safeguard it fluctuate between

the Lockean prerogative model where basic rights can be curtailed in time of emergency and a model where liberty exists only under certain conditions.

2   The *universal democracy* belief system: promoted by a minority of MKs, in this model the State is necessary to defend basic rights and universal values. It does so by preserving the equal distribution of these rights.

Between these two belief systems, the defensive democracy belief system put forward in Erdan's proposition has been the dominant model against the universal democracy one. While imposing itself, the belief system has also been reconstructed in the law-supporters' discourses. Indeed, the defensive democracy belief system that had thus-far referred to a Lockean state where the politics must temporarily and exceptionally balance between basic rights of a minority – of citizens and non-citizens - to the profit of the majority's security has been reframed in a model where the inclusion in the democratic regime becomes a facultative advantage of the individuals who can enjoy citizenship and its rights only if external conditions (the perceived security context) and internal conditions (express clear loyalty to the State) are encountered. Thus, from a defensive democracy balancing rights when needed, the regime model that imposed itself was turned into a conditional democracy that limits the access to the basic rights it provides.

Conclusion

The first objective of this chapter was to demonstrate that the security–liberty paradigm is not satisfying in order to understand the processes that are at work in democracies faced by perceived/existing security threats. The analysis of specific "security" laws in Israel has shown that the security–liberty balance and the consequent notion of a trade-off between rights and security or here, the *defensive democracy* model, was indeed only the policy core of a belief system, where the preservation of the *majority*'s physical security was the central core. In the Israeli case, the liberty–security balance is thus the reflection of a strong majoritarian conception of the regime where the State's first duty is to preserve the majority's physical security, whatever the cost for the minority's basic rights. In the debates under scrutiny, this specific belief system has clashed or coexisted with two other belief systems: the *universal democracy* model, of which the central core is the equitable protection of basic rights and the *defensive ethnocracy* model where the central core is the protection of the Jewish identity of the State. These latter belief systems were both marginal at the time of the analysis, but could be predominant in other circumstances. Had it been the case at the time, the outcome in terms of legislation would probably have been very different. For instance, if the universal democracy belief system had prevailed, it is doubtful that the laws which have been proposed would have succeeded, at least in their present version, as they contravene the belief system's very central core, namely, the equal distribution of basic rights. On the other hand, had the

Table 3.3 Debate structure in 2008

	Supporters	Opponents
Major argument	Useful tool to defend the citizens' security	Take away the most fundamental right of a human being
Other arguments	Regularization of a tool not enough used Fair punishment The enemy of the states do not deserve its protection	There exist enough punishment against criminals Its target is essentially the Arab population
Vision of security	Terror attacks	Not mentioned
Threat perception	Disloyal citizens	Not mentioned
Vision of basic rights	Can be a dangerous tool Have to be deserved	Inalienable
Belief system	Defensive democracy	Universal democracy

defensive ethnocracy model been dominant, the Supreme Court's demand to add humanitarian amendments to the Citizenship and Entry into Israel Law would probably have been disregarded as, in that belief system, the mere presence of non-Jews on the territory is perceived as a threat to its central core (preservation of the Jewish identity of the State).

The imposition of the defensive democracy belief system engendered two major consequences. It first has a direct impact on the legislation and consequently on the Palestinians and the minority's basic rights which have been curtailed with the enactment of the laws. But beyond the impact of the legislation itself, the imposition of the defensive democracy belief system as reconstructed during the debates is of crucial importance for the fabrication of the political regime in Israel. The use and imposition of the defensive democracy model as defined during the debates over the laws engendered – or reasserted – on the one hand, a vision of the regime where physical security of the majority must prevail over the liberties of the minority. On the other hand, the model as reconstructed in 2008 implies that basic rights are not defined as automatically produced by democracy any more but as a rare privilege, which can be granted only if security conditions allow it and if loyalty of the citizens to the State's institution is proven. In that perspective, the defensive democracy has indeed become a conditional democracy where, in order to safeguard the majority's physical security, the very inclusion of citizens in the polity is uncertain.

Deconstructing the debates over security politics as has been done in this chapter thus appears very helpful not only to understand the imposition of specific legislation in the name of security, but also to envisage which kind of political regime is being constructed and reconstructed over time by the legislator. For further research, it would be interesting to confront the belief systems identified in the parliament with other discourses outside of the Knesset, such as those of statesmen, but also of the Supreme Court and journalists, in order to better grasp the dominant belief system in the society in its entirety. More generally, deconstructing debates over other "security" legislations and comparing different national case studies through the approach which was mobilized would be of interest in order to draw more general and transversal conclusions on the place of conflicting belief systems in the elaboration of security politics.

Notes

1 On this topic see Meisel (2005) and Neocleous (2007).
2 See among others section 9 of the US Constitution which raises the possibility of suspending the writ of habeas corpus in time of insecurity; the Canadian Constitution, which allows the government to restrict the Bill of Rights in time of emergency; and the European Convention of Human Rights, which specifies that several rights can be restrained in the interests of "national security, public safety or the economic well-being of the country" (Convention for the Protection of Human Rights and Fundamental Freedoms as amended by Protocol No. 11).
3 See Meisel, Waldron and Neocleous on this issue.
4 "L'objet des politiques publiques n'est plus seulement de 'résoudre des problèmes' mais de construire des cadres d'interprétations du monde."

5 The spouse of a person who is an Israeli national or who has applied for Israeli nationality and meets or is exempt from the requirements of section 5 (1) may obtain Israeli nationality by naturalization even if she or he is a minor or does not meet the requirements of section (5) (1).
6 The States are Lebanon, Egypt, Syria, Saudi-Arabia, Trans-Jordan, Iraq and Yemen (Prevention of infiltration (offences and jurisdiction) law, 1954).
7 Introduced by the Israeli Supreme Court in the 1960s to denote the need for a democratic regime to protect itself from those who want to undermine it from within (Pedahzur 2002: 4), the defensive democracy concept has later been used by the Supreme Court of Israel to designate the need for a democratic state confronted by a state of emergency to find a balance between security and human rights (Barak 2002).
8 In the version of 2005 an age limitation and some other exceptions to the rule determining when the Minister of Interior could grant residence permits were added: medical treatment; working in Israel; and a temporary purpose, provided that the permit to stay for such a purpose shall not exceed the cumulative period of six months. In 2007, another section was added to the law, which established a special committee in charge of assessing the humanitarian aspects of a demand to come to Israel and to make recommendations to the Minister on this basis.
9 In 2003, the Adalah center went to the Supreme Court to challenge the constitutionality of the law. In its ruling, the Supreme Court ruled with 6 in favor against 5, that the law was constitutional. However, it made some recommendations to the government to take humanitarian needs into account. (HCJ 7052/03 Adalah Legal Centre for *Arab Minority Rights in Israel and others* v. *Minister of Interior*, 05–14–2006).
10 This concept is borrowed from Yftachel, who defines the ethnocratic regime as one that "promotes the expansion of the dominant group in contested territories and its domination of power structures while maintaining a democratic facade" (Yiftachel 2006: 3).
11 In September 2006, Bishara and two other Israeli Arab MKs visited Syria illegally. Following this event, the Security services announced they had enough evidence to indict Bishara for crimes, amongst which, aid to the enemy. Bishara then decided to resign from his function in the Knesset.
12 The original bill only proposed to integrate in the definition of breach of trust the illegal entering in an enemy state and the acquisition of citizenship of an enemy state.
13 See, e.g. the proposition of MK Cohen, Vilan and Galon in 2005 and proposition of Ophir Pines-Paz in 2005.

References

Books and articles

Ackerman, B. (2004) "The Emergency Constitution,", *The Yale Law Journal*, 13: 1029–1091.
Barak, A. (2002) "A Judge on Judging: The Role of a Supreme Court in a Democracy," *Harvard Law Review*, 116: 6–160.
Buzan, B., Waever O. and Jaap de Wilde (eds.) (1998) *Security: a new framework for analysis*, Boulder, CO: Lynne Rienner Publisher.
Campbell, D. (1992) *Writing Security. United States Foreign Policy and the Politics of Identity*, Minneapolis: University of Minnesota Press.
Cole, D. (2004) "The Priority of Morality: The Emergency Constitution's Blind Spot," *The Yale Law Journal*, 113: 1763–1800.

72   S. Weinblum

Duez, D. (2008) *L'Union européenne et l'immigration clandestine. De la sécurité intérieure à la construction de la communauté politique*, Bruxelles: Presses Universitaires de Bruxelles.

Huysmans, J. (1998) "Security! What do you mean? From Concept to Thick Signifier," *European Journal of International Relations*, 4: 226–255.

—— (2000) "The European Union and the Securitization of Migration," *Journal of Common Market Studies*, 38: 751–777.

Huysmans, J. and Buonfino, A. (2008) "Politics of Exception and Unease," *Political Studies*, 56: 766–788.

Ignatieff, M. (2004) *The Lesser Evil: Political Ethics in an Age of Terrorism*, Princeton, NJ: Princeton University Press.

Jacskon, R. (2007) "Constructing Enemies: 'Islamic Terrorism' in Political and Academic Discourse," *Government and Opposition*, 42: 394–426.

Meisel, T. (2005) "How Terrorism Upsets Liberty," *Political Studies*, 53: 162–181.

Muller, P. and Surel, Y. (1998) *L'analyse des politiques publiques*, Paris: Montchrestien.

Muller, P. (2000) "L'analyse cognitive des politiques publiques. Vers une sociologie politique de l'action publique," *Revue française de science politique*, 50: 189–207.

Neocleous, M. (2007) "Security, Liberty and the Myth of Balance: Towards a Critique of Security Politics," *Contemporary Political Theory*, 6: 131–149.

Norton, D. and Collins, A. (2004) "US Conflict Behavior and Supreme Court Decision Making: an empirical Analysis of the Crisis Thesis," Paper for the *Annual Meeting of the New York State political Science Association*, April 23–24.

Pedahzur, A. (2002) *The Israeli response to Jewish extremism and violence*, Manchester: Manchester University Press.

Peleg, I. (2004) "Israeli Foreign Policy under Right-Wing Governments: A Constructivist Interpretation,", *Israeli Studies Forum*, 19: 1–14.

Sabatier, P.A. (1987) "Knowledge, Policy-Oriented Learning, and Policy Change: An Advocacy Coalition Framework," *Science Communication*, 8: 647–687.

Sabatier, P.A. and Schlager, E. (2000), "Les approches cognitives des politiques publiques: perspectives américaines," *Revue française de science politique*, 50 (2): 209–234.

Schneider, A. and Ingram, H. (1993) "Social Construction of Target Populations: Implications for Politics and Policy," *American Political Science Review*, 87: 334–347.

Waever, O. (1995) "Securitization and Desecuritization," in R.D. Lipschutz (ed.), *On Security*, New York: Columbia University Press, pp. 46–86.

Waldron, J. (2003) "Security and Liberty: The image of a Balance," *Journal of Political Philosophy*, 11: 191–210.

Yiftachel, O. (2006) *Ethnocracy: Land and Identity Politics in Israel/Palestine*, Philadelphia: University of Pennsylvania Press.

Documents

Citizenship and Entry into Israel law

Government bill 06–04–2003.
First reading of the law 06–17–2003.
Second and third readings of the law 07–27–2003 and 07–31–2003.
Plenary debates 07–20–2004; 07–21–2004.

First reading of the law 05–25–2005.
Second and third readings of the law 07–27–2005.
Plenary discussions 12–19–2006 and 01–15–2007.

Law on citizenship

Bill 1708/17 (amendment 9), 11–13–2006.
First reading of the law, 10–16–2007.
Second and third readings of the law, 07–27–2008.
All sources found on the online Knesset Protocols: www.knesset.gov.il/divrey/qform.asp.

Part II

Citizenship and war

An historical perspective

4 The alien–citizen distinction and the global war on terrorism

Tung Yin and David Abraham[1]

Since the start of the modern civil rights era, the notably harsh laws of citizenship and immigration in the United States (and elsewhere[2]) have experienced some mitigation in the critical distinctions between citizens and aliens (*Graham* v. *Richardson* (1971) 403 U.S. 365; *Fiallo* v. *Bell* (1977) 430 U.S. 787; *Landon* v. *Plascensia* (1982) 459 U.S. 21; *Reno* v. *American Arab Anti-Discrimination Committee* (1999) 525 U.S. 471). Societies became "soft" on the "inside" while grappling with questions of how "hard" to be toward the "outside," the border (Bosniak 2007; Walzer 1983). The retrograde effects of globalization together with our security and imperial obsessions since 9/11, however, have led to a hardening of distinctions both on the inside and toward the outside. Immigration and citizenship have become more Schmittian affairs where the worthy "us" is confronted by the enemy "other." The power of exclusion and especially of deportation has again grown more important (as it was during the Red Scares of the post-WWI and Cold War periods[3]), making citizenship more important.

As the government seeks to undermine constitutional protections in three ways – making it irrelevant who you are, where you are, or whose custody you are in – the benefits of the legal status of "citizen" seem to be in play. At the same time, we know the importance of citizenship as a mechanism for the defense of rights, perhaps especially of minority rights. Indeed, liberal immigration scholars have spent most of the past generation fretting over the discriminatory "bonus" offered by citizenship and have worked "human rights" and "due process" discourses to undermine that bonus (Schuck 1998: 163–175; Bosniak 2007: 77–101). Since 9/11, however, a series of important Supreme Court cases has left us with only a murky sense of what rights apply to whom and where and how much of a guarantee "citizenship" offers.

In this chapter, we review the salient cases and seek to identify some current baselines around these "who, where, and whom" questions. To the extent that they provide concrete answers, Supreme Court decisions are, of course, a primary source of authority. However, we also discuss the government's reaction in many of the key cases, because the government's perception of the political acceptability of its actions is also a useful marker.

Early precedents to the end of the twentieth century

The constitutional challenges posed by military detention of citizens and aliens, and of government action in foreign lands, were slow to develop over the years. Many, though by no means all, of the key decisions arose in the context of wars or armed conflict; others involved immigration regulations. A detailed account of the myriad precedents is far beyond the scope of this chapter, but here we will provide a general sense of the legal landscape that evolved up to the time of the 9/11 attacks.

It is most helpful to consider how citizenship, geography, and individual rights can interact and arise in four different settings: U.S. citizens inside the United States; U.S. citizens outside the United States; aliens inside the United States; and aliens outside the United States. Of course, constitutional law could have (but did not) developed in a way that rendered these distinctions irrelevant, with the Constitution restricting the federal government the same way regardless of whom the government was acting on, and where.

American citizens in the United States are unquestionably covered by the Constitution and the Bill of Rights; the question to be resolved whenever the government seeks to act against the individual is the scope of those rights. Thus, when the Union military proceeded to prosecute and convict an Indiana citizen in a military court for attempting to assist the Confederacy during the Civil War, the Supreme Court in *Ex Parte Milligan* (1866) 71 U.S. 2, 119[4] held that so long as civilian courts were open and functioning, U.S. citizens had to be prosecuted in them, rather than in a military court, for it was "the birthright of every American citizen when charged with crime to be tried and punished according to law." *Milligan*'s expansive rule was later cut back in the German saboteurs case, *Ex Parte Quirin* (1942) 317 U.S. 1 where the Supreme Court permitted the military prosecution of a German soldier with dual U.S.–German citizenship who was captured out of uniform in the United States, on the ground that citizenship did not relieve the soldier of the consequences of violating the laws of war while fighting for an enemy army. And of course, citizenship did not protect 70,000 Japanese-Americans (along with 40,000 Japanese legal residents) from being shipped off to internment camps during World War II based only on their racial ancestry, government discrimination that was upheld by the Supreme Court in the Japanese Internment Cases. This is to say that even for citizens inside the United States, rights are not unlimited.

The question of whether constitutional rights were available for citizens outside the United States – that is, whether, as commentators have put it, the Constitution followed the flag (see, e.g., Raustiala 2009) was spurred in large part by the American acquisition of territories outside what is now the contiguous United States; territories such as Puerto Rico, Hawaii, and others. Unlike North American territories prior to statehood, which tended to have been populated by American settlers and thus to have amassed a degree of cultural and political familiarity with the rest of the country, these new territories were often populated by persons of quite different cultures, for whom American notions of due process, jury trials, and the like might have clashed with indigenous justice (Burnett and Marshall 2001).

The group of cases that collectively addressed this question, the Insular Cases, stand for the proposition that not all constitutional rights are available in U.S. territories, only ones deemed "fundamental" (Burnett 2005, p. 800). These early precedents therefore did not begin to draw sharp distinctions between citizens and non-citizens. They did, however, establish geography as a relevant consideration in determining the scope of rights available to citizens. Later cases, primarily involving U.S. persons tried in military courts overseas in the post-World War II era, eroded the significance of that distinction for citizens, so that today, it is a safe assumption that American citizens generally retain their constitutional rights overseas.

Aliens, on the other hand, have had a more tenuous existence. As recently as World War II, resident aliens who were citizens of enemy nations, though themselves non-combatants, were subject to summary deportation (Gudridge 2003, 2005). The Alien Enemy Act of 1798 gave the President the authority to expel enemy aliens – that is, citizens of countries with which the United States was at war – without any judicial oversight, a power that Presidents Roosevelt and Truman used, even as late as 1946, when hostilities between Germany and the United States had ended, though the state of war had not. The Supreme Court upheld this extended use of the Alien Enemy Act in *Ludecke* v. *Watkins* (1948) 335 U.S. 160. Non-resident aliens were even subject to military prosecution, as in the *Quirin* case involving the German saboteurs. Even after World War II, resident aliens have found themselves virtually powerless to avoid deportation based on having been a member of a disfavored group, such as the Communist Party, with the result that deportation became "a weapon of defense and reprisal" that a state may deploy against suspected adversaries (*Harisiades* v. *Shaughnessy* (1952) 342 U.S. 580, 587).[5]

For aliens outside the United States, the legal rules were even more grim during the twentieth century, for they were deemed to have no judicially enforceable rights at all according to *Johnson* v. *Eisentrager* (1950) 339 U.S. 763. *Eisentrager* continued to cast its shadow long after; during the Clinton Administration in the 1990s, for example, the U.S. Navy intercepted numerous Haitian refugees attempting to enter the country by boat; these refugees were diverted to the U.S. naval base on Guantanamo Bay, Cuba, where they were held until they were repatriated to Haiti. All court challenges to this policy ultimately failed on the grounds that the refugees (obviously not U.S. citizens) were outside the United States and hence no federal court had jurisdiction to hear their cases (see, e.g., *Cuban American Bar Ass'n, Inc.* v. *Christopher* (1995) 43 F.3d 1412; *Haitian Refugee Ctr.* v. *Gracey* (1987) 809 F.2d 794; *Jean* v. *Nelson* (1985) 727 F.2d 957).

Despite their non-combatant status, would-be immigrants have fared no better than enemy fighters overseas. Under what is known as the Plenary Power Doctrine, the Court has abdicated its role of reviewing Congressional regulation of alien immigrants seeking entry into the country. A representative case is *Shaughnessy* v. *United States ex rel. Mezei* (1953) 345 U.S. 206 in which the Supreme Court concluded that an alien once lawfully admitted to the country but who had left in an attempt to visit his dying mother, could be not only denied re-entry to the United States, but also detained indefinitely on Ellis Island, when no other country was willing to admit him.

The 9/11 attacks and the American response

Just about 60 years after the sneak attack on Pearl Harbor, the United States suffered a staggering blow on September 11, 2001, when 19 terrorists from Saudi Arabia, Egypt, Yemen, and the United Arab Emirates hijacked four American passenger jetliners and deliberately crashed three of them into America's twin icons, the Pentagon in Washington, D.C., and the World Trade Center in New York City resulting in about 3000 deaths and considerable humiliation; the fourth plane crashed in a field in Pennsylvania after the passengers fought back and tried unsuccessfully to regain control. Perhaps because of the existence of earlier intelligence reports predicting unspecified attacks, the White House could almost immediately identify the terrorist group al Qaeda as the likely culprit.[6] Roughly translated as "the Base," al Qaeda, led by Osama bin Laden and Ayman al-Zawahiri, aimed to force the United States and other Western nations out of the Middle East (Wright 2006). At the time of the 9/11 attacks, al Qaeda was based in strife-torn Afghanistan and sheltered by the Taliban government – itself previously armed and advised by the United States in a successful effort to topple a progressive secular government supported by the Soviet Union.

On September 17, 2001, Congress passed a sweeping Authorization to Use Military Force (AUMF) that empowered President Bush to launch military strikes against "those nations, organizations, or persons he determines planned, authorized, committed, or aided the terrorist attacks that occurred on September 11, 2001, or harbored such organizations or persons" (*Authorization to Use Military Force* 2001).[7] Less than two months later, the United States attacked Afghanistan with air strikes and limited ground forces fighting in tandem with the Northern Alliance (the Afghan enemies of the Taliban). The Taliban forces quickly abandoned their strongholds in Kabul and Kandahar and morphed into a guerrilla insurgency that persists to the present. A few top al Qaeda leaders, like Mohammed Atef, were killed early on, but bin Laden and al-Zawahiri escaped to remote mountainous regions of Afghanistan.

American and British soldiers and Northern Alliance fighters also captured thousands of suspected Taliban and al Qaeda fighters. In addition, on the home front, the government began rooting out suspected "sleeper cells" – homegrown terrorists – most of whom were prosecuted but a few of whom were also placed in military detention. The disposition of those captured fighters spawned a series of thorny constitutional problems that involved the Supreme Court and Congress on multiple occasions.

In this part, we first provide a descriptive analysis of the practical significance of U.S. versus foreign citizenship in terms of the Bush Administration's initial classification of enemy fighters as enemy combatants subject to military detention or as criminal defendants subject to prosecution in federal courts. As we will demonstrate, the government's classification decisions do not admit of any easily observable set of rules based upon citizenship or geography. Next, we examine the Supreme Court's response to legal challenges brought against the Bush Administration's military detention policies, along with Congress's legislative reaction to some of those court decisions. Finally, we conclude this part by identifying the scope of detainee rights in light of the Supreme Court's recent decision in *Boumediene* v. *Bush* (2008) 128 S. Ct. 2229 and positing theories on how those rights will be further refined under the Obama administration.

The alien–citizen distinction in practice

"Citizenship" and "location of capture" would have served as easily applied, if not entirely legally defensible distinctions, in determining how to treat captured enemy fighters, and would have seemed consistent with precedents such as *Eisentrager*, *Reid* v. *Covert*, and *Quirin*. Any American citizen, regardless of place of capture, could have been prosecuted in a civilian court under various federal criminal laws ranging from providing material support to a designated foreign terrorist organization to treason. Any non-citizen captured inside the United States could also have been prosecuted in a federal court. If captured outside the United States – for example, in Afghanistan – a non-citizen could have been handled through the military system, either for detention as an enemy combatant (in the United States or in situ) or for prosecution in a military commission.[8] To be clear, the point is not that such distinctions would have been the best approach to dealing with captured fighters, nor that they would necessarily have passed constitutional muster. The point is merely that such an approach would have been clearly understood at home and abroad and monitored by existing agencies such as the Red Cross.

In any event, the government's initial forum choices were much less predictable. According to then-Defense Secretary Donald Rumsfeld, about 10,000 persons were captured in Afghanistan during the first several months of armed conflict, and about 1,000 of those were transferred to the U.S. naval base at Guantanamo Bay, Cuba. With one exception, none of these detainees was a U.S. citizen. The one exception was Yaser Esam Hamdi, who was held at Guantanamo Bay until interrogators learned that he held U.S. citizenship by virtue of having been born in Baton Rouge, Louisiana. At that point, the Defense Department moved him from Guantanamo Bay to a Navy brig in Norfolk, Virginia, where he remained in military detention until late 2004 (*Hamdi* v. *Rumsfeld* (2004) 542 U.S. 507). Meanwhile, one other American citizen captured in Afghanistan, John Walker Lindh, was quickly taken into custody by FBI agents and brought back to the United States, where he was indicted in a federal court. Dubbed the "American Taliban" (also "white," "originally Christian," and "rich") by the press, Lindh was afforded a panoply of constitutional and statutory rights, including access to a highly regarded San Francisco defense attorney retained by his father and an opportunity to be tried by a jury of his peers (Gerth, Dec. 10, 2001, p. B3; *United States* v. *Lindh* (2002) 227 F.Supp. 2d 565). The

Lindh trial was surely not going to provide a template for subsequent prosecutions. Hamdi, the swarthy Arab who looked the part of a "real" terrorist, was denied these rights, though the military did allow him to meet with a public defender as a matter of courtesy in the last year of his detention.[9]

With regard to suspected terrorists captured within the United States, the picture was equally unclear. The Justice Department prosecuted numerous American citizens suspected of being involved with, or at least inspired by al Qaeda, typically for providing material support to a designated foreign terrorist organization. Attorney General John Ashcroft touted two high profile convictions of "sleeper cells" – one in Lackawanna, New York, and the other in Portland, Oregon. While the material support prohibition laws have been criticized for their potential overbreadth and inhibiting of free expression, these defendants – like Lindh – were afforded all of their criminal procedure rights. Although prosecutors were put under great pressure to deliver convictions, in form at least, the defendants received real trials.[10]

Not all citizens, however, were handled through the criminal justice system. In May 2002, pursuant to an arrest warrant issued by then-Chief U.S. District Judge Michael Mukasey, government agents detained Jose Padilla as he stepped off an international flight at Chicago's O'Hare International Airport. The government claimed that Padilla had plotted with Abu Zubaydah, reportedly al Qaeda's third-in-command, to construct and detonate a radiological (i.e., "dirty") bomb in an American city. Padilla was taken from Chicago to New York City to be detained as a material witness, but when his court-appointed attorney began to litigate the propriety of his designation as a material witness, President Bush declared Padilla to be an "enemy combatant" and ordered Defense Secretary Rumsfeld to take Padilla into custody. Notwithstanding his American citizenship, Padilla found himself transported to a Navy brig in Charleston, South Carolina. He was not charged with any crime, was denied access to a lawyer, and was kept in solitary confinement in a cell approximately the same size as that given to inmates in Supermax facilities (*Rumsfeld* v. *Padilla* (2004) 542 U.S. 426). Apart from being detained physically on United States soil, Padilla (and Hamdi) were treated essentially the same as non-citizens held at Guantanamo Bay, except that the latter were actually more able to communicate with other detainees.

One non-citizen captured on U.S. soil, Ali al-Marri, was also designated an enemy combatant. A citizen of Qatar, al-Marri had earned his undergraduate degree from Bradley University in Peoria, Illinois, in the 1980s, returned to Qatar, and then re-entered the United States with his family on September 10, 2001, ostensibly to earn a graduate degree at Bradley University. He came to the attention of the FBI after a Guantanamo Bay detainee identified him as a relative. Government agents questioned him in Peoria and then charged him with credit card fraud and with making false statements. After his lawyer began defending against the charges, however, President Bush declared al-Marri an enemy combatant and had the Defense Department take custody of him; he was detained in a naval brig in South Carolina (*al-Marri* v. *Pucciarelli* (2008) 534

F.3d 213, 217). The conditions of confinement were similar to those for the detainees at Guantanamo Bay: nearly total isolation, interrogations, temperature manipulation, and sleep interruptions.

Yet, it was not even the case that all non-citizens were either kept in Afghanistan or shipped off to Guantanamo. Zacarias Moussaoui, a French citizen living in the United States, remains after nearly eight years the only person charged criminally with participation in the 9/11 attacks. Already in federal custody in the United States on immigration charges on September 11, 2001, Moussaoui was subsequently indicted for conspiracy to commit terrorism and air piracy and other related charges based on suspicions that he was supposed to have been the twentieth 9/11 hijacker (Johnston and Shenon, December 12, 2001, p. A1). It seemed incongruous that a non-citizen suspected of such intimate involvement with the 9/11 plot would be treated as a criminal, not an enemy combatant, while a U.S. citizen such as Padilla would not receive similar treatment, particularly since Padilla's alleged activities took place wholly inside the country. Furthermore, another non-citizen, Richard Reid of Great Britain, was not even on U.S. territory when he attempted to destroy a passenger jet over the Atlantic Ocean. Yet he too was indicted on terrorism-related charges and prosecuted in a civilian court, where he eventually pleaded guilty and received a life sentence (Belluck, January 31, 2003, p. A13).

In short, it is difficult to identify or infer any rules regarding the treatment of similarly-situated citizens and non-citizens. Generally speaking, but not always, persons captured in the United States have been prosecuted in civil courts, while persons captured outside have been treated as enemy combatants. In one way, however, the government drew a clear line between citizens and non-citizens: military trials. President Bush's November 13, 2001 executive order authorized the use of military commissions to prosecute non-citizens who are members of al Qaeda, international terrorists, or those who harbored international terrorists (*Military Order of November 13, 2001*).

The Supreme Court decisions

Even if the Bush Administration had taken a more transparent and consistent approach toward its classification decisions, it no doubt would have faced court challenges to its substantive authority to detain persons as enemy combatants. Not surprisingly, then, its opaque policies led to three Supreme Court decisions in 2004 alone, involving Hamdi (*Hamdi* v. *Rumsfeld* (2004) 542 U.S. 507), Padilla (*Rumsfeld* v. *Padilla* (2004) 542 U.S. 426), and Rasul (*Rasul* v. *Bush* (2004) 542 U.S. 466). Collectively, the trio of decisions provided some clarity regarding the respective rights of citizens and aliens, but also left unresolved a number of other questions regarding the rights of aliens as compared to those of citizens. Two years later, in *Hamdan* v. *Rumsfeld* (2006) 548 U.S. 557 the Court answered some more of the unsettled questions, but still left others unresolved. Two years after that, in *Boumediene* v. *Bush* (2008) 128 S. Ct. 2229 the Court took yet another step but continued to leave open some difficult and complex questions.

The two issues in *Hamdi* (2004) 542 U.S. 507, 509 relevant here were whether the President had the legal authority to detain an American citizen as an enemy combatant and, if so, what rights the citizen had to challenge his designation. As to the President's legal authority to detain, the Court noted that the German saboteurs case (*Quirin*) stood for the proposition that citizenship did not relieve one of the consequences of joining the enemy, and that if the United States were entitled to kill Hamdi during armed conflict on the battlefield, it surely could detain him as an enemy combatant (*Hamdi* (2004) 542 U.S. 507, 518–524). The key difference between the state of the law during World War II and the present was the Non-Detention Act (1971). Hamdi argued that no federal law authorized his detention as an enemy combatant and therefore he was entitled to be charged with a crime (with the accompanying rights to counsel and a jury trial) or to be released. The Supreme Court disagreed, concluding that the Authorization for Use of Military Force enacted by Congress on September 17, 2001, constituted Congress's authorization of the President's power to detain American citizens as enemy combatants, despite the fact that the AUMF failed to state explicitly that such power was given to the President (*Hamdi* (2004) 542 U.S. 507, 518–519).[11] However, the Court also concluded that Hamdi was entitled to a hearing in which to challenge his designation as an enemy combatant, and that he was entitled to the assistance of an attorney at this hearing (*Hamdi* (2004) 542 U.S. 507, 533–539).

In *Rasul* v. *Bush* (2004) 542 U.S. 466, 470 the Court considered whether those non-citizen detainees were entitled to file petitions for habeas corpus as a vehicle for challenging their detention. The government had argued that they did not, based on the rule from *Johnson* v. *Eisentrager* (*Rasul* (2004) 542 U.S. 466, 475–476 (citing *Johnson* v. *Eisentrager* (1950) 339 U.S. 763, 777). As in *Eisentrager*, the detainees were aliens held outside U.S. territory. The Court disagreed with the government's argument, based in part on a technical reading of cases decided after *Eisentrager* that the Court viewed as having weakened the precedents underlying *Eisentrager* (*Rasul* v. *Bush* (2004) 542 U.S. 466, 476–479). While *Rasul* may have hinted that the Court intended for the Guantanamo detainees to have more rights than those explicitly identified, it did not have to be read so broadly. Indeed, after *Rasul* was decided, a federal trial judge presiding over a collection of habeas petitions ruled against the detainees on the ground that they were allowed to file those petitions, but as aliens outside the country, they enjoyed no rights that could be vindicated (*Khalid* v. *Bush* (2005) 355 F.Supp. 2d 311).

In *Rumsfeld* v. *Padilla* (2004) 542 U.S. 426 the Court was asked to review Jose Padilla's detention, but declined to do so on what to posterity might appear to be technical grounds. According to the Court's interpretation of its precedents, a detainee such as Padilla who wanted to use the writ of habeas corpus as a vehicle for challenging his detention had to file that petition in a court with jurisdiction over the detainee's custodian. Padilla was being held in Charleston, South Carolina, but his court-appointed lawyer had filed the petition with a New York court, the location of his first detention, ostensibly as a material witness. Therefore, the Court ordered his petition dismissed, but allowed him to refile in the proper court (*Rumsfeld* v. *Padilla* (2004) 542 U.S. 426, 451). This judicial sleight of hand provided the Bush regime with a much more reliably pro-Executive Branch 4th Circuit forum. But it also deprived us all of the key show-down: what rights remain to a U.S. citizen taken inside the United States?

Although their messages are somewhat mixed, the *Hamdi/Rasul/Padilla* trilogy began to break down the distinction between citizens and aliens on a functional basis. While *Hamdi* was something of a defeat for the Bush Adminis-tration, its impact was limited due to its focus on Hamdi's citizenship. If any-thing, it therefore appeared to highlight and heighten the distinction between those with American citizenship and those without. By mid-2004, it was estab-lished that the former had the right to challenge the factual basis of detention with the assistance of counsel. At the same time, however, non-citizens being held at Guantanamo Bay had much less clear rights, as demonstrated by the trial judge who allowed the petitions to be filed but dismissed them for lack of any viable rights to be vindicated (*Khalid* v. *Bush* (2005) 355 F.Supp. 2d 311).

At President Bush's urging, Congress responded to *Rasul* by enacting the Detainee Treatment Act of 2005 (DTA), which, among other things, amended the federal habeas corpus statute in an apparent attempt to eliminate most avenues of judicial review for non-citizens detained at Guantanamo Bay (Detainee Treatment Act (2005)). To be sure, the DTA also regulated the stand-ards for interrogation and treatment of those detainees, but the overall thrust of the statute was to take away the presumptive rights that *Rasul* had given detain-ees independent of their citizenship and to restore the deference to the Executive Branch exhibited in *Eisentrager*. At around the same time, September 2004, the government and Hamdi reached an agreement whereby Hamdi gave up his U.S. citizenship, waived all potential legal claims against the United States relating to his treatment during his years of detention, and promised not to attack the United States or its interests. In exchange, the United States released him to Saudi Arabia (Brinkley and Lichtblau, October 12, 2004, p. A15).

Jose Padilla re-filed his habeas petition in the proper court on July 2, 2004 (*Padilla* v. *Hanft* (2005) 389 F. Supp. 2d 678). Further litigation ensued, and a lower court at one point decided that if Padilla had carried weapons for the Taliban in Afghanistan – as alleged by the government – then it did not matter that he had been captured in the United States as opposed to Afghanistan, because it would mean that he was an active enemy of the United States fighting abroad (*Padilla* v. *Hanft* (2005) 423 F.3d 386). Elaboration and exploration of that argument would have been interesting for the issues being considered here. However, the government abruptly indicted Padilla on terrorism-related charges and transferred him from the custody of the military back to the Justice Depart-ment. Curiously, the criminal charges had nothing to do with the allegations jus-tifying Padilla's military detention; rather, the government accused Padilla of participating in a scheme to raise money and to recruit men for terrorist groups in Chechnya, Bosnia, and other European locations. The case went to trial in an ordinary court[12] in 2007, and Padilla was convicted by a jury, receiving a 17-year sentence of imprisonment (Semple, January 23, 2008, p. A14).

The Supreme Court returned to the war on terrorism in *Hamdan* v. *Rumsfeld* (2006) 548 U.S. 557. Hamdan was believed to have acted as Osama bin Laden's bodyguard and driver, and the Bush Administration designated him for a military war crimes trial. His military-appointed lawyer filed a habeas petition on his behalf, challenging the military's power to subject Hamdan to trial in a military court whose procedures differed greatly from those used in courts-martial, the framework in which allegedly criminal POWs are often (though not always) tried (Jinks 2004, p. 372n.21). When Congress enacted the DTA, however, the government moved to dismiss Hamdan's petition on the ground that the legislature had eliminated their power to hear the case (*Hamdan* v. *Rumsfeld* (2006) 548 U.S. 557, 572). This was consistent with precedents that appeared to vest Congress with the power to take away the jurisdiction of courts to hear certain types of cases, even as to matters that were already pending. These rulings returned non-citizens to the status of having precious few judicial rights The Supreme Court, however, decided to review the case and concluded that Congress had not actually intended to prevent pending cases, such as Hamdan's, from being taken away from the courts (*Hamdan* v. *Rumsfeld* (2006) 548 U.S. 557, 572–585). Although this result was a repudiation of the Bush Administration's legal position, the Court indicated that it was merely interpreting what Congress had enacted. Justice Breyer in particular wrote that all the Court had done was tell the President that Congress had not authorized the military courts that he wanted to use. Nothing prevented him from seeking that authorization explicitly.[13] As we shall see, the cure, the Military Commissions Act of 2006, was as problematic in many ways as the DTA was.

One interesting observation about the outcomes in these four cases is that, in its interpretation of ambiguous statutes, the Court was more lenient toward the non-citizens than it was toward American citizens. This is most clear when one compares *Rasul* to *Padilla*. In *Rasul*, though there was no federal judge based at Guantanamo Bay, Cuba, the Court concluded that Guantanamo detainees could nevertheless seek relief under the federal habeas statute because a court could direct the Secretary of Defense to order a detainee released if he were successful in pursuing his petition (*Rasul* v. *Bush* (2004) 542 U.S. 466, 473–485). Yet, in *Padilla*, the Court did not afford Jose Padilla the benefit of this more relaxed "ultimate custodian" rule, even though under the same reasoning, the Defense Secretary could have ordered Padilla's custodian to release him as well (*Rumsfeld* v. *Padilla* (2004) 542 U.S. 426, 434–442). Consciously or not, the Court took a position at odds from the traditional disfavoring of non-citizens.

After *Hamdan*, Congress passed the Military Commissions Act of 2006 (MCA), which clearly and unequivocally rejected the Supreme Court's interpretation of the DTA. The MCA in essence ratified President Bush's executive order establishing military courts in which to prosecute Guantanamo Bay detainees and reinstated the DTA's elimination of nearly all federal court review of cases involving Guantanamo detainees.[14] In the end, congressional enactment of the Military Commissions Act amounted to no more than a formally legal delegation of unchecked authority, an in-advance indemnification of executive law-breaking (Dyzenhaus 2006).[15] It was a distinct sign that the United States was moving toward a Dual State, where "rule by prerogative" would govern certain, ever-expanding "security" domains while the "rule of law" continued to govern other areas. When Hamdan's military trial resumed, he opted to plead guilty and was given a sentence that amounted to only a few additional months once his previous time in detention was taken into account (Worth, November 25, 2008, www.nytimes.com/2008/11/26/washington/26gitmo.html).

Having pleaded guilty, Hamdan was not in a position to challenge the constitutionality of the MCA, but another group of Guantanamo detainees did. Those cases reached the Supreme Court under the name of *Boumediene* v. *Bush* (2008) 128 S. Ct. 2229 and there, the Supreme Court – for the first time – decided that at least one constitutional provision, the Suspension Clause, covered non-citizens detained outside the United States (*Boumediene* v. *Bush* (2008) 128 S. Ct. 2229, 2243–2262). The Suspension Clause can be read as a grant of power to Congress or a limitation of a pre-existing, assumed power; either way, on its face, it appears to provide that Congress can suspend the right of persons to seek habeas corpus only during times of invasion or insurrection, when required for public safety. The *Boumediene* detainees had argued that the MCA suspended habeas corpus by eliminating most federal court review of their cases, but this argument presupposed that they were to begin with protected by the Suspension Clause. The government again argued that the detainees had no constitutional rights given their non-citizenship status and their location outside the United States. This argument was not foreclosed by *Rasul* and *Hamdan* because both of those cases were decided as a matter of what rights Congress – as opposed to the Constitution – had intended to give to the detainees, and Congress was free to change its mind, as it did with the DTA and MCA. The Constitution, however, sets minimum standards that Congress was forbidden from breaching. The government could prevail in *Boumediene* only if the Constitution did not apply to the detainees, or if it permitted Congress to take detainee cases away from the courts. It could do so only if this was not "suspending" habeas corpus or because it was suspension, but the conditions for suspension were met – namely, that it was a time of invasion or insurrection and that public safety required such action.

The Court ruled in favor of the Guantanamo detainees, deciding that the MCA violated the Constitution because Congress was attempting to suspend habeas corpus without satisfying the requirements of the Suspension Clause; invasion or insurrection threatening the public safety (*Boumediene* v. *Bush* (2008) 128 S. Ct. 2229, 2262–2275). In doing so, the Court necessarily concluded that the Suspension Clause applied to non-citizens outside the country. Instead of a clear statement that the Constitution applied to all persons, aliens as well as citizens and regardless of geographic location, the Court took a more narrow, clause-specific "functionalist" approach. Citizenship and geography were relevant but not dispositive factors. Also relevant was the feasibility of providing habeas corpus to those detainees, including consideration of the burden to the military captors. Given the degree of control that the United States exerted over the naval base on Guantanamo Bay, the Court concluded that there were few practical obstacles to judicial review in the circumstances (*Boumediene* v. *Bush* (2008) 128 S. Ct. 2229, 2259–2262). With such holding, the Court also ducked establishing the precise nature of U.S. control and jurisdiction at Guantanamo.

Aliens and rights at the beginning of the Obama Administration

From the standpoint of counterterrorism efforts, the transition from the Bush Administration to the Obama Administration has proven surprisingly smooth in more ways than one, from retaining Robert Gates as Secretary of Defense to continuing the policy of military detention of captured al Qaeda fighters.[16] At the same time, there have been incremental policy changes, with the result that some past policies might not be reviewed by the courts. Keeping in mind that the government's voluntary cessation of behavior is not the same as judicial prohibition of such behavior, we can still nevertheless identify some concrete answers and some other areas left unsettled.

Who can be detained?

Although some human rights groups have consistently argued that suspected al Qaeda members are not considered soldiers under international law and therefore cannot be subject to military detention, only criminal prosecution, the *Hamdi* decision settles that both citizens and non-citizens can be held under American law without criminal charges if they are deemed the "enemy" under the terms set forth by Congress, because the accumulated historical understanding is that incident to waging war is the authority to detain enemy fighters for preventative incapacitation (*Hamdi* v. *Rumsfeld* (2004) 542 U.S. 507, 517–519).[17] This stance marks something of an inversion from the position held earlier by liberal critics, namely that those captured on a battlefield, no matter if "irregular," should be treated as POWs under the Geneva Conventions and held under humane conditions (such as at American military bases) for the duration.

There are currently no known American citizens being held in indefinite detention as enemy combatants relating to al Qaeda or the Taliban.[18] Since 2002, when Jose Padilla was arrested (or captured), there have been several hundred American citizens indicted on terrorism-related charges. In other words, for the past nearly eight years, all Americans suspected of terrorist links to al Qaeda have been handled by the Justice Department, not the Defense Department (Chesney 2007). At the same time, it is too early to conclude that Padilla was a one-time event and that citizens on the territory of the United States need not worry about being subjected to indefinite detention under military auspices.

What might be gleaned from the *Hamdi* and *Padilla* examples, however, is a sense of the pragmatic obstacles that the government faces in holding its own citizens in military detention. The government refused to allow Hamdi access to a lawyer during most of the pendency of the litigation over his detention, only reluctantly yielding as a matter of grace and then only in the face of sustained legal opposition, opposition that built due to the Bush Administration's extreme legal positions. The Supreme Court's *Hamdi* opinion squarely rejects this restriction, finding that Hamdi *"unquestionably* has the right to access to counsel in connection with the proceedings on remand [challenging his classification as an 'enemy combatant']" (*Hamdi* v. *Rumsfeld* (2004) 542 U.S. 507, 539 (emphasis added)). Thus, any American citizen declared to be an enemy combatant unquestionably has the right to counsel and to challenge such designation. But perhaps even more important than the enumeration of such rights, was the fact that in both cases, especially Padilla's, the Court signaled a willingness to engage in relatively non-deferential review of the government's use of military detention as a counterterrorism tool (*Hamdi* v. *Rumsfeld* (2004) 542 U.S. 507, 517–519; *Rumsfeld* v. *Padilla* (2004) 542 U.S. 426, 430–432). One reason the government chose to shift Padilla back to the criminal justice system instead of continuing to detain him as an enemy combatant may have been a belief that it would fail to satisfy its burden in a hearing of demonstrating that Padilla was in fact the enemy as defined in the Authorization to Use Military Force Joint Resolution (AUMF).[19] Indeed, the conduct for which Padilla was tried and convicted, while related to terrorism generally, was different from that which the government publicly identified as the basis for his initial capture and detention.[20]

With the exception of Ali al-Marri, non-citizen terrorism suspects captured on U.S. soil have also been prosecuted in civil courts. As for al-Marri, after six years of detention in a domestic U.S. naval brig as an enemy combatant, the Obama Administration finally removed him from military detention in March 2009 and sent him back to the criminal justice system to stand trial on federal charges, to which he pleaded guilty in April (Schwartz, May 1, 2009, p. A16).[21] Again, as with the ultimate disposition of Hamdi's and Padilla's cases, the government's ultimate decision to treat al-Marri as a criminal defendant is more usefully understood as recognition of the political obstacles to treating even a non-citizen as an enemy combatant when that person has been on U.S. territory and has not engaged in active violence against the country.

Thus, one might predict with a reasonable degree of confidence that, going forward, terrorism suspects in the United States will continue to be prosecuted as criminal defendants, and not treated as enemy combatants, without regard to citizenship. For persons captured outside the United States, however, citizenship may be a relevant factor in determining whether the Defense Department or Justice Department takes control.[22] It seems, therefore, that the first question to be asked is "where" rather than "who." Only thereafter will citizenship status matter. Of Americans, it would be non-citizen permanent residents returning abroad for jihad or adventure who would be left at greatest risk.

Who can challenge their detention, and for what?

As noted above, it appears unlikely that any persons caught in the United States will be subject to military detention. In the event that some such person were to be detained, both precedent and practice suggest that any person, citizen or not, would be allowed to challenge his detention in a civil court. The government did not dispute the right of Yaser Hamdi, Jose Padilla, and Ali al-Marri to seek judicial review of their detentions. Rather, the substantive nature of the dispute turned on the government's authority to hold them indefinitely without charges. We do not discuss here the netherworld of immigration detention. Recall that after 9/11 the War on Terror began with the arrest and secret detention, not in far away Guantanamo but in the heart of Brooklyn, New Jersey and elsewhere of suspect aliens. The domestic war began promptly with the arrest and secret detention of over 1,200 resident aliens, mostly Muslim. Often, detention was based on civil-immigration violations, but sometimes detention was based on nothing whatsoever. In nearly all cases, detained aliens were neither charged nor even arraigned. Under a so-called Special Registration Program, 80,000 young men from two dozen, mostly Muslim, countries were called into the offices of the Immigration and Naturalization Service for "voluntary" interviews, photos, and other procedures. For 14,000 of them, the reward for cooperation was deportation, mostly on technical grounds that had always been ignored. An unknown number of others were invited for interviews by security agencies from which they did not return for extended periods. Another 50 or so individuals were held as "material witnesses" and temporarily disappeared without ever being charged or called to be witnesses to anything. No one may ever know how many people were detained or rendered overseas (perhaps for torture by proxy), where they were held, for how long, or under what circumstances (Abraham 2008, pp. 259–260 for details and sources).[23]

It is also clear that non-citizens captured and detained outside the United States are not without any constitutional protection, for that argument was foreclosed by the *Boumediene* decision. Whether one understands the decision as being based on individual rights afforded to persons or on limitations on the power of the government, the result is the same: federal courts have jurisdiction to review the government's decision to detain them (*Boumediene* v. *Bush* (2008) 128 S. Ct. 2229, 2243–2262). However, the Court's reasoning in *Boumediene* limited itself to the Suspension Clause. The Court did not rule generally that all constitutional rights were available to the Guantanamo detainees, though such a conclusion would not be inconsistent with *Boumediene*. Read broadly, *Boumediene* could mean a complete repudiation of *Eisentrager*, and with it, guarantee of all applicable Bill of Rights provisions to non-citizens held at Guantanamo Bay. On the other hand, the minimum that *Boumediene* might stand for is simply that the government must justify its decision to detain each person before a civil court. It might be adequate for the government to demonstrate that the detainee was a person or member of a group that "planned, authorized, committed, or aided the terrorist attacks that occurred on September 11, 2001," citing the Authorization to Use Military Force of 2001.[24] Thus, the Executive Branch's continued power to detain depends in some part on Congress's willingness to keep the AUMF extant; should Congress repeal it, the President would find it harder to argue that he has the authority even to satisfy that minimum reading of *Boumediene*.

Still, even at its minimum, *Boumediene*'s ruling has significant implications for detainees. The habeas right carries with it more than the mere formality of filing the habeas petition without any substantive rights. As noted above, after the *Rasul* decision, one federal judge had concluded that all he needed to do was to allow the petitions to be filed before dismissing them on the ground that the aliens had no substantive rights (*Khalid* v. *Bush* (2005) 355 F. Supp. 2d 311). Yet, that decision was ultimately overruled in *Boumediene* (*Boumediene* v. *Bush* (2008) 128 S. Ct. 2229, 2262).[25] In other words, in this context at least the habeas right carries meaningful review of the basis for detention.

There remain broader questions of whether that meaningful review includes other substantive rights, such as the right to counsel. Strictly speaking, these are not criminal proceedings (with the exception of military commissions), so the Sixth Amendment right to counsel is not applicable. Thus far, the courts have not had to decide this issue because major law firms and public interest groups have taken on representation of the Guantanamo Bay detainees on a pro bono basis, and the government has not opposed such representation, though it has insisted on security clearance for those lawyers. Again it is worth recalling that none of this provides solace to resident aliens who continue to face the full force of non-criminal deportation hearings and the generous detention opportunities afforded the government under immigration law.[26]

Who can be tried in a military court?

The German saboteurs case, *Ex Parte Quirin*, decided that the Constitution did not prohibit the prosecution of American citizens in military commissions (*Ex Parte Quirin* (1942) 317 U.S. 1, 37–38). To the extent that *Quirin* remains good law, meaning that the Court will continue to respect its ruling and abide by it, it demonstrates that citizens as well as non-citizens can be subject to military prosecutions. As a practical matter, however, the fact that President Bush's executive order[27] was limited to non-citizens may suggest that it is not feasible politically today to prosecute citizens in military trials. The Lindh episode would seem to substantiate this conclusion, but one cannot know what would have happened if Lindh had either been captured later after the apparatuses and practices had been set up, or if he had been a recently naturalized Muslim American rather than a fair-haired Californian.

Non-citizens, however, continue to face potential military trials. During the presidential campaign, Barack Obama argued against the use of military commissions. Yet, not long after his inauguration, President Obama appeared to reverse course, suggesting that the rules for the military commissions needed to be reformed to make them more fair to the defendants, but that they would continue to be used in appropriate cases (Glaberson, May 16, 2009, p. A1). The improved procedural protections will make the Obama Administration military commissions more closely resemble U.S. courts-martial, thereby reducing the difference in treatment of aliens versus citizens; nonetheless, some differences remain.

Is Guantanamo Bay different from elsewhere?

A final question left unsettled at present is whether the unique degree of control that the United States has over Guantanamo Bay makes it effectively U.S. territory. This is an important issue because if the naval base at Guantanamo Bay were considered U.S. territory, then detainees held there would conclusively have constitutional rights. At the same time, it would mean that non-citizen detainees held elsewhere in the world, such as Afghanistan, would remain in a legal limbo, unsure if they have any right to court review of their detention or any substantive rights.

The United States maintains its naval base at Guantanamo Bay through a lease with Cuba that was signed following the end of the Spanish–American War. Under the terms of the lease, Cuba has no jurisdiction over the land at the base. This means that all crimes committed there are left solely to the United States to prosecute. (By contrast, crimes committed at U.S. bases in other foreign countries are prosecuted either by the U.S. military or by the host nation, depending on the particular Status of Forces Agreement regulating the U.S. military presence.) More importantly, the lease continues until both countries decide to terminate it. Thus, the United States has maintained the naval base over Cuba's objections for more than 40 years (Yin 2005, p. 1061).

Justice Kennedy first suggested in his concurrence in the *Rasul* case that Guantanamo Bay was effectively U.S. soil (*Rasul* v. *Bush* (2004) 542 U.S. 466, 485–488),[28] and the majority opinion expressed sympathy for the argument (*Rasul* v. *Bush* (2004) 542 U.S. 466, 480–481). However, the Court did not rely on this distinction in reaching its decision. Then, in *Boumediene*, the Court even more strongly hinted that Guantanamo Bay was special: "in every practical sense Guantanamo is not abroad; it is within the constant jurisdiction of the United States" (*Boumediene* v. *Bush* (2008) 128 S. Ct. 2229, 2261).

The "Guantanamo Bay is unique" argument is understandably appealing to the Court, because it allows it to assert the power to review the detention of those at Guantanamo Bay without having to concede that non-citizens anywhere can assert all manner of constitutional rights against the U.S. government, including, for example, those seeking entry into the country. But it is also a short-term solution, as the government had essentially ceased transporting captured fighters to Guantanamo Bay in 2002, with the exception of a group of "high value" detainees formerly detained in secret prisons in Eastern Europe. In addition, the "Guantanamo Bay is unique" argument also ignores the situation of hundreds of Taliban fighters detained in Afghanistan.

Indeed, in the early days of the Obama Administration, a federal judge heard a case brought on behalf of persons detained at a military base in Afghanistan. That judge concluded that the detainees, despite being non-citizens clearly outside the United States, had the right to file their habeas petitions (*Al Maqaleh* v. *Gates* (2009) 604 F. Supp. 2d 205). As of this writing, that case is still in litigation on appeal,[29] so this issue remains unsettled.

Conclusion

Given the Supreme Court's incremental steps in checking the executive unilateralism of the Bush Administration, it seems likely that citizenship and geography will continue to play some role in demarcating the treatment of those captured as "enemies" in the continuing anti-terrorism efforts. The backlash against the government's military detention of Jose Padilla suggests (but does not guarantee) that any Americans suspected of being in league with al Qaeda will still be treated as criminal defendants. For aliens, however, the situation remains less clear; those captured outside the United States remain at risk of being classified as enemy combatants. The early indications are that the Obama Administration will moderate some of the extremes of its predecessor, but as of mid-2009, the changes in policy were incremental. Military detention and military prosecution remain aspects of the United States' counterterrorism policy, and it appears that rendition of suspects to other nations will continue (though with more stringent assurances for humane treatment).

As to why there remains so much uncertainty about the legal rights to be accorded aliens, particularly those outside the United States, there are a number of possible reasons. The Court that decided the 2004 trio of cases consisted of three voting blocs: Justices Stevens, Souter, Ginsburg, and Breyer, who generally favored more aggressive judicial checking of the Executive Branch; Chief Justice Rehnquist and Justices Scalia and Thomas, who generally favored substantial deference to the Executive Branch; and Justices O'Connor and Kennedy, who tended to vote more often with the conservative trio than with the liberal quartet, but on more narrow grounds. As a result, the other justices had to compete for O'Connor's and Kennedy's votes by crafting more restrained, incremental opinions than they might otherwise have. One can see Justice Kennedy's influence in the Court's jurisprudence regarding the availability of habeas corpus for aliens not within the 50 states; in *Rasul*, Kennedy concurred in the result but on the more narrow basis that the U.S.'s unique, near-total control over Guantanamo Bay made it effectively U.S. territory. While this was a plausible, even possibly appealing line of reasoning because it addressed only the specific factual issue at hand and limited unintended consequences of a broader ruling, it also left unsettled the status of other places with U.S.-controlled detention facilities, such as Bagram Airbase in Afghanistan.

Additionally, the Court's decisions suggested an initial willingness to defer to Congress as the ultimate branch to enact long-term solutions. Nearly all of the holdings in the 2004 trio of cases were matters of statutory interpretation, meaning that the Court was not construing the requirements of the Constitution, but rather, what an ambiguous federal statute meant; Congress remains free to amend the statute if it believes that the Court misconstrued the meaning of the statute. Thus, in 2004, the Court did not state explicitly that aliens not within the 50 states were nevertheless constitutionally entitled to habeas corpus.[30] Had Congress simply left that interpretation intact, or affirmatively validated it by codifying it in the United States Code, there might have been less uncertainty about the scope of rights available to aliens, for it is easier to conceive of giving aliens statutory rights (which are more easily altered or revoked, if necessary) than constitution rights (which tend to become entrenched). Instead, Congress enacted the Detainee Treatment Act of 2005, which mostly nullified *Rasul*. In turn, the Court construed the meaning of the Detainee Treatment Act favorably toward the detainees in *Hamdan* – again, on statutory interpretation grounds – leading Congress to reassert its authority by enacting the Military Commissions Act of 2006, which sought to undo *Hamdan*. Finally, four years after embarking on this path in *Rasul*, the Court in 2008 ended the back-and-forth in *Boumediene* by basing its ruling on constitutional grounds. The Court could have used this reasoning in 2004 in *Rasul*; its choice to wait to see if Congress would ratify its more restrained reasoning was reasonable, but also contributed to four years of uncertainty.

Now that suspected 9/11 mastermind Khalid Sheikh Mohammed and four confederates have been brought to stand possible trial in New York in a federal court on criminal charges, there may be some increased certainty about the rights afforded aliens when that process is completed.

Notes

1 Tung Yin is Professor of Law at Lewis & Clark Law School. David Abraham is Professor of Law at the University of Miami School of Law. We would like to thank William Nicholson for his extraordinarily capable and dedicated research assistance.
2 In this chapter, we restrict ourselves to the United States. On the mitigation trend internationally, see, e.g., Joppke 2001, 2008; Abraham 2000.
3 On the post-WWI Palmer Raids, see Higham 1963, pp. 229–231; for judicial discussion regarding same, see *Kaplan* v. *Tod* (1925) 267 U.S. 228; *Harisiades* v. *Shaughnessy* (1952) 342 U.S. 580; *Shaughnessy* v. *United States ex rel. Mezei* (1953) 345 U.S. 206; *Galvan* v. *Press* (1954) 347 U.S. 522.
4 For more on the historical circumstances and judicial decisions in this case, see Rehnquist (1998).
5 Of the same order were cases like *Fleming* v. *Nestor* (1960) 363 U.S. 603 where the Court had no trouble depriving a deported non-citizen of his vested property rights in the form of earned social security payments. Deported for the same reason as Harisiades, as a non-citizen, neither Nestor's free-speech rights nor his property rights were quite the same as those of a citizen.
6 On the revelations of the earlier failures of National Security Advisor Condoleezza Rice, see Shenon and Mazzetti (October 3, 2006, p. A18).
7 For a discussion of the sequelae, see Abraham (2008: 259ff).
8 We do not here discuss the Geneva Conventions. Suffice it to say that treatment of POWs is an established and well-regulated area of international law and convention. It is part of American lore that even Nazis could be held as POWs in the American heartland and emerge from the experience as committed democrats.
9 For an argument justifying the differential treatment, on the grounds that it would be even more unfair to treat Hamdi as a criminal defendant because it would criminalize his belief that the United States was his enemy based on the happenstance of his having been born in Louisiana, see Yin (2007).
10 Other, more dubious criminal trials alleging terrorism and terrorist support acts took place around the country. Some, such as occurred in Miami, sometimes appeared absurd. On the Liberty City (Miami) plot to blow up the Sears Tower in Chicago, see Abraham (2008: 268). Others, perhaps less absurd, such as the Ft. Dix pizza delivery conspiracy, arguably were driven more by government provocateurs than by the actual defendants. Nonetheless, these cases adhered in form to domestic rule of law procedures.

Here too, however, the special vulnerabilities of permanent resident aliens should be recognized. In the case of the Liberty City conspiracy, see Semple (December 14, 2007, p. A28) ("The outcome was a significant defeat for the Bush administration, which had described the case as a major crackdown on homegrown terrorists."). Despite the acquittal of one defendant, a legal permanent-resident immigrant, the government moved to deport the exonerated defendant on a seemingly vindictive theory that associating with terrorists is a deportable offense and that, even though he was acquitted by a "beyond a reasonable doubt" standard, the defendant would have lost under a "preponderance" standard, which is all that is necessary for deportability because it is a civil, not a criminal, issue. (See Weaver, February 4, 2008, available at www.miamiherald.com/news/miami_dade/story/405217.html) Ultimately the government succeeded in Immigration Court (*In re Lomorin* [2008] No. A043–677–619).

11 Of course the Authorization was unlikely to have stated such things explicitly because in its entirety it consisted of fewer than 60 words (Abraham 2008: 259).

12 For an argument that Miami is hardly "ordinary" when it comes to the Bush regime and terrorism, being a key site in the disputed 2000 Presidential election as well as arguable state-sponsored terrorism see Abraham 2008: 252–256, 268; Bardach 2006: 88, 91–101. Corral and Chardy (April 21, 2007, p. B3) report that, at the height of the terrorism frenzy, the administration released a convicted terrorist, Luis Posada Carriles, who was responsible for blowing up a plane in midair, killing scores of innocents as well as bombing Cuban hotels, killing a foreign tourist.

13 *Hamdan* v. *Rumsfeld* (2006) 548 U.S. 557, 636 (Breyer, J., concurring) ("The Court's conclusion ultimately rests upon a single ground: Congress has not issued the Executive a 'blank check.' Indeed, Congress has denied the President the legislative authority to create military commissions of the kind at issue here. Nothing prevents the President from returning to Congress to seek the authority he believes necessary.") (internal citation omitted).

14 Military Commissions Act of 2006, Pub. L. No. 109–366, 120 Stat. 2600 (2006) (to be codified in scattered sections of 10, 18, 28, & 42 U.S.C.).

15 In Dyzenhaus's (2006, p. 2039) words: "[T]he legislature will have decided to give the executive what the Bush administration had claimed it could have without legislative authorization." For a similar argument, see Fraenkel 1941, pp. 3–5, 9–10.

16 We do not address here the question of whether and how imperial ambitions are ever rolled back peacefully or willingly. See Johnson 2006; Mueller 2006; Maier 2006; Chomsky 2006.

17 To be clear, the more aggressive legal posture set forth by the Bush Administration – that the President could detain even citizens based on his inherent power as the Commander-in-Chief (Yoo 2005) – has yet to gain widespread acceptance.

18 In 2008, the Supreme Court held in *Munaf* v. *Geren* (2008) 128 S. Ct. 2207, 2216–2228 that two U.S. citizens detained by the Multi-National Force in Iraq, one of whom was convicted in an Iraqi court and faced a death sentence, had a right to seek federal court review of their custody, but also concluded that those same courts lacked the authority to block their transfer to a foreign sovereign's criminal justice system.

19 Authorization to Use Military Force Joint Resolution, Pub. L. 107–40, 115 Stat. 224 (2001) (codified as amended at 50 U.S.C. § 1541). The AUMF provides, in pertinent part, that "the President is authorized to use all necessary and appropriate force against those nations, organizations, or persons he determines planned, authorized, committed, or aided the terrorist attacks that occurred on September 11, 2001, or harbored such organizations or persons, in order to prevent any future acts of international terrorism against the United States by such nations, organizations or persons." Ibid.

20 Again, we do not address here the social and political "Gleichschaltung" function of the original terrorism arrests meant by Attorney General Gonzales and others to legitimate the Bush presidency by creating "national unity and resolve" (Abraham 2008: 259–261).

21 On the al-Marri plea agreement, see Plea Agreement and Stipulation of Facts, *United States* v. *al-Marri*, No. 09-CR-10030 (N.D. Ill. April 30, 2009).

22 Notably, however, in November 2009, Attorney General Eric Holder decided to bring Khalid Sheikh Mohammed, Ramzi Binalshibh, and three other high value Guantanamo detainees to New York to stand trial in a federal court (Savage, Nov. 14, 2009, p. A1).

23 The Ninth Circuit Court of Appeals recently ruled that former Attorney General John Ashcroft may face personal liability for decisions that led to the detention of American citizen Abdulluh al-Kidd as a material witness after the September 11 attacks (*al-Kidd* v. *Ascroft* (2009) 580 F.3d 949, 981 ("Sadly ... even now, more than 217 years after the ratification of the Fourth Amendment to the Constitution, some confidently assert that the government has the power to arrest and detain or restrict American citizens for months on end, in sometimes primitive conditions, not because there is evidence that they have committed a crime, but merely because the government wishes to investigate them for possible wrongdoing, or to prevent them from having contact with others in the outside world. We find this to be repugnant to the Constitution, and a painful reminder of some of the most ignominious chapters of our national history.")). For further analysis of the *al-Kidd* case, see Schwartz, September 5, 2009, p. A10.

24 See Authorization to Use Military Force Joint Resolution, Pub. L. 107–40, 115 Stat. 224 (2001) (codified as amended at 50 U.S.C. § 1541).

25 Specifically, the Court held that aliens being held as enemy combatants at the U.S. naval base at Guantanamo Bay, Cuba were entitled to right of habeas corpus to challenge their detention, by virtue of the Suspension Clause of the U.S. Constitution (*Boumediene* v. *Bush* (2008) 128 S. Ct. 2229, 2262).

26 On government detention and deportation powers, see *Zadvydas* v. *Davis* (2001) 533 U.S. 678; *Shaughnessy* v. *United States ex rel. Mezei* (1953) 345 U.S. 206.

27 Military Order of November 13, 2001, 66 Fed. Reg. 57,833 (November 16, 2001).

28 Specifically, Justice Kennedy opined that

> Guantanamo Bay is in every practical respect a United States territory, and it is one far removed from any hostilities.... In a formal sense, the United States leases the Bay; the 1903 lease agreement states that Cuba retains 'ultimate sovereignty' over it.... At the same time, this lease is no ordinary lease. Its term is indefinite and at the discretion of the United States. What matters is the unchallenged and indefinite control that the United States has long exercised over Guantanamo Bay. From a practical perspective, the indefinite lease of Guantanamo Bay has produced a place that belongs to the United States, extending the 'implied protection' of the United States to it.
>
> (*Rasul* v. *Bush* (2004) 542 U.S. 466, 487 (Kennedy, J., concurring) (internal citation omitted))

29 The United States was granted a motion for an interlocutory injunction on June 1, 2009 (*Al Maqaleh* v. *Gates* (2009) 620 F. Supp. 2d 51).

30 Congress, of course, could in appropriate circumstances, suspend habeas corpus (Rehnquist 1998).

References

Books and articles

Abraham, David, The Good of Banality? The Emergence of Cost-Benefit Analysis and Proportionality in the Treatment of Aliens in the U.S. and Germany, *Citizenship Studies*, 5: 237 (2000).

Abraham, David, The Bush Regime from Elections to Detentions: A Moral Economy of Carl Schmitt and Human Rights, *University of Miami Law Review*, 62: 249 (2008).

Bardach, Ann Louise, Twilight of the Assassins, *Atlantic Monthly*, November, 88, 91–101 (2006).

Belluck, Pam, Unrepentant Shoe Bomber is Given a Life Sentence For Trying to Blow Up Jet, *New York Times*, January 31, 2003, p. A13.

Bosniak, Linda, *The Citizen and the Alien: Dilemmas of Contemporary Membership*. Princeton, NJ: Princeton University Press, 2007, pp. 77–101.

Brinkley, Joel and Eric Lichtblau, U.S. Release Saudi-American It Had Captured in Afghanistan, *New York Times*, October 12, 2004, p. A15.

Burnett, Christina Duffy, United States: American Expansion and Territorial Deannexation, *University of Chicago Law Review*, 72: 797, 800 (2005).

Burnett, Christina Duffy and Burke Marshall (eds.), *Foreign in a Domestic Sense: Puerto Rico, American Expansion, and the Constitution*. Durham, NC: Duke University Press, 2001.

Chesney, Robert, Beyond Conspiracy? Preventative Prosecution and the Challenge of Unaffiliated Terrorism, *Southern California Law Review*, 80: 425 (2007) (conducts an empirical study of the use of material support of terrorist organization charges since the 9/11 attacks).

Chomsky, Noam, *Failed States: The Abuse of Power and the Assault on Democracy*. New York: Metropolitan Books, 2006.

Corral, Oscar and Alfonso Chardy, Posada Terror Case: Posada Is with Family but Unable To Comment, *Miami Herald*, April 21, 2007, p. B3.

Dyzenhaus, David, Schmitt v. Dicey: Are States of Emergency Inside or Outside the Legal Order?, *Cardozo Law Review*, 27: 2005, 2039, 2006.

Fraenkel, Ernst, *The Dual State: A Contribution to the Theory of Dictatorship*. London: Oxford University Press, 1941, pp. 3–5, 9–10.

Gerth, Jason, U.S. Detainee is Questioned, But His Fate is Still Unclear, *New York Times*, December 10, 2001, at B3.

Glaberson, William, Obama to Keep Tribunals; Stance Angers Some Backers, *New York Times*, May 16, 2009, p. A1.

Gudridge, Patrick O., Remember *Endo*?, *Harvard Law Review*, 116: 1933 (2003).

Gudridge, Patrick O., The Constitution Glimpsed From Tule Lake, *Law & Contemporary Problems*, 68: 81 (2005).

Higham John, *Strangers in the Land: Patterns of American Nativism*. New York: Atheneum, 1963, pp. 229–231.

Jinks, Derek, The Declining Significance of POW Status, *Harvard International Law Journal*, 45: 367, 372n.21 (2004).

Johnson, Chalmers A., *Nemesis: The Last Days of the American Republic*. New York: Metropolitan Books, 2006.

Johnston, David and Philip Shenon, Man Held Since August is Charged with a Role in Sept. 11 Plot, *New York Times*, December 12, 2001, p. A1.

Joppke, Christian, Legal Domestic Sources of Immigrant Rights, *Citizenship Studies*, 34: 339 (2001).

Joppke, Christian, Immigration and the Identity of Citizenship, *Citizenship Studies*, 12: 533 (2008).

Maier, Charles S., *Among Empires: American Ascendancy and Its Predecessors*. Cambridge, MA: Harvard University Press, 2006.

Mueller, John E., *Overblown: How Politicians and the Terrorism Industry Inflate National Security Threats, and Why We Believe Them*. New York: Free Press, 2006.

Raustiala, Kal, *Does the Constitution Follow the Flag?: The Evolution of Territoriality in American Law*. New York: Oxford University Press, 2009.

Rehnquist, William H., *All the Laws But One: Civil Liberties in Wartime*. New York: Knopf, 1998 (gives the late Chief Justice's historical account of the *Milligan* and *Quirin* cases).

Savage, Charlie, Accused 9/11 Mastermind to Face Civilian Trial, *New York Times*, Nov. 14, 2009, p. A1.

Schuck, Peter H., *Citizens, Strangers, and In-Betweens: Essays on Immigration and Citizenship*. Boulder, CO: Westview Press, 1998, pp. 163–175.

Schwartz, John, Panel Rules Against Ashcroft in Detention Case, *New York Times*, September 5, 2009, p. A10.

Schwartz, John, Plea Deal Reached With Agent for Al Qaeda, *New York Times*, May 1, 2009, p. A16.

Semple, Kirk, U.S. Falters in Terror Case Against 7 in Miami, *New York Times*, December 14, 2007, p. A28.

Semple, Kirk, Padilla Gets 17 Years in Conspiracy Case, *New York Times*, January 23, 2008, p. A14.

Shenon, Philip and Mark Mazzetti, Records Confirm CIA Chief Warned Rice on Al Qaeda, *New York Times*, October 3, 2006, p. A18.

Walzer, Michael, *Spheres of Justice: A Defense of Pluralism and Equality*. New York: Basic Books, 1983.

Weaver, Jay, Absolved of Terrorism, Haitian Still in Limbo, MIAMIHERALD.COM, Feb. 4, 2008 available at www.miamiherald.com/news/miami_dade/story/405217.html.

Worth, Robert F., Bin Laden Driver to Be Sent to Yemen, *New York Times*, November 25, 2008, *available at* www.nytimes.com/2008/11/26/washington/26gitmo.html.

Wright, Lawrence, *The Looming Tower: al-Qaeda and the Road to 9/11*. New York, Knopf, 2006 (discusses the formation of the terrorist group al Qaeda through the planning of the 9/11 attacks).

Yin, Tung, The Role of Article III Courts in the War on Terrorism, *William & Mary Bill of Rights Journal*, 13: 1061 (2005).

Yoo, John, *The Powers of War and Peace: The Constitution and Foreign Affairs After 9/11*. Chicago: University of Chicago Press, 2005.

Legal authorities

Authorization to Use Military Force, Pub. L. No. 107–40, 115 Stat. 224 (2001) (codified as amended at 50 U.S.C. § 1541)

Detainee Treatment Act of 2005, Pub. L. No. 109–148, § 1005(e), 119 Stat. 2680 (2005)

Military Commissions Act of 2006, Pub. L. No. 109–366, 120 Stat. 2600 (2006) (to be codified in scattered sections of 10, 18, 28, & 42 U.S.C.)

Military Order of November 13, 2001, 66 Fed. Reg. 57,833 (Nov. 16, 2001)

Non Detention Act of 1971, 18 U.S.C. § 4001(a) (1971)

Plea Agreement and Stipulation of Facts, *United States* v. *al-Marri*, No. 09-CR-10030 (N.D. Ill. Apr. 30, 2009)

al-Kidd v. *Ashcroft*, 580 F.3d 949 (9th Cir. 2009)

al-Marri v. *Pucciarelli*, 534 F.3d 213, 217 (4th Cir. 2008)

Al Maqaleh v. *Gates*, 620 F. Supp. 2d 51 (D.D.C. 2009)

Al Maqaleh v. *Gates*, 604 F. Supp. 2d 205 (D.D.C. 2009)
Boumediene v. *Bush*, 553 U.S. __, 128 S. Ct. 2229 (2008)
Cuban American Bar Association, Inc. v. *Christopher*, 43 F.3d 1412 (11th Cir. 1995)
Ex Parte Milligan, 71 U.S. 2 (1866)
Ex Parte Quirin, 317 U.S. 1 (1942)
Fiallo v. *Bell*, 430 U.S. 787 (1977)
Fleming v. *Nestor*, 363 U.S. 603 (1960)
Galvan v. *Press*, 347 U.S. 522 (1954)
Graham v. *Richardson*, 403 U.S. 365 (1971)
Haitian Refugee Center v. *Gracey*, 809 F.2d 794 (D.C. Cir. 1987)
Hamdan v. *Rumsfeld*, 548 U.S. 557 (2006)
Hamdi v. *Rumsfeld*, 542 U.S. 507 (2004)
Harisiades v. *Shaughnessy*, 342 U.S. 580 (1952)
Jean v. *Nelson*, 727 F.2d 957 (11th Cir. 1985)
Johnson v. *Eisentrager*, 339 U.S. 763 (1950)
Kaplan v. *Tod*, 267 U.S. 228 (1925)
Khalid v. *Bush*, 355 F. Supp. 2d 311 (D.D.C. 2005)
Landon v. *Plasencia*, 459 U.S. 21 (1982)
In re Lomorin, No. A043–677–619 (EIDR Krone Processing Center Nov. 20, 2008)
Ludecke v. *Watkins*, 335 U.S. 160 (1948)
Munaf v. *Geren*, 553 U.S. ___, 128 S. Ct. 2207 (2008)
Padilla v. *Hanft*, 389 F. Supp. 2d 678 (D.S.C. 2005), *rev'd*, 423 F.3d 386 (4th Cir. 2005)
Rasul v. *Bush*, 542 U.S. 466 (2004)
Reid v. *Covert*, 354 U.S. 1 (1957)
Reno v. *American Arab Anti-Discrimination Committee*, 525 U.S. 471 (1999)
Rumsfeld v. *Padilla*, 542 U.S. 426 (2004)
Shaughnessy v. *United States ex rel. Mezei*, 345 U.S. 206 (1953)
United States v. *al-Marri*, No. 09-CR-10030 (N.D. Ill. Apr. 30, 2009)
United States v. *Lindh*, 227 F.Supp. 2d 565 (E.D. Va. 2002)
Zadvydas v. *Davis*, 533 U.S. 678 (2001)

5   Citizens at war

Traitors and internal enemies

Ute Frevert

Ever since Thucydides, war has been considered a major challenge to citizenship: It can lead to an expansion of citizenship, but it may also bring about the opposite: a severe curtailment of citizenship. For Pericles as much as for Carnot, who administered the French *levée en masse* in 1793, war constituted a huge project of social inclusion. It epitomized the emotional relationship between citizens and state at the most existential level. By inviting each and everybody to contribute to the war effort, it provided ample opportunity to prove civil allegiance and patriotism. On the other hand, war also imposed serious restrictions on citizens. Furthermore, it called into question who was a good citizen and who was not. Wars gave rise to heightened suspicions and doubts about citizenship. They put people under close surveillance, and more often than not singled out some individuals and groups as internal enemies.

The chapter traces those dynamics of inclusion and exclusion by looking at modern wars in particular. Even though the Peloponnesian War and Pericles' funeral speech gave a fine example of how the logic of inclusion worked, they cannot quite compare to the experience of the nineteenth and twentieth centuries. It is the age of mass warfare, nationalism and total war that sets the stage for something much broader and profounder than what the Ancients had witnessed. Starting with the French Revolution and culminating in two World Wars, the modern period engendered both: unforeseen inclusion and equally radical exclusion of citizenship. It created the figure of the perfect citizen, as well as its opposite: the traitor, the enemy within. Traitors and enemies were most conspicuous during times of war, especially since war became an all-encompassing project. A modern society at war was not satisfied with designing external foes that had to be fought and vanquished. It also needed internal enemies, "bad" citizens against whom the "good" citizens could prove their true worthiness. How those exclusionary politics came about will be demonstrated by looking at three examples: Germany and Britain during World War I, and the USA during World War II.

Citizenship, nationalism, and war

European modernity cannot be understood without the nation-state. Even those historians who stress the ongoing or heightened presence of empires during the nineteenth and twentieth centuries do not deny the growing importance of nation-states. In the mid-nineteenth century, it was above all Germany and Italy whose unification changed the political landscape of Europe. In the wake of World War I, more nation-states appeared on the map, the majority of them in Central and (South-)Eastern Europe. They were the offspring of former multi-ethnic empires (the Russian, Ottoman and Habsburg Empires) that had collapsed during or after the Great War. It can thus be maintained that most nation-states have been born out of war: They were either founded, like Germany and Italy, through wars, or they indirectly benefitted from wars that weakened the central power and thus enabled new states to break away from the center.

Even those states that had assembled and consolidated their "national" territory much earlier than the nineteenth century made use of wars in order to become modern nation-states. In France, the Revolutionary Wars that lasted by and large from 1792 to 1815 served to unify the nation from within, by integrating social and ethnic groups that had hitherto felt very little or distant allegiance to the state. A similar development took place in Spain and Britain where the threat of French occupation or invasion strengthened the relatively feeble bonds of national belonging (cf. for Britain, Colley 1982; Bell 2007).

We can thus distinguish two functions of war in relation to state- and nation-building: War can assist nation-states to be founded, and it can help the process of internal nation-building. It is the latter that calls for a closer analysis, and here we might as well go back to Pericles and the fifth century BC. When he talked to the citizens of Athens who mourned the fallen dead in the war against the Peloponnesian League he did not join in their lamentations. Rather, Pericles offered comfort by presenting the dead as citizen heroes who had acted and experienced citizenship at the highest level. They had sacrificed their lives for their beloved and well-ordered polis, whose excellent constitution had offered them liberty, tolerance, respect and happiness. This sacrifice expressed their pride in being members of such a state and their determination to defend its independence and security by all necessary means. The war thus brought out the best qualities of citizens – qualities that the mourners should discover in themselves and put into action. They should do everything they could to follow the dead heroes' example and help the polis survive, each at his or her own place, though united in grief and pride (Thucydides: 35–46).

About 2,200 years later, French revolutionaries struck a similar tone when they called for the French people to go to war. They were even more explicit when it came to defining each person's particular duty. The decree that the National Convention issued on August 23, 1793 summoned "all Frenchmen" to the "permanent requisition for the services of the armies":

> Young men will go off to fight; married men will forge weapons and transport food supplies; women will make tents and clothing and will provide the service in hospitals; children will shred old linen; old men will be taken to the public squares to offer encouragement to the warriors and to preach the hatred of kings and the unity of the Republic.

This *levée en masse* should last "from this moment until such time as its enemies shall have been driven from the soil of the Republic" (Forrest 1990: 75).

It made clear that the Republic needed the combined effort of all its citizens, regardless of age, gender, and social class. It needed unity in order to triumph over its enemies; at the same time, it created unity through war.

The inclusionary vision of citizenship has never been expressed more poignantly than here. It widely surpassed the legal definition of citizenship that was given in the 1789 Declaration of the Rights of Man and Citizen. The Declaration had reserved full citizenship for men only. Even in revolutionary France, women were not granted the right to vote or hold public office. And even the progressive *Code Civil* from 1804 left married women in a state of dependency and bondage unable to conclude legal transactions, to own property or appear in court. Women were, if at all, second-rate citizens. Only in times of war were they elevated to higher status and addressed as (almost) full-fledged members of the *patrie*.

At the same time, though, war highlighted substantial differences among citizens. The wording of the 1793 decree makes this evident: it starts with young men who go to war, and thus gives priority to their contribution over that of other members of the fatherland. Even if all "services" are considered important, there are some that are more important than others. Without warriors, no war can be led and won.

To be a soldier was therefore judged much more highly than to turn linen into lint or make tents. Someone who risked his life for his nation and actively defended it against its enemies was thought to perform the highest duty, the "crown of duties to the fatherland," as it used to be called in the 1860s. Here again, it was the French Revolution that paved the way for an understanding of active citizenship that was intimately connected to soldiering. By coining the term "*soldat-citoyen*" and by calling the *citoyens aux armes* (in the famous war-song *La Marseillaise*), the Revolutionaries made it clear that they conceived of citizens as those who were responsible for the nation's defence. Since the nation (not the dynastic kingdom) had become a people's affair, it was only logical that it had to be protected by the people instead of by paid mercenaries. It was also believed that men would render this service voluntarily and happily. As every house-owner would gladly and ferociously defend his property, citizens would join the army of their own volition in order to safeguard the achievements of the revolution and the integrity of the nation. Driven by a passionate war propaganda, many in fact did just that. But their numbers soon proved insufficient to feed and sustain the ambitious imperial project. This is why in 1793, the French National Assembly introduced compulsory conscription – military service for all male citizens between 20 and 24 years of age.

Other European countries followed suit, and by 1874, even Russia had joined the club. The rhetoric was surprisingly uniform: Citizens, so it read, were the born defenders of the fatherland. As patriots who loved their country and their nation, they offered their services to the armed forces. In war, they defended their own home and hearth rather than the possessions of a distant ruler. The honor of the nation was their own honor, and if this honor was attacked by an external enemy, the attack also targeted any member of the nation.

During the nineteenth century, citizenship thus became closely associated with serving in the army and going out to war (if necessary). Every young man was compelled to report to the military that decided if he should be recruited or not. Even though the majority of men never served (due to health reasons or to a lack of military demand), their status as citizens was tied to their potential capacity to fight. Governments as well as private individuals and civil organizations tried their best to attach special honours to this status, by semantically elevating military service to a school of patriotism and manliness (Frevert 2004). State law and legal practice also stressed the connection: No man who was eligible for conscription was allowed to emigrate or leave the country for good; if he did so he risked losing his citizenship (Gosewinkel 2001: 169ff., 310ff., 2002: 59–75).

For women, this did not pose a problem since their citizenship was judged to be, at most, of a passive character. Until 1918 in Germany (and 1944 in France), women did not gain political rights (the right to vote and to be elected to parliament, even the right to join political associations was denied to them before 1908). A major argument against granting them full citizenship was their exclusion from military service. That women were not recruited into the armed forces and did not actively participate in warfare, was considered self-evident. When French women petitioned in 1790/91 to enter the National Guard and bear arms, they were met with scorn and derision. With verve, the National Assembly rejected the request in the name of the "natural order": nature had not meant women to give death, but life (Duhet 1977: 117). Later in the nineteenth century, when women started to demand political rights, they were told that they did not deserve them. Liberals and conservatives were united on this point: the right to participate in the politics of a nation belonged exclusively to those prepared to defend that nation with their life and death (Frevert 2004: 118, 208–211).

Inclusion and exclusion: the case of Jewish Germans

The historic link between citizenship and military service gained special impor-tance for those groups and individuals whose citizenship was contested or not granted altogether. Women were a case in point, but also certain ethnic communities. A telling example is given by the USA who since World War I invited new immigrants to join the army and thus gain full citizenship. Those who enlisted became US citizens without having to undergo the lengthy and complicated procedures of naturalization.[1] In this case, war displayed its inclusionary charms: After proving national allegiance in the most convincing way (risking life and limbs), young soldiers from immigrant families were welcomed as respected members of the national community.

The same logic reigned when Prussian Jews were faced, in the 1840s, with royal attempts to Christianize the state. Until then (and since 1814), young men of Jewish faith had been as eligible for military conscription as their Christian compatriots – even if they did not enjoy the same civil and professional rights.

In 1840, however, the new king Friedrich Wilhelm IV tried to undermine Jewish emancipation even further, by exempting all Jewish men from the draft. Faced with this situation, Jewish intellectuals, elders and rabbis filed hundreds of petitions and submitted applications to stop this move. In Prussia, they argued,

> where the army and the people are identical ... every proscriptive approach to the army presupposes a proscriptive approach to the people and the fatherland. We would cease to be completely Prussian, we would once again be the excluded, the separated, only belonging to our country conditionally.
>
> (Allgemeine Zeitung des Judenthums 1842: 200)

For Jewish men, military service was the *entrée-billet* to Prussian citizenship, and they strove hard – and successfully – not to be deprived of it. They had well understood the strategy that lay behind the King's move. To exempt Jews from conscription ultimately meant nibbling off their rights of citizenship, even if the latter were already painfully infringed. It would have enhanced Jewish vulnerability in a state that still struggled to grant them full citizenship and equal civil rights.

By 1869, legal and civil equality was eventually established. Anti-Jewish prejudice, however, lingered on, and got even more aggressive after the German Empire was founded (through war) in 1871. While the Prussian army in the 1840s was a relatively low-key institution, its reputation grew out of bounds after the German victory over France. To belong to the army and to rise in its ranks became a major obsession among young men, particularly for those who belonged to the ambitious middle classes. Jews were no exception – but they again faced serious obstacles. Only very few Jewish men were accepted as professional officers or promoted as reserve officers in the Prussian army. Young Walther Rathenau, for example, who was born in 1867 to a well-to-do Berlin family, and was murdered as foreign minister of the Weimar Republic in 1922, ardently hoped to become a career officer. When he learnt that this was virtually impossible for an unconverted Jew, he joined the army as a regular soldier striving for the title of a reserve officer. This was denied to him, however, just as it was to Willy Ritter Liebermann von Wahlendorf. He, too, left the army in frustration. Although his family connections were excellent, and despite his membership in an elitist student corps, his cavalry captain's anti-Semitic stance even denied him promotion to lance-corporal (Frevert 2004: 160ff.). Such cases prove that Jews – although fully emancipated citizens – were not welcome in the higher echelons of Prussia's most cherished institution. Even if they performed the same patriotic duty of citizenship and served in the army, they would not make it to the upper ranks. Anti-Semitism was omnipresent in the Prussian officer corps, and backed by the Emperor. Jews were considered as among the main enemies of the new German nation-state, next to Catholics, Socialists, and Poles. They were not to be trusted to be loyal citizens of the Reich, since their nationality was disputed. Anti-Semites were outspoken about their deep distrust towards Jewish citizens who, for them, were either racially unfit to be true

Germans, or belonged to an international, cosmopolitan brand of people that lacked national feelings and patriotism. In 1886, Jewish students complained openly that broad sections of the German population considered them as "strangers" and not as equal citizens. Although they pledged to prove that "we can be Jews and Germans in the truest sense of the word," those proofs did not convince those who thought otherwise (quoted in *Juden in Preußen: Ein Kapitel deutscher Geschichte* 1981: 253. See also L.F. Swartout 2003: 148–166).

Suspicions as to the internal enemy gained new and further momentum when it came to war, in 1914. In the beginning, though, everybody praised the inclusionary effects of war. The Emperor himself took the lead and proclaimed national unity ("I know nothing of parties any more, I know only Germans"). Jewish organizations, as much as Catholics or Protestants, declared their willingness to defend the fatherland by all means. Zionists no less than those who identified themselves as "German citizens of Jewish faith" implored the "Jewish youth" to prove that they belonged to the "best sons of the Fatherland" by "taking up arms with flying colours" (*Juedische Rundschau*, No. 32: 1). Many felt that the war presented an opportunity to once and for all demonstrate their trustworthiness and national loyalty and finally overcome the prejudices of those who denied them "justice" and respect.[2]

These hopes, though, did not come true. Despite the proclaimed domestic truce (*Burgfrieden*), anti-Semitic slurs were quick to start. When the war did not go as expected and did not bring victory home within a few months, the initial enthusiasm of the middle classes quickly faded away. Social tensions increased, mainly about allegations of an unequal share in the war burden. Suspicions particularly targeted Jews; rumors spread that they were working against the German war effort: they acted as war profiteers by pushing prices up, and, even more odiously, they shirked military service at the front. Anonymous complaints were sent to various branches of military government. Commanders took them seriously and urged the War Ministry to intervene. Initially, the latter kept its distance and showed no reaction. In 1916, however, the situation got more urgent. Faced with serious shortages of men and supplies, the Supreme Command pressed for more inclusive recruitment measures. The War Minister now ordered all military commands to carry out a census of Jews serving in the military. In parliament, this was justified as a means to "probe reproaches against Jews" without any "anti-Semitic intentions whatsoever." Many parliamentarians from liberal and leftist parties thought differently, though. They vehemently criticized the *Judenzählung* as motivated by anti-Semitic prejudice, and warned of its discriminatory effects. Jewish representatives were particularly infuriated. Eminent banker Max Warburg voiced his indignation and urged the Imperial Chancellor to intervene on behalf of Jewish soldiers. Others spoke about their bitterness and disappointment and deplored the dramatic social split caused by the War Ministry's move (Angress 1976: 77–146, 1980: 117–135; Hoffmann 1997: 89–104, 256–260).

Even if the *Judenzählung* did not deal the ultimate blow to Jewish Germans' expectations of justice and integration (Sieg 2003: 201–216, 2001), it highlighted the conflicts experienced by a society at war. Instead of fostering national unity, as promised at its outset, war increased the tensions that had plagued society before. The quest for total inclusion was soon reversed and gave way to politics of exclusion. Those politics were carried out on many levels: Social groups and individuals pushed for them, and eventually (and reluctantly) the state joined in. Rather than holding its ground and keeping the "home fron'" intact, the government allowed for special groups to be singled out and suspected of harming the national cause. It was the collective that was targeted, not individual transgressors. Every Jewish citizen came under suspicion – for being Jewish and not Christian. The internal enemy had got a face, and was no longer allowed to hide behind the shelters of legal citizenship.

As everybody knows this was not the final chapter of Jewish Germans' exclusion. But few know that the final chapter actually started with excluding Jewish Germans from military service. When the National Socialist regime reintroduced general male conscription in 1935 (after it had been banned by the Versailles treaty in 1919), it deliberately exempted all men of "non-Aryan descent." Only "German men who belonged to the political nation (*Staatsvolk*)" were eligible to serve in the army. To be a soldier was considered the "privilege and honourable right" of "Aryans"; Jews did not qualify. Their "race" and their "blood" dismissed them from membership in the national community (*Volksgemeinschaft*) and from participating in the institution that was considered (next to the Nazi party) the most important mainstay of the new German state (Foertsch 1935: 49–60).

This principle of exclusion was made public in September 1935 when the government openly declared Jews as aliens. At the Nuremberg Party Rally, new laws were passed in order "to protect German blood and German honor" and to reserve full citizenship for "Aryans" only. Those of non-Aryan "blood" were deprived of political rights; they were not allowed to hold public office and could be – and were to be – excluded from ever more civil rights. The laws defined Jewishness in purely racial terms and maintained that "full Jews" were those with three Jewish grand-parents. Conversion was no longer acknowledged as an excuse. While Imperial Germany had accepted baptism as the *entrée-billet* into the "good" society (including the reserve officer corps), Nazi Germany only cared for race and blood.

It was telling that even before the Nuremberg Laws were officially passed, the law that reintroduced military conscription had already made the same provisions. It thus highlighted and anticipated the exclusionary effects that went along with the new racial definition of citizenship. And it drew attention to the fact that military service and active participation in warfare was again deemed to be the "most noble" right and duty of citizenship. In this respect, the Nazis continued a venerable tradition that found a strong backing in German society. It did not come as a surprise, then, that Jewish Germans protested vehemently against being excluded from this tradition. The Jewish veterans' organization immediately published a declaration that held on to the "Jews' unalienable right to serve Germany with weapons under general conscription. We consider this duty of honour as our highest good, next to the right to our homeland [*Heimat*]" (Müller 1987: 189).

A year later, 69-year-old Ludwig Goldstein sat down in Königsberg to write his autobiography. He devoted a whole chapter to his military experience that he gained as a conscript in the early 1890s. He spoke extremely fondly of the year that he spent in the Imperial army, even though he did not omit his captain's constant rants and raves. On the whole, however, he remained utterly "thankful for the military education and formation of my personality (*des ganzen Menschen*)." And he looked somewhat bitterly at his military documents that "did no longer matter nowadays, since the modern musterroll renounces 'non-Aryans'" (Geheimes Staatsarchiv Berlin-Dahlem 1936: 64f.). The chapter of Jewish Germans' citizenship was about to be closed.

Citizens of foreign descent: "once a German/Jap, always a German/Jap"

While the case of Jewish Germans represents a particularly dramatic experience of exclusion, it is not the only case. The internal enemy could and did have many faces, and Germany was not the only country that carried out politics of exclusion. All modern nation-states that entered war at some time or other, found it difficult to deal with "new" citizens, i.e. immigrants from other countries who had acquired citizenship in their chosen homeland.

Emigration and immigration had become a major phenomenon in Europe since the second half of the nineteenth century. Although most emigrants headed for North and South America, a substantial minority chose other European countries. Thus, the number of Germans living in England and Wales nearly doubled between 1861 and 1911. About half of them settled in London where they developed a dense network of German social clubs and associations. Most of them did not apply for British citizenship as this generally did not offer any extra benefits.[3]

So they had to register as "aliens" after Britain declared war on Germany in early August 1914 – which about 50,000 or so did. In comparison, about 6,000 people counted as naturalized citizens of German descent. Although they generally enjoyed the full privileges and rights of British subjects, they now came under increasing attack. Conservative and right-wing organizations waged a relentless campaign against "hyphenated Anglo-Germans" and demanded to revoke naturalization for all Germans who had acquired British nationality during the past 30 years. A member of the House of Lords declared in 1916 that naturalization made no difference for Germans: "Once a German, always a German." In the Commons, a Unionist MP referred to the "call of the blood" that transformed even seemingly loyal citizens of German descent into dangerous spies. After the press had expressed fears about Germans in public service, the government eventually decided that it would only employ sons of natural-born British or Allied subjects (Panayi 1991: 63, 65, 67–69).

The witch-hunt against all things German also targeted the royal family who in 1917 changed their German name of Sachsen-Coburg-Gotha to Windsor;

Prince Louis of Battenberg – who because of anti-German accusations had resigned from his position as First Sea Lord – became the Marquis of Milford Haven and assumed the surname of Mountbatten. Sir Eyre Crowe, Assistant Under-Secretary at the Foreign Office who was fiercely anti-German nevertheless found himself attacked because of his German mother and wife. A feminist journal pointing out his "double link with Germany" protested "against staking the safety of the British Empire and of our Allies upon the loyalty of this man." Golf clubs excluded naturalized Germans from frequenting their courses (Panayi 1991: 194, 199).

In sum, naturalized Germans (and Austrians) were put under enormous social, economic and political pressure. Their loyalty to the British crown was called into question or altogether denied. As in the German case against Jews, the war radicalized animosities and suspicions that reached back to earlier decades. They reflected anxieties and insecurities about the nation's own standing and identity – German fears of internal diversity as much as British fears about threats to their country's role as the world's powerhouse.

The fears that came to the fore in the USA after the country entered World War II had to do with race. It is the story of how the USA treated citizens of Japanese descent after 1941 – a well-known story since President Reagan officially apologized about it in 1988. While American citizens of German descent were not targeted at all and German "enemy aliens" were treated relatively mildly (only 7,000 were arrested of whom 2,300 were interned), Japanese-born citizens were dealt with much more harshly. Starting in February 1942, about 120,000 people, two thirds of them holding American citizenship, were evacuated from the West Coast and interned in government camps. Although confidential reports maintained that 90–98 percent of Japanese Americans were absolutely loyal to the United States, the US army held different views. And it managed to convince the Roosevelt administration that immediate action was necessary.

For General John DeWitt, commander of the Western Defense, "*the Japanese race is an enemy race* and while many second and third generation Japanese born on US soil, possessing US citizenship, have become 'Americanized', *the racial strains are undiluted*" (Muller 2007: 17; Daniels 1993: 216–238). Military experts on Japanese psychology stressed that "among the Japanese, loyalty follows families" rather than citizenship: "Citizenship is a Western concept. In the minds of the Japanese there is the belief that once a Jap always a Jap" (Muller 2007: 19, 43, quote from a 1943 training lecture for field investigators in the Army Service Commands). As a consequence, young men of Japanese descent were declared to be unacceptable for service in the armed forces (although the army soon started to enlist volunteers with Japanese language skills from the camps) (Muller 2007: 22f., 32f.). The policy of mass exclusion only ended in January 1945 when the government decided to replace it with a program of individual exclusion. This move was fostered by growing criticism within the political elite, a change in military concerns, and growing dissent among those interned on the grounds of their Japanese descent.

Conclusion

The general pattern that has emerged through those examples is obvious. Modern wars that involve nation-states have a tendency to become total wars. They aim at including all members of the nation and enlist them in various functions. Political propaganda has it that in modern wars, one nation confronts another nation. The "cabinet wars" of the early modern period have pitched professional armies against each other; the "people's wars" of the nineteenth and twentieth centuries were fought by whole nations, represented by citizen-soldiers. Military service is from now on considered a major (male) duty, and honor. It offers a perfect way to demonstrate one's sense of belonging, and is closely connected to political and cultural notions of citizenship. Prussian Jews in the 1840s were equally convinced of this link, as were African American soldiers serving in World War I: "When we have proved ourselves men, worthy to work and fight and die for our country, a grateful nation may gladly give us the recognition of real men, and the rights and privileges of true and loyal citizens of these United States" (Barbeau and Henri 1974: 7, see Grossman 1993: 169–190).

Wartime promises of and quests for inclusion go along, however, with heightened suspicions about citizens' loyalty and national allegiance. This became obvious as early as in 1792–1793 when the French Revolution faced serious political conflicts with neighboring states. The Revolutionary Wars not only triggered off bouts of wild xenophobia; they also put enormous pressure on those French citizens who were suspected as potentially disloyal: aristocrats, but also members of other political factions. Similar hunts for the internal enemy can be observed in most war societies. They target social and political groups as much as religious and ethnic communities. When war broke out in 1914, the German government had prepared orders to arrest leading social democrats whose loyalty was deemed unclear. Under the Second Red Scare starting in 1947, the US government conducted four million investigations as well as 12,000 hearings by loyalty boards in order to detect communist sympathies among federal employees and job applicants (Muller 2007: 1, 136ff.).

Hot and cold wars thus lend themselves to internal rifts and exclusionary politics. The latter are, above all, conducted against foreigners who happen to be citizens of enemy states. They are treated harshly in all belligerent countries. Here, World War I marked a novel stage of development, with hundreds of thousands of civilians being held in internment camps all over Europe and the USA. While the French government's decision in 1870 to intern 30,000 Germans was met with international outrage and successful pressure to release them within three weeks, Germany, Britain and Russia all detained massive numbers of enemy subjects between 1914 and 1918 (see Stibbe 2006: 5–19. As to the 1870 war, see Spiropulos 1922: 46. As to the novel dimensions of WWI, see the case studies by Nagler 1993: 191–215; Nagler 2000; Cesarani and Kushner 1993; Lohr 2003; Jahr 1999: 297–321). Internment, forced repatriation, deportation and expropriation were, so to speak, normal ways of dealing with "enemy aliens" after war was declared. As until 1949, international law offered no formal protection for civilians under enemy control (apart from the rights of populations living in occupied territory), governments did as they chose to do.[4]

The politics of exclusion did not stop here, however. Even people holding formal citizenship found their rights questioned and their loyalty disputed. Looking at practices in different countries with different political regimes and cultural self-understanding, those politics show remarkable structural similarities. Democracies seem to be as sensitive to fears about citizens' political allegiance as less democratic societies. Right-wing conservatives display markedly stronger reservations and suspicions than liberals who are less often drawn to political or racist exclusion. As a general rule, societies that cling to a "thin" notion of liberal citizenship and stress individual liberty rather than strong normative commitments, tend to be less concerned with potential defectors in times of crisis. In contrast, societies that favour a "thicker" concept of republican citizenship, that constantly worry about their internal cohesion and demand continuous proofs of allegiance, are obsessed with the figure of the traitor and internal enemy which gains exceptional urgency during a war (see Boveri 1961, and the interesting case study on France in Bavendamm 2004. As to notions of liberal versus republican citizenship, see Schuck 2002: 131–144; Dagger 2002: 145–158).

It is an interesting question to what degree different concepts of citizenship influence the way citizens are treated during wars. Are countries that grant citizenship predominantly on grounds of blood relationship (*ius sanguinis*) more or less doubtful about their citizens' trustworthiness than those that follow the *ius soli*, i.e. the principle that those who are born in their territory gain citizenship? The case studies presented in this chapter do not show any marked differences. States like the USA that adhere to *ius soli* are as vulnerable to suspicions of betrayal as states like Germany that mostly follow *ius sanguinis*. The extreme example of Japanese Americans after 1941 suggests that the rule of *ius soli* can invite greater doubts as to the trustworthiness of born nationals.

Furthermore, it has to be stressed that those doubts always concern collectives. A whole group – the Jews, the Germans, the Japanese – comes under attack, and individuals are judged negatively because they are seen as belonging to this very group. The negative judgment does not rest on individual actions and personal conduct. It rather focuses on identity and identification, on belief and emotion – on, so to speak, essentializing and totalizing notions of belonging that do not allow for individual choice and variation. The legal principle that every person has to be judged according to what he or she actually does or has done gives way to a regime of social, ethnic and political stereotyping and prejudice.

This regime plays out on several levels. In modern nation-states, accusations and witch-hunts against allegedly disloyal citizens emanate from social and political groups rather than from government agencies. The age of the political mass-market is characterized by a great number of associations, parties, and pressure groups that try to channel public opinion and mobilise support for their aims. They increasingly use modern communication (press, radio etc.) to spread and popularize their message. In Britain during World War I, it was above all the right-wing press that pushed for stronger action against Germans who had acquired British nationality. In Germany, anti-Semitic associations and individuals sent in complaints about Jewish shirkers and war profiteers. These (mostly anonymous) letters built up pressure on military commanders to take action. The federal government, though, was initially not inclined to listen to those demands. The administration's foremost goal was to keep the domestic peace and stop internal strife. Only when the military and economic situation deteriorated, could it be compelled to give in. As soon as the Jew Census was formally ordered, though, social anti-Semitism gained a much higher reputation. By putting its Jewish citizens under special vigilance, the German government formally acknowledged and justified anti-Semitism and accepted it as a guideline of exclusionary politics.

A similar development took place in the USA after 1941. Here again, it was the state's decision to take action against its citizens of Japanese descent that made all the difference. Even if those citizens (as much as their fellow-citizens from China) had already encountered numerous instances of racial prejudice in their daily lives and local neighborhoods, official politics had remained a neutral stance. But when the army convinced the Roosevelt administration to target Japanese Americans, prejudice turned into persecution and formal exclusion. While social discrimination and prejudice could be individually dealt with, political discrimination and exclusion had much more dramatic and lasting consequences. They induced a deep sense of alienation and left Japanese Americans with a collective feeling of shame and disrespect that was hard to overcome after the war ended. It even served to strengthen the ties within the Japanese community and thus propelled a tendency that ran counter to the declared goals of American immigration politics.

As a general rule, state intervention into the rights and duties of citizenship thus acquires a much higher importance than any individual or social attack. As citizenship is above all a political concept, official infringement does much greater harm than measures of social othering. Even if social or democratic citizenship, i.e. the free participation of citizens in the various institutions and organizations of civil society, constitutes a major element of belonging, political or republican citizenship can be considered the foundational block of civil rights and inclusion. Whenever this foundation is questioned or targeted, civil liberties and the rule of law (*Rechtsstaat*) are in trouble.

As history shows, wars make it easier for anti-liberals to attack the foundation and single out certain groups for exclusion. It depends on the strength and vivacity of their critics whether those attacks prove successful. Democracies usually comprise a great number of groups and individuals who are sensitive to civil rights and protest against any violation brought about by other groups or, ultimately, the state. Even in a semi-parliamentary state like Imperial Germany, there were many (non-Jewish) liberals and social democrats who fiercely criticized the Jew Census of 1916 and attacked the government for its non-declared anti-Semitism.

Another important safeguard may, of course, be found in the legal system. Wherever strong legal institutions are enshrined controling the state's handling of civil rights, the latter are usually in good hands. Without a constitution that states those rights, and without an independent Supreme Court that makes sure that civil rights are not curtailed by other citizens or by the government, the state of things may be much worse – especially in times of war.

Notes

1 196 American Law Reports, federal, 365 (originally published in 2004).
2 In 1913, when Germany celebrated the one-hundreth anniversary of the Leipzig battle of nations, a major Jewish newspaper had bitterly complained that Jews "as Prussian citizens and sons of the German Fatherland" were not treated "according to our worth, to our will and to the fulfilment of our duty" and that they were "put last" (*hintangesetzt*) compared to "sons" of other faiths (*Allgemeine Zeitung des Judentums*, 77, 1913).
3 To become a British subject, one had to reside within the Empire for at least five years, needed a "good character" and an "adequate knowledge of the English language," and had to take the oath of allegiance. Aliens who chose not to apply for British citizenship could hold property in the same way as British subjects could, but they were not allowed to vote or hold municipal and parliamentary office. See Panayi 1991: 61f.
4 In Stibbe 2006 it is mentioned that this calamity was redressed by the 1949 Geneva Convention on Human Rights that was meant to protect non-combatants during wars.

References

196 American Law Reports. Federal. 365 (originally published in 2004).
Allgemeine Zeitung des Judentums (1842) vol. 4, no. 14, April 2.
Allgemeine Zeitung des Judentums (1913) vol. 77, no. 11, March 14.
Angress, W.T. (1976) "Das deutsche Militär und die Juden im Ersten Weltkrieg," in *Militärgeschichtliche Mitteilungen*, vol. 19.
Angress, W.T. (1980) "The German Army's *Judenzählung* of 1916. Genesis – Consequences – Significance," in Leo Baeck Institute Yearbook, vol. 33.
Barbeau, A. and Henri, F. (1974) *The Unknown Soldiers: Black American Troops in World War I*, PhiladelphiaL Temple University Press.
Bavendamm, G. (2004) *Spionage und Verrat: Konspirative Kriegserzählungen und französische Innenpolitik, 1914–1917*, Essen: Klartext.
Bell, D.A. (2007) *The First Total War: Napoleon's Europe and the Birth of Warfare as We Know It*, Boston: Houghton Mifflin.
Boveri, M. (1961) *Treason in the Twentieth century*, London: Macdonald.
Cesarani, D. and Kushner, T. (eds.) (1993) *The Internment of Aliens in Twentieth Century Britain*, London: Frank Cass.
Colley L. (1982) *Britons: Forging the Nation*, New Haven, CT: Yale Uuniversity Press.
Daniels, R. (1993) "From Relocation to Redress: Japanese Americans and Canadians, 1941–1988," in P. Panayi (ed.), *Minorities in Wartime: National and Racial Groupings in Europe, North America and Australia during the Two World Wars*, Oxford: Berg.
Dagger, R. (2002) "Republican Citizenship," in E.F. Isin and B.S. Turner (eds.), *Citizenship Studies*, London: Sage.
Duhet, P.M. (1977) *Les femmes et la révolution 1789–1794*, Paris: Flammarion.
Foertsch, H. (1935) *Wehrpflicht-Fibel*, Berlin: Offene Worte.
Forrest, A. (1990) *The Soldiers of the French Revolution*, Durham, NC: Duke University Press.

Frevert, U. (2004) *A Nation in Barracks: Modern Germany, Military Conscription and Civil Society*, Oxford: Berg.

Geheimes Staatsarchiv Berlin-Dahlem, HA XX, Handschrift 7: Dr. Ludwig Goldstein (1936) *Heimatgebunden. Aus dem Leben eines alten Königsbergers*, October 31, vol. 2, Königsberg.

Gosewinkel, D. (2001) *Einbürgern und Ausschließen: Die Nationalisierung der Staatsangehörigkeit vom Deutschen Bund bis zur Bundesrepublik Deutschland*, Göttingen: Vandenhoeck & Ruprecht.

Gosewinkel, D. (2002) "Citizenship and Naturalization Politics in Germany in the nineteenth and twentieth centuries," in Daniel Levy and Yfaat Weiss (eds.), *Challenging ethnic citizenship: German and Israeli Perspectives on Immigration*, New York: Berghahn.

Grossman, J.R. (1993) "Citizenship and rights on the Home Front during the First World War: The 'Great Migration' and the 'New Negro'," in P. Panayi (ed.), *Minorities in Wartime: National and Racial Groupings in Europe, North America and Australia during the Two World Wars*, Oxford: Berg.

Hoffmann, C. (1997) "Between integration and rejection: the Jewish community in Germany, 1914–1918," in J. Horne (ed.), *State, society and mobilisation in Europe during the First World War*, Cambridge: Cambridge University Press.

Jahr, C. (1999) "Zivilisten als Kriegsgefangene. Die Internierung von 'Feindstaaten-Ausländern' in Deutschland während des Ersten Weltkrieges am Beispiel des 'Engländerlagers' in Ruhleben," in R. Overmans (ed.), *In der Hand des Feindes: Kriegsgefangenschaft von der Antike bis zum Zweiten Weltkrieg*, Cologne: Böhlau.

Juden in Preußen: Ein Kapitel deutscher Geschichte (1981) ed. Bildarchiv Preußischer Kulturbesitz, Dortmund: Harenberg (foundational document of the Jewish student fraternity Viadrina).

Judische Rundschau (1914) No. 32, August 7.

Lohr, E. (2003) *Nationalizing the Russian Empire: The Campaign against Enemy Aliens during World War I*, Cambridge, MA: Harvard University Press.

Müller, K.-J. (1987) *Armee und Drittes Reich 1933–1939*, Paderborn: Schöningh.

Muller, E. (2007) *American Inquisition: The Hunt for Japanese American Disloyalty in World War II*, Chapel Hill: University of North Carolina Press.

Nagler, J. (1993) "Victims of the Home Front: Enemy Aliens in the United States during the First World War," in P. Panayi (ed.), *Minorities in Wartime: National and Racial Groupings in Europe, North America and Australia during the Two World Wars*, Oxford: Berg.

Nagler, J. (2000) *Nationale Minoritäten im Krieg: "Feindliche Ausländer" und die amerikanische Heimatfront während des Ersten Weltkriegs*, Hamburg: Hamburger Edition.

Panayi, P. (1991) *The Enemy in our Midst: Germans in Britain During the First World War*, New York: Berg.

Schuck, P.H. (2002) "Liberal Citizenship," in E.F. Isin and B.S. Turner (eds.), *Citizenship Studies*, London: Sage.

Sieg, U. (2003) " 'Nothing more German than the German Jews'? On the Integration of a Minority in a Society at War," in R. Liedtke and D. Rechter (eds.), *Towards normality?* Tübingen: Mohr.

Sieg, U. (2001) *Jüdische Intellektuelle im Ersten Weltkrieg: Kriegserfahrungen, weltanschauliche Debatten und kulturelle Neuentwürfe*, Berlin: Akademie Verlag.

Spiropulos, J. (1922) *Ausweisung und Internierung feindlicher Staatsangehöriger*, Leipzig: Rossberg.

Stibbe, M. (2006) "The Internment of Civilians by Belligerent States during the First World War and the Response of the International Committee of the Red Cross," *Journal of Contemporary History*, 41, pp. 5–19.

Swartout, L.F. (2003) "Mut, Mensur und Männlichkeit: Die „Viadrina", eine jüdische schlagende Verbindung," in M. Hettling *et al.* (eds.), *In Breslau zu Hause? Juden in einer mitteleuropäischen Metropole der Neuzeit*, Hamburg: Dölling und Galitz.

Thucydides, *The Peloponnesian War*, II.

6 Limited war, limited citizenship

The case of veterans in the People's Republic of China

Neil J. Diamant

Liu Junmin and the strange case of the ten-year revoked disability pension

In August 1965 the Bureau of Civil Affairs of Yishui County (in Shandong Province, Eastern China) issued a report to provincial authorities vouching for the full restoration, with back pay, of the pension provided to a 47-year-old disabled veteran named Liu Junmin, who despite being wounded in 1942, had had his pension revoked since the end of 1955. The Yishui letter was the culmination of a two-year investigation surrounding the circumstances of his injury and the cancellation of his pension. It also included a healthy dose of self-criticism. "Our bureau," it noted, "has direct responsibility for Liu's case." Lackadaisical implementation of party policies, sloppy investigation and "a bias towards oral testimony" were all cited as the main causes for the ten-year pension hiatus (Shandong Provincial Archives [SA], A20–1–432: 2).

In all likelihood Yishui officials were unenthusiastic about copping to these deficiencies, but their hand was forced by other investigations into the case. According to an investigation by a team of six officials, Liu Junmin's case began in 1944, when he was in a security detachment attached to *The Masses Daily*, the newspaper of the provincial Chinese Communist Party (CCP) committee. While pulling guard duty in the town of Beiguan, Liu was "shot by a special agent," causing numerous wounds to his torso and leg. In September 1946, Liu returned home and was elected a member of his village party committee during land reform. The village was evacuated during a Nationalist offensive in 1947, but he returned in the spring of 1948. In August of that same year he was "introduced" to the Party by a fellow villager – Ma Jie – and other cadres. In 1951, he was given a certificate confirming that he was officially disabled and deserving of a fixed pension. By the end of that year, Liu was the secretary of the village's party branch. In 1953, however, he was expelled from the CCP, and in 1955 he lost his disability payment.

This turn of Liu's political fortunes resulted from the testimony of a fellow veteran in his unit, Yang Changxue. Yang charged that Liu's injury was not the product of being "beaten by a special agent," but was a "self-inflicted wound" designed to remove himself from harm's way. Liu, he charged, "betrayed the revolution." As "proof," Yang told village party members that Liu's wound was "top-down, on a slant, and began in the interior part of the leg"; this would not have been possible if someone standing in front of him attacked him. Yang's testimony was seemingly confirmed by another member of the unit. Ma Jie, the village cadre, noted: "If he was treated unjustly, why didn't he say anything for 10 years?"(SA A20–1–432: 4).[1] Faced with these two accounts – a war injury caused at night with no eyewitnesses and a self-inflicted wound – the special investigation team now faced the task of disproving one of the versions.

As it turned out, this proved fairly easy to do. After two days they ascertained that there was no proof that the wound's origin was on the inside of the leg, or that it was self-inflicted. Three other members of his security unit testified that "no one at *The Masses Daily* said anything about a self-inflicted wound; everyone said a special agent did it." As early as September 1963, even Yang Changxue, who lodged the accusation, said that he "never heard of any leader disagreeing with the agent story," but decided that Liu's injury was fake "on the basis of the sound of the gun" and the position of Liu's body vis-à-vis the shell casing, which the investigation team recreated to show that the wound could only have come from the outside. The other "proof" – that Liu's decade-long wait for justice was itself evidence of his guilt – was also challenged. Liu claimed that he did in fact report the case to the county government and "talked to the township chief and others," who all confirmed that it was very difficult for Liu to pursue his case because "he had a hard time walking, and needs money and free time." The outcome of the investigation was now clear: Liu was framed by Yang Changxue. But why did he do this?

Under pressure from investigators, Yang admitted to fabricating the whole story because of a personnel vendetta against Liu. Access to medicine and illness, however, were at its core. According to Yang's confession, back in the early 1950s he had gone to Liu's village when the latter was the party secretary in order to procure medicine for his ill son. Liu was at the local pharmacy when Yang came in. Yang asked that Liu cover the cost of the medicine, but Liu did not intervene on his behalf. Even though the pharmacy agreed to give him credit for the cost of the medicine, Yang was incensed: "We were once together in the army, and now it's as if he doesn't even know me." The medicine did not help, however, and Yang's son died. Distraught, he vowed to Liu: "Your leg will be my retribution! Your disability is fake! Just wait until the CCP has a purge!"(SA A20–1–432: 7).

In pursuing his vendetta against Liu, Yang Changxue found an ally in Liu's political rival in the village, Ma Jie. It was Yang who told Ma Jie that Liu "faked his injury." According to the testimony by a former township chief, there were two factions in the village: Ma Jie's faction was on the ropes; Liu's was ascendant. Ma, however, was politically ambitious – "he really wanted to be an official" – but his background was problematic: he had been a bandit during the war. When this piece of information was exposed, Liu and others requested that Ma be expelled from the party. Higher levels of the CCP, however, disapproved this action. When village officials deliberated whether to restore Ma's status, Liu was among those who decided against it. Since that time, Liu told investigators, "He has a grudge against me." In sum, the investigators concluded, "It was all Yang Changxue's personal revenge and Ma Jie's ability to take advantage of the situation to cause him harm." In 1955, Liu was expelled from the party. To kill two birds with one stone and to prevent Liu from "creating pressure," they also decided to discontinue his disability payments; the paperwork for this was wrapped up in 1955 and authorized by the regional party committee, even though they lacked this authority. The Provincial government never authorized revoking his pension or his "revolutionary disabled soldier" status (SA A20–1–432: 24).

Liu's saving grace was that he happened to serve in a security detachment to the province's most important newspaper, *The Masses Daily*, whose literate officials stepped in to prod other agencies to reopen the case. From 1963–1965, two editors at *The Masses Daily*, Huang Fengxian and Zhu Min, repeatedly intervened on Liu's behalf. Huang and Zhu jointly wrote a letter to the Bureau of Civil Affairs in December 1963 with a blow-by-blow account of Liu's version of events; after writing to Provincial Civil Affairs and not receiving a response, Huang accompanied Liu to their office to talk with them face to face. Another newspaperman called Yishui County Civil Affairs to figure out what went wrong. A year passed and the matter was still unresolved, so they wrote another letter to provincial Civil Affairs, and Zhu procured a letter about proper administrative procedure from the newspaper's party committee and sent it to the provincial CCP party committee. "According to the [unspecified] regulations," it noted, "disability status and pension are generally not revoked as a disciplinary measure, and only sometimes for criminal offenses." Because Liu was never prosecuted for a criminal offense, "his pension should not have been revoked." In 1965, a special investigation team finally was formed, the witnesses located and the truth uncovered. Justice, however, was fleeting. A year after his pension was restored, the Cultural Revolution broke out. The government offices that handled pensions were pulled into the turmoil.

This case, which I found in the Shandong Provincial Archive, is puzzling for a number of reasons. First, given its chronology covering the mid-1950s to the mid-1960s, it should not have happened in the first place. Liu Junmin had a very difficult time regaining his revoked pension despite the fact that several nationwide campaigns had taken place to elevate the status of the military and military personnel. By 1965, many Chinese were aware of the good deeds of Lei Feng, a People's Liberation Army (PLA) soldier who accidently died and was held up as a model for national emulation after the party "discovered" his diary in which he effusively praised Chairman Mao. In addition to reading about Lei Feng, many Chinese experienced the militarization of many institutions, particularly in the education system. Students conducted drills, learned how to shoot and studied about the sacrifices of revolutionary martyrs. Liu Junmin, despite his military background, benefitted very little from this. Second, the Chinese state is often portrayed as a strong one – a state "able to get things done" – with a leadership capable of imposing its will on the population. Redistribution of land (in land reform) in the early 1950s, the enforcement of the one-child per-family policy since 1978, and, more recently, the rapid growth of the economy all give the state a formidable presence. But if the state did have high capacity, how did it happen that Liu's pension was *illegally* revoked, he was ousted from power, the medicines that should have been available for Liu's nemesis Yang Changxue's son were not, and local officials organized unauthorized attacks against him? If it had not been for Liu's ad-hoc connection to *The Masses Daily*, no investigation would have taken place. Finally, how was it possible that someone like Ma Jie – a bandit-turned-party secretary – successfully asserted claims to high political status, entered the CCP, received the support of district-level officials and then conspired, successfully, to dispute the legitimacy of an injury to a PLA soldier? If military success has been such an integral part of the CCP's legitimating national narrative (the party claims to have defeated the Nationalists, Japan, the United States, India, and Vietnam), why was Liu Junmin vulnerable to political predation and administrative malfeasance?

In this chapter I argue that Liu's difficulties are best understood as a manifestation of the failure to foster what I call "martial citizenship," which I define as either sympathy, respect, appreciation or a willingness to accord higher status (particularly by elites), to individuals who served a state in a military capacity.[2] Liu Junmin's case, I suggest, was part and parcel of a larger failure to respect veterans and implement policies that would have helped them secure a respectable place in the polity. Liu certainly was not an isolated case. An analysis of petitioning in one Shandong county between 1953–1965 found that quite a few disabled veterans experienced comparable problems (Haiyang xian zhi 1987: 649), and an internal party document from the early 1960s noted cases of local cadres, not unlike the district official in Liu Junmin's case, "beating up, taking revenge upon and causing the suicides of disabled veterans and members of military and martyr families" (SA A20–1–332: 1). Only several years after the establishment of the PRC, a period when the state was supposedly experiencing its "honeymoon years" (Cheng and Selden 1994: 646), veterans of the successful revolution compared themselves to "dirty socks that are tossed aside after use" (Qingpu District Archive [QA] 48–2–105: 136) while others called veterans "scum," and "used and discarded goods" (Shanghai Municipal Archive [SMA] B168–1–628: 47; B168–1–607: 50). If we use James Burk's notion of citizenship as "whether we enjoy recognition and respect *from our fellow citizens* as *worthy* members of the political community" (Burk 1995: 503) the treatment of veterans at the hands of their own state and fellow citizens does not indicate that this concept was particularly meaningful in China.

The significance of China's inability to significantly raise the status of the military and its personnel can hardly be overestimated, particularly when we compare the status of veterans in China to those in many other countries. Even though scholars have often emphasized the role of law and legal institutions in the elevation of marginal groups in society, there is a substantial body of evidence from democracies and non-democracies alike that military service during wartime has played an equally important, if not greater, role, in promoting citizenship, particularly if we understand this concept in terms of respect and appreciation rather than formal rights – the doffing of a hat, as it were.[3] Particularly in Continental Europe after French revolutionaries, thinking that "war was to be a total effort, in which all members of the community had a role," showed the world the power of a conscripted citizen-army (Forrest 2006: 14) full citizenship status for males was very closely connected to military service, which was defined as a patriotic political commitment (Geyer 1993: 152–153). The basic premise was that citizenship could be *activated* and *proven*, and social respect possibly attained, *if* men demonstrated courage and comported themselves with honor in difficult circumstances. In the United States African-Americans, Native Americans, and other minority groups based their claims to citizenship using this military-based principle (Sitkoff 1997: 74; Johnson 1999: 29, 33; Shaffer 2004; Franco 1990: 129; Britton 1997: 181).

This relationship between war, patriotism, and citizenship status is also relevant in non-democracies. In Meiji Japan, for example, the 1873 law requiring military service of young men also led to the conferring of rights as well, since a "blood tax" on people could not be demanded in the absence of a constitutional system (Hackett 1964: 336, 350). Research by Joshua Sanborn on late Czarist Russia and the early Soviet period demonstrates that the army high command, worried about the security of their country, argued for a very broad extension "of military service and citizenship" by means of the Universal Military Service Law (passed in the 1870s). As late as 1894, military officials argued for the "citizen-building role of the military," since few institutions besides the military would be able to weaken "tribal differences" among Russians (Sanborn 2003: 9, 12, 18). It was also the military, not intellectual elites, which argued for a conception of citizenship in which people can and should expect something in return from the state for their military service. The claims were fairly basic: soldiers wanted the state to take care of their families while they were away, "respect" their contributions, and grant them privileges in relation to their "nonwarrior fellow citizens" (ibid.: 5, 50).

China, I suggest, was noticeably different in this respect. Many political elites failed to respect veterans for their military contributions even during the periods when such respect was more likely to emerge – the early years of the state, during war, propaganda campaigns, and protracted periods of international tension. Wartime military service, which led to a gradual rise in the status of more marginalized citizens in many places in the world, has not produced a similar effect in China. Moreover, many institutions that emerged during and in the immediate aftermath of war, such as welfare, insurance schemes, pensions and the like (Keegan 1976: 220–221; Porter 1994: 179–191; Colley 1992: 304) have been notably lacking in China, even in the rural areas from which the People's Liberation Army (PLA) draws most of its recruits. Whereas warmaking has been crucial to state-making and the expansion of executive powers in Europe, the United States and the former Soviet Union, in China the central state frequently fights a losing battle against entrenched local officials, is often flustered by its inability to gather basic information on the economy and the environment, and has difficulty enforcing international agreements to which it is obligated, as well as many domestic policies; most peasants, for instance, have more than one child. To explain why so many veterans were poorly treated, the low status of the military, as well as the "larger" difficulties with welfare institutions and state capacity, we must look at the *type* of wars China has fought over the last century. Unlike the former USSR, Israel, Japan, the United States, many countries in Western Europe and Taiwan, South Korea or Singapore, China has never fought as a *nation-in-arms* in a highly legitimate or total war against a clear foreign foe, nor has it ever experienced anything close to near universal conscription. As a result, the historical connection between mass war and citizenship, mass war and the status of the military and between war and veterans' status, has not been forged in China.

These are large claims that appear, on first glance, to fly in the face of much of the conventional narrative about the rise of the Communist Party (on the strength of its nationalist credentials), the legitimizing function of its wars, and the status of the military. This narrative, I suggest, ignores several common-sensical questions raised China's twentieth-century history. China's revolution, unlike those of the United States, USSR, France, Turkey and most other nation-states, was based in the countryside, and so the overwhelming majority of its veterans were therefore peasants (Meisner 1982: 177; Shichor 1996: 338). As much as intellectual elites talked and wrote about the need for a stronger state, very few joined the military in a combat role (Waldron 2003: 257). War did not produce a "leveling affect" or much sympathy for veterans among educated elites; the relationship between Liu Junmin and the journalists at *The Masses Daily* was ad-hoc and did not last longer than his problem. Neither the Nationalists, who governed China between 1928 and 1949, nor the CCP were strong enough to implement a nationwide draft; prior to 1949, China was internally divided, and the Korean War took place too soon after the establishment of the PRC to institute a well-organized draft. Moreover, given the length and complexity of China's revolutions and wars (1911–1949), it makes sense that someone like Ma Jie, the former bandit, could claim credit for their eventual successes – thereby diluting veterans' claims to martial citizenship. Finally, given that China fought most of its wars against *former allies* (the United States was allied with "China" in WWII; India in the 1950s; the USSR until the late 1950s; and Vietnam until the mid-1970s), it stands to reason that many people would dispute their sagacity and legitimacy, and therefore the authenticity of the "chips" veterans hoped to cash in. Martial citizenship in China, I suggest, was mainly limited by the composition of the military (resulting from the rural-to-urban dynamics of the revolution, elite bias against military service and the lack of a draft), and the length, complexity and questionable legitimacy of its wars.

To illustrate both the weakness of martial citizenship in China and my arguments about its primary causes, in what remains of this chapter I take a close look at two policy areas that had a decisive impact on military personnel. In the first, I examine policies about *place*. Given that most veterans were peasants, how did the state treat their quest to translate martial-based claims for citizenship (respect and appreciation) to *urban citizenship* – a city residence card? I then turn to policies about *status*: what impact did state propaganda and policies about the legitimacy of the Korean War and veteran identity have on the views of ordinary citizens towards military service and veterans? How did ordinary people and local officials react when veterans claimed that they deserved more respect and better treatment based on their wartime contributions?[4]

Policies of place

Service to a state or a revolutionary cause rarely goes unacknowledged, even if the motivations for such service have been less than altruistic. In the contemporary United States, for example, veterans receive a host of benefits, even if many join the armed services because of limited career options. Requiring "pure motives" as the quid pro quo for benefits would be impractical (how would impure motives be discovered?), counterproductive (it would deter people from serving), and unfair; pure motives, after all, are not expected of any other sector of society that benefits from government largesse.

Just as wars have been endemic to human civilization, so too have demobilizations of the armies fighting those wars. Demobilization, in turn, frequently has been associated with granting those who fought for the state some sort of reward (material and/or symbolic) for service, which is most always defined as "patriotic." Historically, one of the most common and attractive has been the land grant, sometimes accompanied by cash payments. By some indications, the Roman Empire established the precedent for this, at least in the West. Soldiers discharged from service after the Second Punic War (218–201 BC) received various sizes of land grants in Italy as part of the consolidation of Roman power on the peninsula (Goldsworthy 2006: 29, 156, 254). By Caesar's time (101–44 BC), it was "almost taken for granted" that if a general wanted to enhance the benefits for his men, it would be in the form of land grants. Intending "to satisfy the discharged veterans," he provided each soldier 5,000 *denarii*, more than a soldier would earn if he "served a full 16-year term in the army," and more than he expected. In the fall of 46 BC, he began his program "to provide farms for his veteran soldiers," a compensation plan that required a great deal of effort and involved surveyors, investigators and staff to hear "pleas from interested parties" (ibid.: 473–474). He also confiscated land from vanquished enemies (like Pompey) and their supporters for this purpose (Keppie 1983: 55; Goldsworthy 2006: 473). After Caesar, land confiscations to benefit veterans became even more widespread and aggressive. Under Augustus, 18 cities, many known for their "proven fertility," lost land "for the benefit of veterans." When land was not enough for veterans in a town, the Emperor took from adjacent ones by force (Keppie 1983: 60–61, 89). In all forms of settlement, veterans were allowed a significant degree of autonomy, as befitted their martially-gained status as "citizens" of the empire. Settled "in strict military formation," they had their own leaders and spokesmen, and were able to maintain a "spirit of comradeship" in their colonies (ibid.: 110).

This model of veteran settlement – land, political patronage, and community – proved exceptionally resilient in military demobilizations in the West. In Great Britain, for example, some 4,000 veterans and their families were resettled in Nova Scotia in 1749, and in 1763, after the Seven Years War, veterans were settled in Quebec, Florida, and Grenada (Reese 1992: 39, 42). In the United States until quite recently, land grants were also the principle way the government rewarded veterans. The Continental Congress and some of the colonies promised bounties of land for military service during the Revolution. The Military Land Bounty Acts of 1811–1812 "set aside a special military tract between the Illinois and Mississippi Rivers" (Black and Hyson 1944: 3). Land grants were also offered to veterans of the War of 1812, the Mexican War and various conflicts with Indians in the 1850s; by 1855, "any veteran of any war from the Revolution on, or his heirs, could obtain a warrant for 160 acres of land anywhere in the surveyed public domain" (ibid.). According to one study of veterans in agriculture, land was both "available" and "almost universally desired" (Taylor 1945: 48).

This cursory survey allows us to point to some initial differences with China, another major empire of the pre-modern world. China, like Rome, was very concerned with border security since it was surrounded by other powerful groups. Unsurprisingly, soldiers who waged war on behalf of the emperor were often forced to resettle in border regions, where they set up fortifications in strategic areas, pushing out the local population. Other components of the Roman model, however, were not adopted. In China, political leaders *did not* conceive of land grants as a reward for a veterans' military service, as something that was *owed* to the veteran for having rendered an important service to the government. Furthermore, ex-soldiers had no say in the matter of their residence, unlike the West where soldiers could choose to settle on the land, or not. In other words, China shared with Roman-style military colonization only its *strategic rationale*, not the underlying sense of reciprocity, gratitude, and recognition of elevated social and political status.

The absence of this "spatial" dimension of martial citizenship can be seen quite clearly in China's policy towards its veterans after capturing power in 1949. Even though very large areas of the countryside were ravaged by war and many families torn apart, and despite the Communist Party's reputation for policy oscillations during the 1950s and 1960s, its resettlement policy for veterans was remarkably consistent: veterans were either "collectively demobilized," or "resettled in their native place" (*yuan ji an zhi*). In the former scenario, entire regiments were immediately "civilized" and sent to work in collective farms or in fledgling industries in some of the harshest environments in the country. Usually bachelors, these veterans worked in railway construction, opening up agricultural wasteland, oil exploration, and other large-scale civil engineering projects. In 1950, for instance, a unit of 20,000 soldiers became a "construction brigade" in the arid and virtually barren Northwest (but an area rich in oil). In Qinghai province, veterans were the "main" workforce; 2,000 were assigned to one well alone, constituting some 70 percent of the workforce (Republic of China, Ministry of Defense 1957: 33).

Most veterans, however, were just sent back to their original village. At least officially, there were some exceptions to the *yuan ji an zhi* policy: veterans who had a special technical skill and could find an employer willing to hire them might be able to attain urban residence. The origins of this policy are not clear – it is probably based on dynastic precedents of demobilizing armies – but the main thrust of it was quite similar to the collective demobilization policy: disperse veterans and keep them as far away as possible from the capital, cities, and industrial centers – in other words, places associated with status and wealth. Veterans were not given any choice in the matter, and, for most all of them, moving back to the countryside was an extremely unattractive option. Unlike many of their land grant counterparts in the West, they *did not* want to settle down, farm, and live a quiet life. In China, veterans' expectations of martial citizenship was infused with notions of *urban citizenship* (in Chinese, the original word for a city person, *shimin*, was also used to mean "citizen") since this connoted higher pay and status. The *yuan ji an zhi* policy contradicted this aspiration.

On the face of it, the *yuan ji an zhi* policy made sense: why wouldn't soldiers want to go "home"? But in the context of the war-torn and poor countryside this regulation was a stupendous simplification. Take the concept of "native" for instance. Wars frequently lead to social dislocation, refugee flows, and long-term family separation. Did "native" mean where one was born, or where one lived for many years during the war? "Place" could be equally problematic. Wars also lead to physical destruction – entire villages were bombed by the Japanese during the occupation. On the surface, "resettlement" appears to be a simple concept, but it was not. Wars in China resulted in massive civilian casualties. How could a veteran who returned to an empty or damaged home be celebrated as a war hero? None of the inevitable chaos of war, let alone rural veterans' desire for urban residence, was taken into consideration. Equally problematic, there is little evidence of deliberation about the policy's potential effectiveness, dangers or complexities. In all of the time he spent writing theoretical and other instructions from his relative safe haven in Northwest China, Mao did not devote a single essay to veterans as a group. Nor can I find evidence of input from local experts on the Chinese rural economy, as was the case in many Western countries in the run-up to major legislation affecting rural-bound veterans.

County and provincial-level gazetteers, much like the hundreds of documents reiterating this basic regulation, give us a rather glossy and uncomplicated summary of how *yuan ji an zhi* was implemented. For instance, the Civil Affairs section of Anhui's provincial gazetteer notes that, from 1950–1958, the province took in 224,344 veterans, among whom 198,448 (88.5 percent) were returned to the countryside from which they came (Anhui sheng zhi: minzheng zhi 1993: 140). In Shandong Province, approximately 50,000 demobilized soldiers arrived in the first six months of 1957. Of these, "the absolute majority" returned to the countryside, generally close to 80 percent (Republic of China, Ministry of Defense 1957: 13, 33).

Archival records, on the other hand, flesh out the more problematic aspects of this policy. Leaving aside for the moment the question of whether or not veterans "assigned" to work in agriculture actually *stayed* in the countryside in the short or long term, the general thrust of the data suggests that a very large majority of them returned to the countryside. If this was the case, it would mean that only a minority of rural veterans could secure positions in the local political structure and have political power. To veterans, this would be a double blow, since, in addition to "becoming a peasant," returning to the countryside after service without any increase in power and status was a serious "loss of face." In Yelong Township in Qingpu, veteran Dong Jianliang told officials at a 1957 meeting:

> Civil Affairs doesn't educate the cadres and peasants enough, so when we returned here and had to go back to farming, they all look down upon us, thinking that we're all good-for-nothings. There's great pressure on us, which makes us very depressed. It's hard for us to work. That's why we request job transfers.
>
> (QA 48–2–105: 4)

Pressure also came from family. According to a national-level report, families wrote their sons and husbands to "stay in the army or work for the government, just don't come home" (SMA A54–2–49: 40).

Gazetteer and other data bear out veterans' minority status in local political administration and the limited opportunities for upward mobility – a predicament that surely affected the political fortunes of Liu Junmin, whose story began this chapter. In Yi County, Hebei Province, 21 percent of returned veterans had positions at the village and township levels (Yi xian zhi 1991: 360) with a similar figure in Jinzhai County in Anhui (Jinzhai xian zhi 1992: 527). In Qingpu County (1951), only one of the 38 returned veterans was a village chief, two were militia platoon leaders and one-third were militiamen (QA 48–2–31: 30). Undoubtedly, these fortunate veterans were grateful to the CCP and viewed their military experience very positively, but it appears that most were less lucky and could not secure political jobs, especially those with power.

The failure of the state to accommodate veterans' demand to reward martial citizenship with urban status and/or political status back in the village had severe repercussions. Facing political discrimination in the village and attracted to higher wages being offered in urban industries, many veterans picked up and left the countryside. Urban officials wrote in condescending tones toward these veterans. Rarely did they use a neutral term such as "moving" or even "migrating." Instead, veterans were almost always described as "aimlessly" or "recklessly wandering" (*mangmu wailiu*) into cities. "Wandering" into cities was particularly acute in Shanghai as well as in less well-off areas. Shandong Province, on China's eastern seaboard, was one of the main areas of conflict in the recent wars against Japan and the Nationalists. After the wars, thousands of veterans refused to go home, spilling into near and faraway cities. Deeming the problem of *mangmu wailiu* "very serious," officials wrote in 1953, "Almost every large city in the country has veterans from Shandong who are blindly (*mangmu*) looking for work," with most of them concentrating in the north

(SA A20–1–109: 48). Certainly the numbers suggested that a large-scale movement of veterans was underway; in a three-month period in 1954, close to 3,000 veterans departed the province and "headed northeast," often after having sold off their farm material and personal possessions (*Shandong xingzheng gongbao* 1954: 13). This meant, of course, that they were destitute when they arrived in cities.

More serious than leaving the countryside of the city, however, were more aggressive confrontations between rural veterans and urban officials. In the early 1950s veterans were reportedly "very angry" when confronted by the police and other authorities demanding documents and information (SMA B1–2–1519: 4). One veteran simply could not fathom why they, victors of the revolution, would now be denied to right to live where they pleased: "Now we have a unified government, so we should be able to go wherever we want!" Some – by one 1953 account the "majority" (SMA B168–1–61: 125) – flat out refused to leave, "convinced that it will be easy to find a job" (SMA B1–2–1519: 4).

When trickery and "talking back" did not do the trick, veterans were willing to adopt more confrontational tactics. In Shanghai circa 1957, they took their bedding to the reception offices of local authorities and refused to leave (SMA B168–1–633: 102). In Qingpu in the mid-1950s, veterans made repeated visits to the Bureau of Civil Affairs, often getting into heated arguments with its officials (QA 48–2–27: 47; QA 48–1–35: 15). To each other they said, "You're a fool and idiot if you don't fight with government officials," and when reprimanded for their behavior remarked, "Party, Government – I don't give a damn!" (QA 48–2–156: 21). Some threatened suicide (SMA B1–2–1519: 4), and others did kill themselves (SMA B168–1–600: 111). Some violence was not self-directed: reports mentioned veterans who "beat cadres" and "create disturbances" (ibid.).

The politics of status

The restrictions placed on veterans' efforts to "cash in" on their military service to achieve urban status was not the only way martial citizenship was limited in China. Equally if not more important to veterans was social and political recognition of their status in everyday interactions with officials and ordinary people. The case of Liu Junmin, violence, and suicides may very well suggest that some of their problems can be traced to the lack of a consensus about the value of their military service and the wars they fought. According to the Communist Party's version of history, veterans were considered (to use Augustus' title) "first citizens" owing to their contributions to the party and state. Was it the case that many others disagreed entirely with this assessment?

Archival documents, however, greatly complicate this picture, in what amounts to a near-alternative version of reality. Given space limitations, two examples will have to suffice: popular views about the Korean War, and the extent to which a military record trumped "bad" class background (landlord, rich peasant, capitalist and the like).

China, like all states during wartime, tried to mobilize public opinion in support of the war in Korea when it broke out in 1950. Officials fanned out in neighborhoods and villages to teach ordinary people about "patriotism" and why the war was both necessary and legitimate. This was not easy: the meaning of "patriotism" was not well-understood (the term in Chinese, *aiguo zhuyi*, or "love of country-ism," was borrowed from Japanese), and many people were aware that the United States helped defeat Japan in WWII. In 1951, for example, there was a short-lived campaign to get Shanghai residents to sign "patriotic compacts" in support of the war, but reviews of these efforts noted that the campaign failed to materialize in 40–50 percent of firms; in an investigation of 950 work units, "empty and vague" compacts were found in 600 of them (SMA C1–2–362: 29). When these compacts were signed, it was often a *pro forma* affair. In one firm, investigators asked workers what the compacts were actually about but "no one could remember." In "very many firms," patriotic compacts simply became a method to discipline a fairly unruly workforce; patriotic compacts morphed into "labor contracts": workers promised to avoid "dozing off" and "eating whenever we feel like it" (SMA C1–2–362: 30).

The more serious propaganda effort – the campaign to "Resist America and Support Korea" – yielded similar results: implementation was shoddy and people's reactions ambivalent. According to a draft of a summary report, the campaign unfolded reasonably well in "universities and hospitals" but "hardly anything was done in private firms; what is done stops at the cadre and activist level and doesn't go any further" (SMA C1–2–361: 31). In the industrial sector, workers and managers both thought the campaign diverted attention from production and was a waste of time (ibid.: 35). An internal report from a district level party committee found that its members "generally don't care about current affairs," and "see propaganda work as a burden"; "very many" presented it as nothing more than a "production drive" (SMA A22–2–45: 54).

As much as ex-post-facto investigations revealed "unbalanced development" in the campaign, investigators probably were more startled when they encountered local cadres and ordinary workers' reactions to the various protagonists in the war, namely, their own government, North Korea, the USSR, and the United States. In one district, many people were confused by the campaign to go to war with the United States. A woman surnamed Cao said, "I only understand resisting Japan, not resisting the US and supporting North Korea"; another said, "Why go to war with the United States?" (SMA A22–2–45: 98). Ordinary workers were similarly "confused" according to investigators, who summarized their views after extensive interviews (SMA C1–2–361: 33; SMA A22–2–25: 55):

The United States is attacking North Korea, not us, so why go to war?

Penicillin is American, and even at its worst the US isn't nearly as bad as the Japanese devils.

The US is better than Japan; in the past they gave us flour and milk powder.

The USSR wants China to "carry the bridal carriage" [do the hard work, while the bride gets all the glory]; they want China to burn and they'll come in to reap the millet.

North Korea's in a war and wants us to fight but we shouldn't. What will we do if they decide to attack Shanghai? Their army is very tough.

Given these views of the war, perhaps it should not be very surprising that those who returned from Korea expecting better treatment would be very disappointed when encountering a less-than-warm reception. During the latter period of the Korean War in Shandong Province veterans and former POWs staged "uprisings" against the Communist Party because of poor treatment, in particular, the lack of access to land (it had been distributed to others while they were away at war), medicine for chronic illnesses and pain, and women who would marry them (SA A20–1–41: 69).

If veterans who had served honorably in Korea experienced difficulties securing status on account of people's dim view of the war, those who fought against the Japanese (sometimes heroically) with the Nationalists but after 1945 engaged the PLA, but later surrendered and fought with them (Chinese history is full of rapidly shifting political alliances) experienced even greater difficulties. There were quite a few of these veterans: among 200 veterans who arrived in Shanghai in 1950–1951, roughly 27 had served with the Nationalists "for a long time"; some were officers with a "complicated" political history (SMA B168–1–600: 108). A 1952 analysis of the social and political background of 2,105 veterans in Shanghai showed that 70 percent were "volunteers" for the Korean War, 6 percent left the Nationalist Army on their own accord and were absorbed into the PLA during the latter phases of the Civil War and almost one-quarter were pre-1949 POWs who were "re-educated" (SMA B168–1–607: 53).

But even these veterans were not as problematic as some of those who joined the PLA from urban areas after 1949, since they were more likely to have had extensive contact with the Nationalists, who controlled cities prior to the Communist takeover. According to the Interior Minister, these veterans were even more problematic than former POWs and Nationalist soldiers (*Minzheng jianbao*, 24 May, 1956: 2). Which of these identities were more salient? Could someone who fought against Japan with the Nationalist Party be recognized for this patriotic contribution? Could a veteran who fought against the United States in the Korean War but whose father was a landlord be treated with respect? In the former Soviet Union during WWII, the answer to this was fairly clear. As noted by the historian Amir Weiner, mass war reduced the significance of class status. By 1944, social origins were no longer the "dominant criteria of sociopolitical status"; bad class or family background was redeemed through wartime exploits, while non-combat service was marginalized (Weiner 2001: 8, 60, 68–69).

Until we have access to more archives, it will be impossible to answer these questions conclusively, but the general pattern suggests that "civilian" party officials either flatly refused to recognize, or at least pretended to refuse to recognize when it served their interest, "problematic" veterans' contributions (to fighting the Japanese or the United States), focusing instead on their anti-Communist history or "class purity" as the most important method of evaluating political worthiness. In 1951, a report noted, veterans with "complicated" backgrounds languished without land, jobs or housing for as long as a year; some lived in guest houses and subsisted on welfare (SMA B168–1–600: 115) and in villages some of these veterans were immediately placed under surveillance (SMA B168–1–607: 49). In 1952, the Shanghai government noted that "it is impossible to solve" employment problems facing those with "complicated histories" and that the government could not support them with aid indefinitely (SMA B168–1–605: 79), a problem that continued well into the late 1950s, as enterprise personnel directors, either by themselves or jointly with the local party committee, refused to hire veterans with complicated pasts. Stress was endemic among these veterans, as was poverty and anger at local units for ignoring the "spirit" of state policies and directives from the Minister of the Interior that veterans' past problems should be "separated" from current ones, and their own personal problems from those related to their families (SMA B127–1–820: 28).

Crime and suicide statistics reveal some of the personal repercussions from "problematic" social and political histories. In a 1957 investigation of 40 suicide cases occurring between 1955–1957, 12.5 percent were caused by stress and anxiety stemming from "political history problems" (SMA B168–1–633: 78) while some 25 percent of 135 criminal cases involving veterans in 1956 resulted from the politicized charge of "counterrevolution," the second largest category after theft (36 percent) (SMA B168–1–517: 139). The categories of "counterrevolution" and "problematic history" incorporated a wide range of experiences, but mainly referred to veterans who were in the Nationalist Party at some point, had kin in Hong Kong or Taiwan, or suspect class background (*Minzheng jianbao*, 24 May, 1956: 2).

What the experiences of these veterans suggest is that the cultivation of martial citizenship requires a significant amount of simplification, or *narrative simplicity*. Veterans in China had a difficult time securing citizenship based on their martial contributions because China's wars (against the Nationalists, Japanese, and Americans) were too complicated. Some of those who claimed martial citizenship (like Ma Jie, in the opening story) were bandits who supported the CCP; others were members of the Nationalist Party, and yet others had fought with the CCP, but other family members did not. As a result, martial citizenship could not successfully contend with other forms of claiming rights and status, such as serving in a union, a youth league, or being a land reform "activist." This situation was quite different than in the USSR, where, as noted earlier, martial citizenship trumped class considerations, the US (where front-line combat soldiers had the highest status after WWII), and Vietnam, where veterans, unlike their CCP counterparts, are permitted to produce literature that both speaks to their experience and even is critical of war (for instance, Bao Ninh's *The Sorrow of War*, 1996). All of these countries were, at some point, nations-in-arms, had mass conscription and fought wars that were considered more legitimate (and less complicated) than those in China.

Conclusion

One unfortunate problem in the study of Chinese politics is that much of the basic terminology we use to explain events there is extracted from the Western political experience. Whether we do this for pedagogical reasons, or to explain things in terms that our Americanist and Europeanist colleagues will understand, we often resort to terms such as nationalism, patriotism, citizenship, institutions, state-building, democracy, and rights. For instance, the Communist Party's rise and political victory has been attributed to its nationalism and legitimacy, the frequent resort to petitioning and lawsuits is explained in terms of "rights consciousness," "political institutions" have been evoked to account for its recent economic success, and there is a burgeoning literature on "democratization" despite any evidence that China has moved in that direction. The view that PRC veterans were well-treated is epiphenomenal to this larger issue.

The main problem with these conceptual transplants is that so many of them can be traced historically to *wars*, and specific *types* of wars, which China did not experience. As noted in the introduction, mass wars, citizen armies and generals-turned-politicians have been a driving force behind citizenship (as far back as Rome), patriotism and nationalism, and state-building. In modern China, however, armies belonged to political parties, the country was never a nation-in-arms, most of its wars were limited wars or border conflicts (guerilla warfare, Korea between 1950–1953, India in 1962, USSR in 1969, Vietnam in 1979), there were no "citizen-soldiers," the Nationalists or the CCP did not institute conscription, its wars were often controversial and complicated, and neither the Nationalists nor CCP experienced the centralization of political power that results from mobilizing a country for war. Given this history, perhaps it is not all that surprising that many policies regarding veterans were discriminatory and only partially enforced, that the center was often ignored by localities, that many veterans had a difficult time claiming patriotic credit and "citizenship" status for their military service, and that registration for the draft was problematic. The problems that Liu Junmin and other veterans faced, I suggest, are symptomatic of far deeper problems in the Chinese state and society – in particular, its weak capacity, shallow legitimacy, and inability to provide an avenue for more respect and status through military service – service that the state itself deems to be highly patriotic.

Notes

1 In rural China, the administrative hierarchy, starting from the bottom, is as follows: village, township, district, county, province, Beijing. In urban China, the district is one-level below the municipal government.

2 This definition avoids the issue of formal "rights," since China, like many other non-democratic countries, does not conceive of higher status in these terms.

3 Measuring citizenship in terms of formal rights is problematic because rights are frequently unenforced or only partially enforced.

4 It should be noted here that most all of the data for this chapter comes from CCP archives in Shanghai, Shandong, and Qingpu (a rural county near Shanghai). All were in Chinese and translated by the author. Further elaboration of the argument and documentation can be found in Neil J. Diamant, *Embattled Glory: Veterans, Military Families and the Politics of Patriotism in China, 1949–2007*, (Lanham: Rowman and Littlefield, 2009).

Bibliography

Archives in the People's Republic of China and The Republic of China on Taiwan

Shanghai Municipal Archives (SMA), China
Qingpu District Archives (QA), China
Shandong Provincial Archives (SA), China
Bureau of Investigation (Ministry of Defense), Taiwan

Local Gazetteers and Bulletins (xian zhi/gongbao)

Anhui Province, Bureau of Civil Affairs, 1993
Haiyang County, Shandong Province, 1987
Yi County, Hebei Province, 1991
Jinzhai County, Anhui Province, 1992
Shandong xingzheng gongbao, Shandong Province
Minzheng gongbao (various dates), Shanghai

English language sources

Bao, N, and Phan T, trans. (1996) *The Sorrow of War: A Novel of North Vietnam*. New York: Riverhead Trade.
Black, J. and C. Hyson (1944) "Postwar Soldier Settlement." *Quarterly Journal of Economics* 59, 1: 1–35.
Britton, T. (1997) *American Indians in World War I: At Home and at War*. Albuquerque: University of New Mexico Press.
Burk, J. (1995) "Citizenship Status and Military Service: The Quest for Inclusion by Minorities and Conscientious Objectors." *Armed Forces and Society* 21, 4: 503–529.
Colley, L. (1992) *Britons: Forging the Nation, 1707–1837*. New Haven: Yale University Press.
Forrest, A. (2006) "La Patrie en danger: The French Revolution and the first Levée en masse." In Daniel Moran and Arthur Waldron, eds., *The People in Arms*. Cambridge: Cambridge University Press, pp. 8–32.
Franco, J. (1990) "Patriotism on Trial: Native Americans in World War II." Ph.D. dissertation in History Department, University of Arizona.
Geyer, M. (1993) "War and the Context of General History in an Age of Total War." *Journal of Military History* 57, 5: 145–163.

Goldsworthy, A. (2006) *Caesar: Life of a Colossus*. New Haven: Yale University Press.

Hackett, R. (1964) "Japan." In R. Ward and D. Rustow, eds., *Political Modernization in Japan and Turkey*. Princeton: Princeton University Press, pp. 328–351.

Keegan, J. (1976) *The Face of Battle: A Study of Agincourt, Waterloo and the Somme*. New York: Viking.

Keppie, L. (1983) *Colonisation and Veteran Settlement in Italy, 47–14 BC*. London: British School at Rome.

Meisner, M. (1982) *Marxism, Maoism and Utopianism: Eight Essays*. Madison: University of Wisconsin Press.

Porter, B. (1994) *War and the Rise of the State: The Military Foundations of Modern Politics*. New York: Free Press.

Reese, P. (1992) *Homing Heroes: An Account of the Reassimilation of British Military Personnel into Civilian Life*. London: L. Cooper.

Sanborn, J. (2003) *Drafting the Russian Nation: Military Conscription, Total War and Mass Politics, 1905–1925*. Dekalb: Northern Illinois University Press.

Shaffer, D. (2004) *After the Glory: The Struggles of Black Civil War Veterans*. Lawrence: University of Kansas Press.

Shichor, Y. (1996) "Demobilization: The Dialectics of PLA Troop Reduction." *The China Quarterly* 146: 336–359.

Sitkoff, H. (1997). "African-American Militancy in the World War II South." In Neil McMillan, ed., *Remaking Dixie*. Jackson: University of Mississippi Press, pp. 70–92.

Taylor, C. (1945) "The Veteran in Agriculture." *Annals of the American Academy of Political and Social Science* 238: 48–55.

Waldron, A. (2003) "Looking Backward: The People in Arms and the Transformation of War." In Daniel Moran and Arthur Waldron, eds., *The People in Arms*. Cambridge: Cambridge University Press, pp. 256–262.

Weiner, A. (2001) *Making Sense of War: The Second World War and the Fate of the Bolshevik Revolution*. Princeton: Princeton University Press.

7 Soldiers' violence and the dialectics of citizenship and victimhood in contemporary Israel

Yaron Ezrahi

Introduction: the rise and decline of the ethos of the citizen-soldier in modern Israel

The main focus of this chapter is the processes that have been eroding the ideal of the citizen-soldier which prevailed in the early decades of the State of Israel. I shall argue that the moral status of the Israeli army within the larger society has been declining not only due to the role the army has played in enabling the divisive settlement movement in the occupied territories, but also by the fact that Israeli soldiers have increasingly come to embody the replacement of the Zionist ethos of republican citizenship by a contemporary version of the exilic ethos of the Jews as permanent victims. I shall also argue, among other things, that one of the most instructive symptoms of the weakening of the civic–republican ethos in post 1967 Israel has been the deepening split between nationalist and liberal norms for the uses of military force and the sharp rise in the tendency of the state and its official – including military – spokesmen to keep the army above politics by attributing publicly controversial massive or brutal uses of military force in the encounter with armed and unarmed Palestinians to pathological deviance of individual soldiers.

Perhaps the most powerful expression of the democratic-republican ideal of the citizen-soldier in antiquity is found in the *Funeral Oration* of Pericles in which the leader stressed the close association forged in Athens, 2,500 years ago, between the admiration for the warrior citizens who sacrificed themselves in defending their city and their pride in Athens' democratic form of government. The ethos of this tradition was appropriated and contextualized eventually in numerous distinct and often rival political and legal traditions. In the early sixteenth century, Machiavelli, who had reflected extensively on the political experience of Athens and Rome, considered the role of the citizen-soldier in defending freedom from external and internal enslavement, as perhaps the most important legacy of antiquity. For Machiavelli, soldiers' discipline and solidarity are fungible, convertible into assets of civic republican life. Although he usually favored a regime based on mixed constitutions, he valued most the existence of a virtuous public-regarding citizenry, as one can infer from his analysis of the Roman Republic in his *Discorsi* (Machiavelli 1950). Because for Machiavelli the republican ideal associated patriotism, a civic militia, and civic political service, he also objected to the use of mercenary armies.With the rise of modern individualism and the evolution of democratic conceptions of citizenship, the patriotic idea of the virtuous citizen-soldier has been converted in nationalistic republics into an ethos of self-sacrifice for the independence of a nation whose group solidarity is cemented by a combination of the primordial bonds of ethnicity, religion, language and common memory. In more liberal-democratic societies the emphasis has been rather on defending the freedom of a society, conceived mostly as a voluntary association of law-abiding free citizens.

By contrast to the solidarity forged by nation states, in liberal democratic societies, the uses of force in war have been constrained by the ability of soldiers to imagine themselves as members of a wider international human society, which includes their adversaries. In the course of time this dual membership, in a local collective and the transnational human community, has been translated into a host of norms, expectations and rules – enunciated by military codes and international bodies – for tempering the use of force in violent conflicts. Obviously, national group solidarity unchecked by individual human empathy between individuals serving in adversary armies would tend to be associated with less restrained uses of force. In Israel the split between these two types of orientations has, as will be shown below, posed difficulties in stabilizing an acceptable national army code.

As is well known, cases of brutal conduct by some IDF (Israel Defense Forces) soldiers in military conflicts are not a recent phenomenon. The misperception of shocking cases of brutalization by Israeli soldiers as just a recent phenomenon reflects, to a large extent, decades of a functional historical amnesia supported and sustained by a massive culture of denial boosted by the epic narrative of the heroic return of the Jewish people to its homeland. Many democracies created by ruthless revolutionary violence have tended to gloss over that early stage, proceeding soon after a successful revolution or revolt to "edit" memory and control violence by the law. Israel is no exception. Hannan Hever, for example, has pointed out the tendency of Hebrew literature to conceal or repress references to violence, particularly to brutal violence that was involved in the very act of establishing a "Jewish State" in this region (Hever 2002). These efforts at constitutionalizing the use of force by Israelis have been only partially successful, however, in controlling the flourishing illegal subculture of violence unleashed by the settlement project in the occupied territories.

The split between contesting orientations towards the legitimate use of collective force

Looking back one can discern, since the Six Day War of 1967, the consolidation and articulation of two deeply divergent orientations toward the use of force. The first consists of elements of the Zionist ethos of the new Jew as an armed soldier and of the ideal of settling the land, as well as religious and nationalistic imaginaries of Greater Israel. These elements have increasingly merged following the 1967 War in support of the movement to settle the occupied territories, begetting justifications for a concept of force as a means to control disputed lands and subordinate their natives – usually Arab villagers. Buttressed by the growing political fusion of nationalism and religion since the 1977 winning coalition of Likud and the National Religious Party, this approach has rationalized an increasingly assertive and often aggressive use of physical force in the occupied territories and during Israel's wars.

The second orientation has consisted of a range of milder attitudes toward the use of physical force ranging from widespread indifference, through moderate support for a nonideological conception of force as necessary merely for keeping order and backing a negotiated settlement with the Palestinians, to strong objection to a prolonged occupation and the use of force to sustain it. I wish to argue that this division, by politicizing the perceptions of what appears as appropriate or excessive application of military force, inevitably weakened key cross-ideological and cross-party underpinnings of the ethos of the Citizen-Soldier as a national ethos of a "people's army" in Israel as a democratic republic. While in moments of national emergency and in response to gruesome acts of Palestinian terror waves of national solidarity blurred the distance between these opposing approaches, the antagonism between maximalist and minimalist orientations toward the use of military force has put the army in a precarious, vulnerable position. In the context of the controversial settlement project and the difficult task of protecting a zealous Jewish settlers' population while being responsible also for the welfare of the resisting Palestinians, incidents of brutal uses of force tended, as we shall see, to be attributed to ideology or psychology, to extremists on the right or to deviant individuals.

I would like to suggest that what seems to have changed in the course of time is not so much the degree of social denial of, or tolerance toward, excessive and even brutal uses of force by some Israeli soldiers, but the terms of this denial and of the rationalizations of such conduct. As one would expect, since the grip of common republican-democratic civic ideals which legitimate citizens' motivation to use military force and make sacrifices have weakened over time, the normative vacuum which was created has been filled by alternative values; by a strained combination of the values of right-wing mission-oriented nationalism, left-wing reservations concerning the massive use of force, and a liberal and psychological focus on the mental state and welfare of soldiers as individuals. In this state of affairs, explaining away controversial instances of brutal soldiers' violence in terms of psychological or social pathologies was congenial for keeping the army relatively clean and sustaining in the minds of many Israelis of left to center affiliations a watered-down version of the earlier ethos of the army as a heroic people's army defending the whole nation. But with the passing decades, with the army's entanglement with the repressive practices of the occupation and the asymmetric protection of the settlers has increased, the status of the IDF in Israeli society has continued to decline.

The settlement movement and the radical politicization of military violence

From the October 1973 Yom Kippur War through the First Lebanon War (1982), the Two Palestinian Intifadas (1987–1993, 2000–2004), the Second Lebanon war (2006) to the Cast Lead Gaza operation (2009), the IDF's controversial military performances have only reinforced a growing social ambivalence towards the army, symbolized by the state commissions of inquiry established following some of those wars, as well as the charge, repeated annually, that the IDF is taking too large a part of the national budget. At the same time the difficulties of continually protecting the image of the people's army as a defense army, against its continual degradation as the army of occupation, were compounded by the increasing role of the electronic mass media in exposing the violence of Israel's wars and the clashes between Palestinians and army-backed settlers in the occupied territories. Against the background of the growing impact of the electronic mass media exposing both the violence of the wars between Israelis and Palestinians, as well as the intense interest of the local and international media in shocking and scandalous stories of soldiers' brutality, the army has discovered that often the arguments of security or necessity do not work. This realization led the army, fearful of entanglement in the political conflicts between liberal-left and religious nationalist orientations towards the uses of the national military power, to resort to languages devoid of the political connotations of siding either with the party that condones the more massive use of force or with the liberal-democratic spokesmen who condemn it.

This fear of using the politically loaded language of either camp encouraged the army and the society at large, including some supporters of the maximalist approach to the use of force, to frame brutal soldiers' violence in the supposedly neutral, scientific psychological language of individual pathologies and personality disorders, in the language of legal violations, or in the language of unintended human error represented by such expressions as "collateral damage." Below I shall treat mostly the uses of the psychological, as an alternative to the moral and political, discourse on violence.

Obviously, for soldiers coming from the wide circles of the Israeli left and the political center, the occupation and the repressive control of the Palestinians have encouraged a political reading of the motives behind the application of massive force against the latter. At the same time, for soldiers coming from nationalist and national-religious backgrounds, believing that the lands taken in the 1967 war were liberated, attempts to criticize the use of massive force in order to consolidate control and enable eventual annaxetion have been usually construed as unpatriotic leftist attitudes. The general public support for the use of massive military force to cope with external threats to the entire country, during the early decades of statehood, was partly replaced by an increasingly strenuous split between indifference and criticism from some sectors of the society, and religious-nationalist enthusiasm from others. Both of these responses have lacked an all-national appeal sufficient to support endorsement of the use of violent military force in the occupied territories by the entire country. This is largely the reason why settlers tended often to bridge the gap between what they wanted done and what the army was ready to do by their own violence (see Ezrahi, forthcoming).

The fragmentation of the Israeli conception of legitimate collective military force

Israel, therefore, is in many respects a mixed case. Difficulties in sorting out the relative weight of potential causes of brutal violence, such as psychological-personality factors, social background, ideological or religiously induced stereo-types of the enemy, fear provoked in particular situations or hatred stemming from solidarity with comrades wounded or killed by the other side, render gener-alizations based on available cases almost untenable. At the end of the first decade of this century, the controversy around the Goldstone Report accusing the IDF of committing war crimes during the Gaza operation of 2009 reveals the dimensions of the political divisions that have been problematizing attempts to keep the IDF out of politics. In such controversies clarity is the first victim of confusion between the languages of material causal accounts, legal arguments, and ideological-rhetorical contests.

I would like to suggest, however, that particularly in the context of the occu-pation, a confused sense of purpose experienced by the Israeli army due to the government demand that it handle simultaneously problems of national defense and maintain order in the occupied territories, has made its own contribution to the expansion of both "privatized" and ideological accounts of excessive, illegit-imate uses of force. Blurring the mission of the IDF to handle external threats with police tasks of keeping order among the occupied civilian Palestinians has only accentuated the ambiguities between police tasks of "crowd control" or arrest of suspects, for example, and "fighting the enemy." This resulted in a failure to respect differences between civic police codes for handling civilians and military codes for the application of force in handling external enemies (see Ezrahi 1997: 207–235). Altogether, the contradiction between civil police and military norms for the use of force and the missions of controlling Palestinians and protecting often violent settlers in the occupied territories, were a principal cause of the growing ambivalence inherent in the mandate of the state to send young Israelis to serve in combat units. The occupation has been experienced by many soldiers as a moral no-man's-land, an environment of normative instabil-ity, incompatible with the early certainties of the ethos of the people's defense army.

The repeated attempts in Israel to refresh and articulate an army code of ethics are of course symptomatic of the normative instability with regard to the framing of Israel's military force in the post 1967 War era. It has affected not only the difficulties of internalizing the military code but also the country's entire educa-tional system. In addition to such constraints, even if it were properly internalized by soldiers and officers, the usefulness of the army code of ethics is very limited as a tool for guiding soldiers when and how to restrain the excessive use of force. Abstract formulations of principles and schematic standardization of complex battlefield situations usually remain irrelevant in real situations. Moreover, the code rarely addresses the problems posed by its own contradictory demands from soldiers who are instructed for instance to both respect human life and at the same time to unyieldingly pursue their military missions until decisive victory.

The record shows that despite partially successful attempts to develop international and national mechanisms for imposing sanctions on gross violations of such military codes of ethics, which severely restrict the use of force mostly to the narrow goal of self-defense, the ultimate test of the virtue of the modern democratic citizen-soldier is a test of individual personality, the capacity and inclination of the individual to imagine himself a member of both a national and an international community and to balance intra-group considerations by a measure of human inter-group considerations based on appreciation of the universal value of human life. Obviously, such a capacity to balance often competing commitments usually depends upon early exposure to humanistic values in the contexts of family, school and society, which in the Israeli case does not usually extend to children and youth studying in orthodox, ultra-orthodox or nationalist educational institutions. Nevertheless, one could have expected that in light of the increasing rise of individualism in modern Israel, particularly since the 1970s, the respect for the humanity and the life of individuals not just by virtue of their membership in one's own group could have positive spillover effects on soldiers facing their enemy in diverse conflict situations as individuals (Ezrahi 1997). Such a process no doubt occurred with respect to some soldiers. Its significance was moderated, however, since, as revealed during the second Lebanon War and the Gaza operation, the rise of individualism intensified Israel's collective sensitivity to Jewish war casualties and has ironically increased the willingness to use more lethal force in confronting enemy soldiers and suspect civilians, in order to minimize risks to Israeli soldiers.

It is indeed intriguing that both liberal and religious – or secular – nationalists could at times (like in the case of the 2009 Gaza operation) converge in supporting maximalist uses of force against armed and, consequently in this case, unarmed Palestinians, for vastly different reasons. The former were motivated mostly by a reluctance to take high risks in an urban guerrilla war and spare the lives of IDF soldiers, whereas for the latter the resort to maximalist military measures reflected almost missionary enthusiasm to destroy the enemy.

While for Israeli nationalists the original epic narrative of Israel's wars and liberation, that was thickened following the 1967 War by religious political messianism, was always communal, for liberal and democratic Israelis it was also an epic romantic narrative of the unique qualities of a new kind of individual Jew, of the emergence of citizens-warriors-poets, as they were described in *Scrolls of Fire* (Kovner 1981). Now, what under the global and local influence of materialistic neoliberal individualism has come to replace this former idealization is, as we shall see in some detail, a pathetic preoccupation with the mental health of soldiers before or after the war, or the draft dodging of hedonistic urban Israeli youth.

When for many soldiers fighting is not inspired by a self-evident hegemonic democratic ethos of defending the people's freedom that can accommodate diverse conceptions of the military mission, when the social glue that bonds the social fabric of combat troops partly erodes in the face of divisions between critics and supporters, like in the case of Israel, unruly individual soldiers are more likely to have leverage to act outside even the watered-down, ambiguous norms of the army code. Moreover, in such situations soldiers who act brutally in both combat and noncombat situations can nevertheless expect that at least many of their comrades would lie in order to protect their friends.

As I intimated above, such conduct relates also to the effects of bureaucratization, to the difficulties of preserving the powerful pre-state highly ideologically charged voluntaristic civic culture, a culture of disciplined individuals that the state of Israel inherited in its early decades from the pervasive voluntarism of *Yishuv* (the pre-state Jewish community). Within the framework of the newly established, largely bureaucratic state, and its large population of immigrants from nondemocratic societies, the culture of civic voluntarism and individual responsibility has been widely substituted by "bureaucratic logic" (see Handelman 2004). Except for voluntary service in elite combat units, for the larger group of soldiers voluntarism was substituted by legal conscription sanctioned by penalties for draft dodging.

Whereas the voluntaristic component continued for a few decades to link soldiering, individual agency and virtuous citizenship, virtuous citizenship has come to be associated more with republican values of group solidarity and sacrifice than with notions of individual responsibility as a dimension of being a member of a civic association of free individuals. Obviously, only on the basis of such a sense of individual responsibility could internal mechanisms of self-restraint be cultivated and eventually relied upon to control the excessive use of force and the brutalization of the Israeli soldier in the course of the conflict.

From citizens-soldiers to heroic victims

The gradual erosion of the Israeli individual civic agency of the earlier period was symbolized, in recent years, by the expression "rosh katan" meaning "small head" or a deliberate avoidance of personal responsibility. As I intimated above, the most disturbing social symptom of this process has been the substitution of moral by psychological vocabularies for addressing the experience of soldiers in the battlefield. In a study published in *Israel Studies*, Yoram Bilu and Eliezer Witztum have discerned in the 1970s the first signs of a shift from collective to more individualistic modes of mourning fallen soldiers (Bilu and Witztum 2000). They linked this process with a tendency towards the "de-glorification" of war and army service and an increasing shift from focusing on the role of soldiers as defenders of the state, to a preoccupation with the mental health of soldiers who suffered from Combat Stress Reaction (CSR) and, in the late 1980s and especially during the 1990s, with the traumas of war and Post Traumatic Stress Disorder (PTSD). This process was accompanied, as shown in a study of "psychology and war in contemporary Israel" by Edna Lomski-Feder and Eyal Ben Ari (2007), by the increasing deployment of psychologists, social workers and other care professionals in the military. Furthermore, the psychological disempowerment of the soldiers in the regular army was also augmented by a rising involvement of parents with their children-soldiers in the course of military service, thus enhancing a process of "infantilizing" soldiers as children. While the central role of families in national campaigns for releasing their children-soldiers from captivity – like in the case of Gilad Shalit – is perfectly understandable, it also demonstrates the significant weight achieved in the context of the Israeli army by parent–child, relative to soldier–state, relations. One can add to that the significant number of youth who were allowed to avoid military service on grounds of mental or family difficulties. Most instructively, Bilu and Witztum, Ben-Ari and Lomsky-Feder and others have indicated that focusing on the mental and emotional health of soldiers and the emergence of the category of "psychological war casualties" in Israel has come to compete with, and increasingly replace, the focus on ethical principles of military conduct, what was often called in the early days the commitment to the "purity of arms." Obviously, framing soldiers' conduct in therapeutic psychosocial language tends to replace the focus on soldiers' resiliency as individuals facing adversity by a focus on their vulnerability as objects, as potential or actual patients. Such orientations can easily diminish the perceptions of individuals as active agents capable of hard choices, while encouraging their perception as passive, as people belonging to categories of "weak populations," susceptible to the manipulations of non-democratic hierarchical authority, often disguised as a caring authority.

Psychosocial attitudes, observes Vanessa Pupavac, entail "the erosion of conceptualization of the citizen as an autonomous rational subject" (Pupavac 2001). Apparently in the context of the Israeli army a category such as "weak soldiers" is likely to be associated with the undermotivated soldiers who tend to come from social groups which characteristically denounce the occupation or are thoroughly ambivalent toward putting their lives on the line except in clear cases of self-defense. By comparison, the category of "strong soldiers" would be characteristically attached to highly motivated and even over-motivated soldiers, coming from low social economic strata, often the same social, economic and religious strata for whom the military has a crucial role in the realization of an ideological or religious vision, identity building or social mobility. To reiterate, in the larger context of the contested place of arms and physical force in modern Israel, attitudes toward high as against low motivations for employing violence against the Arabs have been thoroughly politicized, visibly projecting onto the army the political antagonisms in the wider society.

Curiously enough, the declining celebratory attitudes towards Israeli citizen-soldiers in recent decades enabled a partial reengagement and reframing of exilic forms of the mourning of powerless Jews, killed in pogroms, as heroic victims. Bilu and Witztum note the traditional utilization of the term *"Kedoshim,"* meaning "holy ones," associated with the Jewish concept of *"Kiddush ha'shem"* (dying for the sanctification of God) to commemorate fallen soldiers (sometimes also civilians) as martyrs. They aptly observed also the common use of this semi-religious (non-Zionist) language in relation to both Israeli soldiers and Holocaust victims. In all these cases, what is usually glorified and commemorated is the passive heroism of victims, not the assertive heroism of warriors (see Quint 1992). Ironically, of course, if in the case of Holocaust victims, mostly unarmed and often leaderless Jews were facing the overwhelming ruthless force of the Nazi army, in the case of Israeli soldiers the warrior ethos has been challenged by the psychological and moral dilemmas of facing often unarmed and extremely weak and vulnerable civilian Palestinians. In particular since the first *intifada*, the sheer condition of armed IDF soldiers in uniforms facing stone-throwing youths and protesting women was sufficient, as I already indicated above, to melt down the grounds of military heroism. The exilic heroism of the powerless Jew managed, however, to penetrate the vacuum created by a weakened Zionist ethos of the new Israeli and spread into the general Israeli consciousness, creating another kind of aura mixed with compassion to soldiers treated as psychological casualties, as soldiers turned into patients. Rabbi Avichai Ronsky, who served as Chief Rabbi of the IDF some time before and during the Gaza Operation, took an opposite course, trying to inspire the soldiers to fight hard and mercilessly by lending religious meaning to combat. While it certainly worked out for soldiers who were trained in special religious pre-army schools and the religious army framework of Yeshivot Hesder, the Rabbi and his methods appeared too controversial to become a likely model for the rest of the army of the IDF.

I would like to suggest then that to a considerable extent this development has been actually undermining perceived discontinuities sought by Zionism between diasporic and Israeli orientations toward resistance and death of serving soldiers. The early Zionists expected that the creation of a Jewish state would end the condition of the Jews as victims and "return them to history" as agents. But in the course of more than six decades of statehood, and especially during the last three decades, the exilic mentality of victimhood, against which Zionism reacted, recaptured the Israeli public mind with a vengeance. One can construe in this context the separation wall built by former Prime Ministers Ariel Sharon and Ehud Olmert to divide Israelis and Palestinians as a complementary unconscious symbolic reenactment of the old Ghetto mentality. Another symptom of this change has been the aforementioned tendency, most salient during the 2009 army operation in Gaza, to protect the lives of combat soldiers no less, and even more, than, the lives of Israeli civilians.

From citizens-soldiers to "ontological victims"

These developments point to an increasing tendency of Israelis, like Diaspora Jews, to perceive themselves as what I would like to call "ontological victims," a kind of "essential" victims, a trend that consistently ignores the possibility that their own actions participate as causes in creating the very situations they perceive as threatening. Ontological victims do not perceive themselves as acting but always as reacting. A paradigmatic expression of the ethos of ontological victimhood can be found in the famous statement of former Israeli Prime Minister, Golda Meir, when she said "I am ready to forgive the Arabs for killing us but not for making us killers." (I thank Yoel Elizur for reminding me of Golda Meir's quote.) Ironically the Arabs are here super-agents, not only responsible for their own actions, but for ours as well. (In contemporary Israel this orientation is manifest, among other things, in the difficulty experienced by a large part of the public of perceiving the occupation as a cause or a provocation that triggers waves of violence against Israelis as well as the widespread difficulty, noted by Jose Brunner, of perceiving the Palestinians as victims and as a people also suffering from Post Traumatic Stress Disorder (Brunner 2004).) We can see then that the extent to which the uses of the category of "psychological casualties" are narrow or wide, exclusive or inclusive, obeys in fact a political logic. Brunner aptly notes further the persistent political dimension of the social construction of trauma by Israelis.

This tendency is naturally linked with the Israeli inclination to view almost all wars – at least in their beginnings – as wars of necessity not wars of choice. Usually when public criticism during or following a war is directed to the government or the military, it concentrates on tactical errors or failures to anticipate an emergency, or effectively wage a war, not so much on the very justification of taking the risk of going to war. Now the self-perception of many Israeli Jews as permanent essential victims, reinforced by the spread of the frame of Post Traumatic Stress Disorder beyond those directly involved or affected by violence, has been deepening the disempowerment of the very core of critical and potentially resistant citizenry. Brunner notes a similar process of extension in his study of the politics of psychic vulnerability indicating the subtle processes by which, especially after 9/11 2001, the ascription of trauma in other countries, even beyond the USA, has begun to spread from direct victims of terror to the larger group of the others who were psychically wounded by merely observing it on television. Clearly the symbolic "victimization" of the entire population following a major terror event helps establish the state as a patron guardian of a disempowered vulnerable citizenry, thus paving the way for canceling basic civil liberties in the name of protecting, and caring, for the public.

If this trend continues – reinforced further by waves of panic produced by pandemics like swine flue – we may see in the future the emergence of institutions and policies which recall some science fiction visions of the state as a kind of collective therapeutic instrument that feeds on turning citizens into child-like patients. There are of course many precedents to the "medicalization" of the conduct of dissidents in order to silence or delegitimate moral or ideological opposition. Michael Heyd observed that already in the seventeenth century religious enthusiasts who were often also political radicals were regarded as ill individuals who lost their capacity to reason. In his *A Question of Madness*, the Russian dissident Zhores Medvedev recorded the uses of psychiatry to incarcerate and dope Soviet dissidents treated as mentally ill. In democratic societies judges often limit the attribution of criminal actions to involuntary psychological causes in order to protect the very concept of criminal responsibility (Heyd 1995; Medvedev 1971). Admittedly the spread of the diagnosis of Post Traumatic Stress Disorder to millions is a more subtle and less salient process. But in undermining civic agency its long-term effects on the viability of liberal or social democracy are bound to be very grave.

Conclusion

The above discussion offers a complex picture of the relations of soldiering, force and citizenship in modern Israel. I argue that the early republican ethos of the Israeli soldier-citizen as a member of the "people's army" has been weakened and with it civic constraints on normless violence, which has come to be socially attributed either to particular individuals or groups suffering from psychosocial disorder or to individuals or groups expressing excessive religious or ideological enthusiasm to fight for their visions. More generally, a tendency to tolerate or conceal glaring examples of brutal violence by Israeli soldiers is influenced in contemporary Israel by the self-perception of Israelis as victims, whose acts against the enemy are mere reactions to concrete threats of physical obliteration. The shadow of the Holocaust, the human costs and military setbacks of the 1973 Yom Kippur War and other violent confrontations with Arabs, the terror in Israeli cities, the Kassam missiles over southern Israel, the second Lebanon War and the perceived threat of nuclear Holocaust triggered by Iran, have cumulatively accentuated and accelerated this process. Obviously a state in which spreading fear and a sense of collective victimhood are the most effective means for mobilizing votes is prone to blur the crucial distinctions between deterrence, selective moderate uses of weapons of first resort, uses of heavier weapons of second resort and, finally, the massive uses of weapons of last resort. Such a tendency to ignore boundaries between degrees of applied military force at macro-level is bound to render such boundaries looser at the level of encounters between individual soldiers as well.

One cannot ignore, however, the simultaneous counter-effects of the deglorification of the Israeli army and a rather dramatic general decline in the willingness of contemporary youth to put their lives on the line in fighting imagined and even real enemies. Contemporary forms of materialistic or narcissistic psychological individualism and youth culture, as well as a series of dramatic failures to achieve the goals of military actions or translate them to visible political assets, may very well reduce future prospects for popular support of wars and increase the political costs of "normal" wars and brutal uses of force. What in the case of Israel remains worrisome today, is that unlike the Athenian citizen-soldiers of the time of Pericles who were proud – albeit for a short time – to be the soldiers of a democracy, Israeli soldiers-citizens have a few shared reasons beyond internal unit camaraderie and ethnic solidarity to feel proud to be the soldiers of Israel as a democracy that defends freedom, equality, and the rule of law at home. Whereas nobody can predict the net results of the countervailing trends and forces that clash in contemporary Israel, the tendency of citizens and soldiers disempowered by their own self-perception as victims responding to necessity may, as of this writing, seem the more powerful trend. In the final analysis, as long as this trend persists, the dialectics of citizenship and victimhood in contemporary Israel will continue to indicate a deep weakness in Israeli political culture.

References

Bilu, Yoram and Witztum, Eliezer. 2002. "War-Related Loss and Suffering in Israeli Society: An Historical Perspective," *Israel Studies* 5: 2, 1–31.

Brunner, Jose, 2004. "Die Politik der Traumatisierung. Zur Geschichte des verletzbaren Individuums," *WestEnd: Neue Zeitschrift für Sozialforschung* 1, 7–24.

Ezrahi, Yaron, 1997. *Rubber Bullets, Power and Conscience in Modern Israel*, Berkeley: The University of California Press.

Ezrahi, Yaron, 2000. "1977," in Elie Barnavi and Saul Friedlander, eds., *Les Juifs et le XXe Siecle: Dictionnaire Critique*, Paris: Calmann-Levy, pp. 782–789.

Ezrahi, Yaron, forthcoming. "The Occupation and the Israeli Democracy," in Daniel Bar-Tal and Itzik Schnell, eds., *The Israeli Occupation of the West Bank and the Gaza Strip: Implications for the Occupying Society*.

Handelman, Don, 2004. *Nationalism and the Israeli State*, Oxford: Berg.

Hever, Hannan, 2002. "A Map of Sand: From Hebrew Literature to Israeli Literature," *Theory and Criticism* 20 (Hebrew).

Heyd, Michael, 1995. *"Be Sober and Reasonable:" The Critique of Enthusiasm in the Seventeenth and Early Eighteenth Centuries*, Leiden: Brill.

Kovner, Aba, ed., 1981. *Scrolls of Fire: A Nation Fighting for its Life; Fifty Two Chapters of Martyrology*, Jerusalem: Keter (Hebrew).

Lomsky-Feder, Edna and Ben-Ari, Eyal, 2007. "Trauma, Therapy and Responsibility: Psychology and War in Contemporary Israel," in Aparna Rap, Michael Bolling and Mobika Boeck (eds), *The Practice of War – Production, Reproduction and Comminication of Armed Violence*, London: Berghahn Books, pp. 111–131.

Machiavelli, Niccolò, 1950. *The Prince and the Discourses*, New York: Modern Library.

Medvedev, Zhores, 1971. *A Question of Madeness*, New York: Borzoi/Alfred Knopf.

Quint, David, 1992. *Epic and Empire*, Princeton: Princeton University Press.

Pupavac, Vanessa, 2001. "Therapeutic Governance: The Politics of Psychosocial Intervention and Trauma Risk Management,", *Disasters* 25: 4, 358–372.

Part III

Citizenship, war and the rights of women and ethnic minorities

8 Indian Muslims and the war on terror

Reflections on their citizenship status

Ornit Shani

The notion of a Muslim threat to the integrity of the nation has intermittently been at the centre of political contestations in India. This projection of Indian Muslims as a threat to the nation is perplexing. Since the partition of the subcontinent into India and Pakistan in 1947, India's Muslims have persistently experienced inadequate access to vital state resources like employment and education. They have become among the most alienated groups within the body of Indian citizenry (Prime Minister's High Level Committee, henceforth Sachar 2006). Their adversities, however, did not find expression in separatist tendencies, or in political radicalism. India is the third biggest Muslim country in the world after Indonesia and Pakistan. Despite their large numbers (13.4 percent of the population), Indian Muslims have not for the most part mobilized around a Muslim party, nor have they tended to identify with Pakistan's support of Kashmiri secessionism (Ministry of Information and Broadcasting 1951; Noorani 2003: 102–106).

The major internal challenge to security in India is, in fact, posed by Naxalite (Maoist) violence, which has a major presence in about 170 of India's 604 districts. The Indian Ministry of Home Affairs recorded 7,806 incidents of Naxalite violence across 13 states resulting in 3,338 deaths between 2004–2008 (Ministry of Home Affairs 2009: 171). Over the same period 8,022 incidents of violence in Jammu and Kashmir resulted in the death of 1,909 civilians and 806 members of the security forces (Ministry of Home Affairs 2009: 6). Outside Jammu and Kashmir and the Northeast, however, only 26 incidents of "Islamic terrorist attacks," including the November 2008 Mumbai attack, were recorded between 2000–2008. These resulted in the deaths of 904 civilians and 41 security forces members (Institute of Conflict Management 2009). Most of these incidents appear to have been initiated and conducted by foreign Islamic organizations, like the Pakistan-based Lashkar-e-Taiba. Domestic organizations, especially members of the Student Islamic Movement of India, are though to have been associated with six of the incidents.[1]

Muslims in India, particularly from the mid-1980s, have regularly been at the receiving end of violence directed against them by members of militant Hindu organizations. Communal violence has grown since then in the context of the rise of the Hindu nationalist movement, which positioned itself in opposition to

Islam and Muslims, and sought to redefine India as a primarily Hindu state. Between 2007–2008, the Ministry of Home Affairs accounted for 1,337 incidents of Hindu–Muslim violence across India. These resulted in 219 deaths, overwhelmingly of Muslims. Over the same period 47 people died in 367 incidents of Hindu violence against Christians (Ministry of Home Affairs 2009: 48–49). The most deadly violence against Muslims in recent years took place in the state of Gujarat in February–March 2003. Aided by senior state officials, members of militant Hindu organizations killed 2,000 people, with unofficial estimates putting the death toll at closer to 5,000. Most of the victims were Muslim. The carnage was sparked after two train carriages transporting Hindu religious volunteers caught fire, resulting in the death of 58 passengers. The provenance of the fire was unknown. Before a formal investigation had even been initiated, and despite conflicting accounts about its cause, state officials, among them the Chief Minister Narendra Modi, declared it an organized Islamic terrorist attack (Varadarajan 2002: 5–8; Shani 2007: 170–171). In the aftermath of September 11, the discourse of the War on Terror as well as the main legal provisions for its conduct, the Prevention of Terrorism Act (POTA), was readily employed against Muslims. Indeed, anti-terror laws in India from the 1980s have often singled out Muslims (Singh 2007: 53–54), stripping them of basic democratic citizenship rights, even though home-grown Islamic terrorism only accounts for a small percentage of terror attacks. In contrast, the large-scale violence against Muslims by militant Hindus was seldom dealt with under these laws.

If, on the whole, Muslims in India did not endorse secessionist politics, and did not mobilize politically along religious lines, why and how was a prolonged narrative of a "Muslim threat" sustained for so long? This chapter explores the persistence of such a notion within the Indian polity. It advances the proposition that the "Muslim Problem," and the neglect of Muslims' citizenship played a role in the processes of state building in India. This conception enabled the new state to contain significant threats to its integrity, particularly from persistent and deep caste and class conflicts.

Of the various deep social conflicts that have challenged India since its independence, the "Muslim problem" was the least threatening to the integrity of the nation. The main issue at the heart of this problem lost its raison d'être with the partition of the subcontinent into India and Pakistan in 1947. "The vital and most important problem," which in Jawaharlal Nehru's view was pending against the ability of a free democratic India to "stand together," was "the appalling poverty of the people" (Nehru 1948: 11). Poverty alleviation and development was the key challenge, since "Political democracy", Nehru stated, "is not enough. It must develop into economic democracy" (Nehru 1985: 18). The lower and backward caste Hindus (approximately 60 percent of India's population) form the vast majority of India's poor. Poverty rates among Muslims in contemporary India are also high. They generally perform poorly in relation to other socio-religious communities, like the lower and backward castes (Sachar 2006). Muslims in India are also divided by caste, or caste-like groupings (e.g. Ahmad 1980: 7;

Singh, G. 1980: 6; Hasan 1997: 8; Sikand 2001: 288; Sachar 2006: 192–194). Among Indian Muslims 40.7 percent (5.5 percent of the general population) are estimated to be lower and backward castes. Thus, in effect, the Muslim minority in India is a member in a large group of Hindu caste minorities that together represent just under two thirds of the population and the majority of India's poor.

In the allocation of state resource, as well as in the construction of membership claims in the nation, the Indian state fragmented its poor majority along religious and caste lines. In its conceptualization of Muslim citizenship, the state divorced religion from caste, construing and homogenizing Muslims only in terms of a religious minority. Conversely, in the citizenship construction of the lower and backward caste Hindus, the state conflated religion and caste. This fusion contributed to the making of a composite religious Hindu majority, glossing over deep caste–class divisions among Hindus. In so doing, the state, in the making of its citizenship regime forestalled the potential threat to its integrity from caste and class unrests.

In order to understand this process, how it transpired in the Indian democratic context that was guided by a strong secular ethos, and its functions for state building, this chapter examines the construction of the Indian citizenship regime as a result of a dynamic interplay between four emerging conceptions of citizenship. Each of these conceptions contributed to the construction of Muslim citizenship in terms of a religious minority, thus perpetuating a notion of a Muslim threat to the secular nation, as well as a limit on the possibility of their attaining full membership in the nation. Even though Muslims experienced a denial of their citizenship, they could nonetheless find enough scope for inclusion between the four alternative frameworks for membership in the nation.

The chapter is divided into two parts: the first presents the conception of a Muslim problem within the Indian polity, and questions the basis for such a conception, by briefly examining the predicament of Muslims' citizenship. The second part discusses the four conceptions of citizenship that emerged within the Indian polity, and analyzes how the four-fold citizenship framework sustained a notion of a Muslim threat, and operated to deny Muslims' citizenship, thereby also containing other, more acute social threats to the integrity of the nation.

The Muslim "threat" and Muslim predicament

India gained independence following the partition of the subcontinent into two states in the context of what was conceived as an intractable religious antagonism. Pakistan was proposed as a Muslim homeland. India, by assertion or default, was for the Hindus. The then 45 million Muslims who remained in India were required to demonstrate the sincerity of their choice and to prove their loyalty (Pandey 1999: 610; Sirnate 2007: 232–233). Against the background of violence and the need to deal with the growing numbers of refugees, Sardar Vallabhbhai Patel, the then Deputy Prime Minister of India and Home Minister, urged Muslims in November 1947 to "search their conscience and ascertain if they are really loyal to this country. If they are not let them go to the country of their allegiance" (Ministry of Information and Broadcasting 1967: 9). In a speech in Lucknow in January 1948 he stated that "mere declarations of loyalty to the Indian Union will not help them at this critical juncture. They must give practical proof of their declaration" (Ministry of Information and Broadcasting 1967: 64; Guha 2007: 365).

The distrust of Muslims at the time also began permeating to the bureaucracy. Some official memoranda in the early years after partition dealt with the issue of Muslims as "a problem of governance" and as a potential fifth column; in some government administration units lists of Muslim employees were prepared and their loyalty was questioned (Guha 2007: 365–368; Zamindar Fazila-Yacoobali 2007: 91, 112). Muslims in the bureaucracy were targets of suspicion if they had relatives in Pakistan, which many Muslims from the partitioned areas did. (Zamindar Fazila-Yacoobali 2007: 226).

Whether Muslims in India were trustworthy citizens, and whether they were, or could be, "Indian enough" would became a lingering issue within the Indian polity. From the mid-1960s the Muslim problem was mainly perceived in terms of the question of the assimilation of Muslims in the mainstream of the nation. A government official diagnosed this problem at the time as "an emotional one, and it largely exists because of the unwillingness of the Muslims to integrate themselves into the country" (Chagla 1962).

In this official view, Muslims were standing apart, refusing to integrate and insisting on their minority causes. This perception was expressed in official representations of Indian Muslims. For example, less than 1 percent of the 1,742 documentaries produced between 1948 and 1972 by the film division of the Ministry of Information and Broadcasting "had anything to do with the presence of Muslims in India." The little that was produced presented an understanding of Muslims as "special minorities set apart from the national mainstream in one way or another" (Roy 2007: 53). Generally, Muslims were represented and remembered by "stereotypical images" that attempted to capture fixed "innate differences" (Amin 2004: 95; Roy 2007: 64).

The charge that "Muslims, with a few exceptions, are anti-national and harbour extra-territorial loyalty to Pakistan" (Dave 1990 II: 11), and that they are not Indian enough culminated in the mid-1980s with the rise and growing popularity of Hindu nationalism. The Hindu nationalist movement, which sought to redefine India on the basis of Hindu values and ethos, positioned itself in opposition to Islam and Muslims, and rallied around the claim that the Muslim minority threatened Hindus and that Muslims were appeased by the state. Its rise was accompanied by intensifying communal violence in large parts of the subcontinent. On the fiftieth anniversary of India's independence, L. K. Advani, a senior leader, sometime the president, of the Hindu nationalist Bharatiya Janata Party (BJP) appealed to the Muslims of India to "purge every trace of the Two-Nation theory from their mindset" and in effect suggested that "they [still] need to be Indianised" (Noorani 2004).

A prolonged narrative of a Muslim threat to the nation was sustained, and claims that Muslims were appeased by the state came to the fore in the 1980s, although there had been no real basis, material or ideological, for such perceptions. In fact, Indian governments did not show much interest in their Muslim citizens. The publication of the Report of the Prime Minister's High Level Sachar Committee on the Social, Economic and Educational Status of the Muslim Community of India, in November 2006, was presented as the first "systematic effort since independence to analyze the conditions of religious minorities" (Sachar 2006: 2). The committee was established in March 2005 partly to make up for the "lack of authentic information about the social and economic status of Muslims" (Sachar 2006: v).

In truth, Indian governments have had a reasonably good understanding of the predicament of their Muslim citizens. In May 1980, Indira Gandhi's government constituted a Prime Minister's High Power Panel to probe into the economic disabilities of minorities and other weaker sections. The panel, chaired by Dr. Gopal Singh, studied, in the main, data for the 1970s and early 1980s, and submitted its report in June 1983 (Report of the High Power Panel on Minorities (henceforth Singh, G.) 1983). The Gopal Singh Committee wrote in its Report that "there are those who believe that Muslims have been the victims of the discriminatory implementation of the various developmental schemes" (Singh, G. 1983: 14). The Committee hoped that its recommendations, for example, on education, would "enable [Muslims] to become useful citizens" (Singh, G. 1983: 26). But the report was shelved and was not presented before the parliament until August 1990, when its recommendations were rejected (Khalidi 2006: 43). The Sachar committee consulted the Gopal Singh report, but made no reference to it in its report. One of the Sachar committee members suggested to me in an interview that the reason was that the "Gopal Singh report was mainly based on perceptions and rhetoric rather than good data." He added that the Gopal report created a "gloomy picture" and was therefore shelved by Indira Gandhi. Indeed, the Gopal Committee report, in the words of one of its members, indicated that the plight of Muslims "was worse than that of the scheduled caste [former untouchables]" (Zakaria 2004: 210). The Gopal Singh report may not have used as sophisticated data as the later Sachar committee, but the conclusions of both reports with regard to basic features of allocation of state resources for Muslims, are similar.

Muslims, according to the Sachar Report, are generally at a significant disadvantage in their mean years of schooling, attendance levels, dropout rates, and completion of matriculations and graduation in relation to their share in the population and when compared to other minority groups, Scheduled Castes (SCs), Scheduled Tribes (STs) and Other Backward Classes (OBCs) (Sachar 2006: 54–76, 84–86).[2] The literacy level among Muslims in 2001 was 59 percent below the national average of 65 percent (Sachar 2006: 52). Despite an expansion of educational access since independence, their rate of progress has been slow. The findings of the Gopal Singh Report also showed that the rate of Muslim school enrolment fell short (Singh, G. 1983: 20–21).

Admission to government jobs, particularly at the high levels of the bureaucracy, is another measure of Muslim access to state resources. The presence of

Muslims between 1971 and 1980 in the elite and highly competitive Indian Administrative Service (IAS) was found by the Gopal Singh Committee to be 2.9 percent of the total intake, except for two years, when it reached between 6.3 percent and 7.5 percent (Singh, G. 1983: 31). The Sachar Committee found that the presence of Muslims in the IAS in 2006 was 3 percent, of whom 2.3 percent secured their position as direct recruits through competitive examination. The rest were promoted from state services (Sachar 2006: 165–166).

Between 1971 and 1979, Muslims were recruited into the federal Indian Police Service only in five out of those nine years. In 1973, for example, out of a total recruitment of 116 candidates there was only one Muslim. The average recruitment of Muslims over this period amounted to a mere 2 percent (Singh, G. 1983: 31). In 2006, according to the Sachar Report, the share of Muslims in the Indian Police Service was 4 percent, of whom only 2.7 percent were appointed on the basis of direct recruitment through competitive examination (Sachar 2006: 165–166). The Muslim share in the armed services was even lower. In the Air Force only 1.2 percent of the pilots were Muslim, 1.8 percent of the flight controllers, and 1.2 percent of group captains. Among commanding officers in the Central Reserve Police Force across India, 2.6 percent were Muslim. In the "Group A" service level in the Central Reserve Police, Muslim males constituted 3 percent and females 4.2 percent (Sachar Committee papers 2006 File 32/V: 34). There have never been formal legal impediments to Muslims being enlisted in the armed forces or the police.

Some Muslim population in India appear to be systematically disenfranchised. The Sachar Committee identified a number of reserved assembly constituencies for the SCs that had Muslim majority populations. In Uttar Pradesh (UP), for example, there were eight reserved constituencies with a Muslim majority. In three of them the Muslim population was more than double that of the SCs (Sachar 2006: 269–270).[3] There were similar cases in Assam, Bihar, Jharkhand, Rajastan and West Bengal (Sachar Committee papers 2006 File 86: 2–3).

Muslims are divided by castes. The Sachar Report presented in detail the main features of caste divisions among Muslims in India e.g. Ashrafs, Ajlafs and the very low caste Arzals, and Gopal Singh recognized this as well (Sachar 2006: 192–194). The Sachar Report also defined a category of Muslims OBCs in some of its data. Official recognition of castes among Muslims had already been made in 1955, when the first Backward Classes Commission, which was appointed to determine the criteria for the identification of groups, other than the SCs and STs, that should be treated as socially and educationally backward submitted its report. The Chairman of the Commission, Kaka Kalelkar disclaimed in a letter of dissent the Commission's recommendation to use caste criteria for determining backwardness. He linked his objection to the ramifications it might have on religious minorities and their rights. "In practice," he wrote,

their [Muslim] society was more or less caste-ridden.... Muslims came forward to prove that except for the four upper castes, namely Sheikh, Syed,

Moghul and Pathan, all the other Muslim castes were inferior and backward. They told the Ministry of Education and the Backward Classes Commission that caste is rampant among them.

(Government of Gujarat 1983: 24–26)

Only from the 1980s and 1990s were a few Muslim groups recognized as backward caste entitled to limited reservations in government jobs and educational institutions. The Sachar Committee (just as the Gopal Committee had done before it) examined the socio-economic status of Muslims in relation to the lower and backward caste Hindus. Its findings on the caste dimension among Muslims, however, had no bearing on its recommendations. The Report addresses "the Muslim community of India" (Sachar 2006). Thus, the Sachar Report, which was produced for the government with the aim of formulating "policies and programmes to address the issues relating to the socio-economic backwardness" of Indian Muslims (Sachar 2006: v), perceived Muslims in terms of religion without ultimately taking into account the implications of their internal heterogeneity. This approach, from the viewpoint of the state, epitomized the ramifications of the evolving Indian citizenship and the position of Muslims within it.

Muslims within the Indian citizenship regime

Citizenship is a key institution that sets the terms of engagement between individuals, social groups and the state and forms the basis for attaining membership and a sense of belonging in the social body and the state. It is also a mechanism for determining how prospective diverse groups should be delimited, and defines the boundaries of exclusion. In a single polity, several conceptions of citizenship, corresponding to different conceptions of membership claims, may coexist (Shafir and Peled 1998: 411; 2002: 3–7). Discussions of citizenship conventionally focus on tensions between the liberal and ethno-national notions as a basis for granting and conceiving of citizenship (Yashar 2005: 38–40). Shafir and Peled expanded this to a three-fold framework, distinguishing between liberal, republican and ethno-national conceptions of citizenship (Shafir and Peled 1998: 408–427; 2002, 3–7).[4] Each of these citizenship conceptions represents different paradigms for state resource allocation. The liberal conception of citizenship views the individual as the bearer of a package of rights, designed to protect her personal liberties. On the face of it, the liberal conception of citizenship is the most inclusive and universalistic. The republican citizenship concept, in turn, contains the notion of a common good that is prior to the individual citizen and her choices. Rights are granted in accordance with the contribution of citizens to the common good. The collectivist nature of the republican conception of citizenship creates scope for a strong sense of solidarity, a sense of belonging and security. In turn, it is less tolerant toward group grievances. As such, a republican citizenship conception can be exclusionary toward groups and individuals who are not perceived to be conforming to, or advancing the defined common good. In the ethno-nationalist notion of citizenship the nation is founded on blood ties. A descent group defines membership in the nation.

In this analysis of a three-fold framework citizenship is defined from the viewpoint of the state, and becomes an end in the making of the state. The paradigmatic question is the extent to which the state protects the life of individuals, certain collectives in pursuit of a shared good, or a community tied by blood. In India, however, we can distinguish a fourth dominant conception of citizenship. As an institution for membership claims within the political organization of the state, citizenship may also imply a notion of membership of the state *in* the society, whereby power is invested in the people. In this view, the state is above all a coercive entity. To ensure genuine self-government, a minimal control of and interaction with the state is desired. The non-statist citizenship conception thus places emphasis on the agency of the citizen and her capability to govern her life. The citizen carries, first and foremost, duties rather than natural rights. Among her basic duties are the responsibilities to actively oversee the way she is governed, to self-help and to resist and challenge injustices. Citizens' rights can therefore only emanate from duties. In the non-statist citizenship conception, the relations between the state and society are not built upon an artificial institutional system that is based on a consensus of values and universal rights, shared common good, or ethnic origins, which ultimately enforce consent. The non-statist conception is predicated on enabling dissent and tolerating the existence of social antagonisms and conflicts. In India, I contend, this notion of the *non-statist* citizen exists, whose ideational and institutional basis can be extrapolated most prominently from M.K. Gandhi.

In Gandhi's ideal, society would not relinquish power to a central state. The underlying structure of the relationship between the individual and the state would be composed of innumerable villages. "Every village will be a republic … having full powers. It follows, therefore, that every village has to be self-sustained and capable for managing its affairs even to the extent of defending itself against the whole world" (Gandhi (henceforth CWMG), Vol. 91: 325). The state will not be organized as "a pyramid" but as "an oceanic circle of villages whose centre is the individual" (CWMG, Vol. 91: 325). The Union state is not dissolved, but true independence lies in a village unit that is "economically and politically as autonomous as possible" (CWMG, Vol. 91: 371; Vol. 82: 406–407). This, according to Gandhi, is the road to true democratic self-rule. And true democracy is what promotes the welfare of the people. Gandhi called it *sarvodaya*, or progress for all (CWMG, Vol. 81: 37; Gandhi 1954: 3–4). For such a democracy, citizens were required to be vigilant and involved with the government. In the Gandhian *non-statist* citizenship conception, "submission to the state law is the price that a citizen pays for his personal liberty. Submission, therefore to a State law wholly or largely unjust is an immoral barter for liberty" (Gandhi 1954: 114). A citizen, therefore, has an "inherent right" to civil disobedience (CWMG, Vol. 25: 391–392). A notion of resistance and dissent is embedded into this citizenship conception. In a Gandhian perspective, the method of dissent should be non-violent. Gandhi's citizenship notion competed with and was in a continual interplay with the liberal, republican and the ethno-nationalist conceptions of citizenship that were also rooted in the pre-independence era, as contending visions of the India to be. Through the concurrent interactions and the resulting tensions between these four predominant notions the Indian citizenship regime evolved. At various times, one or the other of these citizenship notions gained dominance.

An ethno-nationlist citizenship conception gained currency in the context of partition. This citizenship conception held fast to the two-nation theory – Pakistan for the Muslims and India for Hindus – and seemed compatible with the actual making of India. Some members of the Constituent Assembly even demanded an ethnic definition of citizenship for India. Dr. P. S. Deshmuk, for example, proposed that an Indian citizen, among other things, should be "every person who is a Hindu or a Sikh by religion…" (Constituent Assembly Debates (CAD), Vol. IX: 352). "I think that we are going too far in the business of secularity: does it mean that we must wipe out our own people … that we must wipe out Hindus" (CAD, Vol. IX: 354).[5] The political language of ethno-nationalism persistently questioned Muslims' loyalty to the country, and called Muslims to "search their conscience," and "go to the country of their allegiance" (Ministry of Information and Broadcasting 1967: 9). This citizenship conception did not leave much scope for Muslims to become members in the nation. But soon after partition they did not have much choice. The Pakistani government began curtailing the access of Muslims from India, concerned that the new state could not support more Muslim refugees. By January 1, 1952, the deadline for acquiring Pakistani citizenship, Indian Muslims officially became foreign to the Pakistani state (Zamindar Fazila-Yacoobali 2007: 70–75, 176–177).

Against the background of a prevailing ethno-nationalist discourse in the aftermath of partition Gandhi's oft-repeated stance was "let there be no Hindu, no Parsis, no Christians and no Jews. We should realize that we are only Indians, and that religion is a private matter" (CWMG, Vols 98: 68; 96: 267). Gandhi's deep commitment to communal harmony appeared to be a counterweight to ethno-nationalist sectarianism. Although communal unity was a cornerstone of Gandhi's idea of India, it was paradoxically Gandhi who unwittingly played a role in stoking an ethno-nationalist conception of citizenship and embedding it into the mainstream in 1932, long before the demand for the recognition of Muslims in India as a nation was raised by Muhammad Ali Jinnah. At the time, when the proposal was made to grant the Scheduled Castes (SCs) separate electorates and incorporate them as a distinct minority group on the basis of civic and political rights, Gandhi insisted on incorporating the SCs on the basis of religion, as Hindus (Gould 2004: 17–19). Gandhi is reported to have said that a "separate electorate will create divisions among Hindus so much that it will lead to bloodshed. Untouchable hooligans will make common cause with Muslim hooligans and kill [upper] caste Hindus" (CWMG, Vol. 56: 466). The citizenship claims of SCs were now bound up with the claims of all Hindus.

The conflation of religion and caste in the ethno-nationalist construction of the nation marked the limits of the Gandhian citizenship conception. In relation to caste, religion was not, as Gandhi's rhetoric suggested, a personal matter divorced from politics. On the contrary, religion formed part of the basis for a harmonized social order that created unity of cultural diversity. In his Sarvodaya (progress for all) programs Gandhi championed the removal of untouchability, yet ultimately conceived upliftment only within the purview of the Hindu caste system as an order of equality and harmony (Dalton 1967; Omvedt 1973; Parekh 1991). Indeed, the underpinning language and rationalization of Sarvodaya schemes for the poor in the first two decades after independence were imbued with Hindu idioms (Harris 1998: 332). It is not surprising therefore, that Muslim participation in those schemes was minimal. Moreover, in the context of the mass violence and the displacements Muslims experienced during the first years after partition, they needed the state as the guarantor of their safety. By 1949 many Muslims, especially returning refugees, became stateless. Their legal status was not adjudicated until November that year, when citizenship provisions were introduced ahead of the enactment of the constitution (Zamindar Fazila-Yacoobali 2007: 76, 106). Under these circumstances the non-statist conception of citizenship had little appeal to most Muslims.

Many Muslims could find viable prospects in the liberal conception of citizenship. An individualist liberal notion of citizenship was integral to the enactment of the constitution in January 1950. India was defined as a democratic republic, and its founding legal document assured fundamental rights to all individuals guaranteed by equal protection against state action. The liberal conception of citizenship provided, on the face of it, equal membership in the state to all its citizens. The question of whether Muslims were "Indian enough" became irrelevant within the liberal framework. This citizenship conception enabled Muslims to devise a political strategy for membership in the nation. A liberal paradigm allowed them a relatively smooth shift from being a nation within a nation, as they were defined by the ethno-nationalist conception, to becoming a minority. The constitution guaranteed the protection of religious and cultural rights of its minorities, which a liberal notion of citizenship can tolerate within the private sphere. The reservations for the SCs and STs were the exception. These differential citizenship rights introduced a tension in the constitution between a commitment to equality, on the one hand, and the scheduling of special quotas for some groups, on the other. It posited some contradictions for policy makers. Yet even those differential rights could be read, and have been interpreted by the courts as religious and cultural rights of minorities among Hindus. Thus, for the purpose of reservations, the SCs and STs were conceived as "those groups who because of their low ritual status in the traditional Hindu hierarchy and their spatial and cultural isolation were subjected to imposition of disabilities and lack of opportunity" (Galanter 1991: 122). The judiciary enforced this designation on the grounds that "acceptance of a non-Hindu religion operates as a loss of caste" (ibid.: 315).

The interlinking of religion and caste within the liberal conception contained the lower castes within the category of Hindus, while offering these marginalized groups some preferential treatment in access to state resources. Within the liberal field Muslims were able to make what appeared to be cultural identity claims over, for example, the protection of Muslim personal law and the status of Urdu. This left untouched the question of their socio-economic backwardness. Indeed, liberalism provides only limited scope for socio-economic claims and redistribution measures. Group-identity claims within a liberal citizenship conception, in turn, perpetuated a growing sense of the "problem" of the assimilation of Muslims in the mainstream of the nation, as such demands sometimes appeared to promote a "minority cause." Moreover, within this liberal conceptualization Muslims were sometimes even seen to be liable to their own predicament: due to "conservative, social and cultural ethos and their tendency to remain aloof" (Singh, G. 1983: 14). This view could vindicate governments, as they were shirking responsibility for their Muslim citizens.

Within the republican, collectivist notion of citizenship Muslims had in principle an alternative future within the nation after independence. A collectivist citizenship drive and a definition of a common good seemed essential to overcoming the grand task of creating social cohesion after partition. In this conception of citizenship, economic growth within a framework of equity – development – defined the common good, putting the "national interest" in line with the interests of the state. Development was, after all, the most vital problem that free India had to address. In this republican vision, led by Jawaharlal Nehru, massive and active state redistributive mechanisms would keep Indian democracy viable. Accordingly, the government embarked on central planning, as the means of achieving this end. By 1954 the parliament had passed a resolution adopting "a socialistic pattern of society" as the objectives of economic and social policy to ensure "that there is equitable distribution of the national wealth" (Planning Commission 1957: 12).

In the republican conception of citizenship Muslims could become Indian if they invested themselves in the efforts for the country's planned economic development; and if they prioritized the "needs" of the nation state over their individual or group rights. The republican rhetoric of planning offered a share in the nation for each of its citizens. It required the bringing of all citizens into a "mainstream," glossing over divisions. This meant that the viability of this conception of citizenship hinged on the state's ability to deliver on development with equity, and its ability to perceive diversity in socio-economic, rather than religious and cultural terms. But for the most part, the state defined Muslims in religious terms and excluded them from membership in groups that qualified for preferential treatment for social uplift within a framework of development with equity. The Fourth and Fifth Five-Year Plans (1969–1979) were the first to state that their main thrust was directed "towards ameliorating the conditions of the backward sections of the society"; and "spreading the impetus and benefits of economic growth to the weaker sections," especially "tribals, Harijans (SCs) and backward communities" (Planning Commission). Muslims were not included in the list of beneficiary groups. But based on their socio-economic predicament, Muslims should have been considered part of the majority of India's "weaker sections," rather than as a religious minority.

Overall the state fell short in its efforts to deliver development with equity through central planning. Consequently, by the mid-1970s, the republican conception of citizenship was called into question by a non-statist citizenship drive, which emphasized people's power and social change through non-cooperation. This emerged in the context of broad economic and social unrest, largely over the frustrated promises of development, which found expression in broad social movements such as the Nav-Nirman agitation in Gujarat, and the JP Bihar movement for social justice and against corruption.

The declaration of emergency rule (1975–1977) could be seen as an extreme attempt to restore a republican vision in crisis. It was justified by Indira Gandhi as a means of "removing the difficulties which have arisen in achieving the objective of socio-economic revolution, which would end poverty and ignorance." Her rationale was that India's democratic institutions "have been subjected to considerable stresses and strains and that vested interests have been trying to promote their selfish ends to the great detriment of the public good" (The (forty-second amendment) Act 1976: 1). Indira Gandhi attempted to reinstate the republic, devising a program for speedy implementation of fundamental social reforms. The stated aim of the emergency was to make up for earlier failures to distribute resources to the poor and improve their livelihoods. Paradoxically, the poor, and among them Muslims in particular, were those who suffered most harshly the injustices inflicted by the emergency (Tarlo 2003: 130–146).

After the emergency republicanism weakened, taken over by the growing prominence and balancing act between ethno-nationalism and liberalism. This change in balance occurred in the context of growing assertions of the lower and backward castes, disillusioned with their scope for development. In some ways, as long as the republican discourse predominated, the political power of these Hindu marginalized groups was limited. Now, the lower and backward castes began creating their own parties and power bases. Political alliances between lower and backward caste groups and Muslims emerged as well. For example, in Gujarat the Congress party established the KHAM caste alliance in the mid-1970s, with the idea of promoting itself as the advocate of the oppressed groups. KHAM was the acronym for Kshatriyas, Harijans, Adivasis and Muslims, who together formed about 55 percent of the population of the state. This was an alliance of economic classes that could potentially upset the social and political order. In UP the emerging Bhartiya Kranti Dal (BKD) party, which was led by Charan Singh, a member of a backward caste community, appealed directly to the common economic interests of the peasantry from the backward classes. By the 1970s Singh constructed the AJGAR political alliance, an acronym for Ahir (Yadav), Jat Gujar and Rajput, which covered a wide range of OBC and intermediate castes. In 1984 the Bahujan Samaj Party (BSP) was founded on the tenet of bringing social transformation and economic emancipation to the SCs, STs, OBCs and other minorities such as Muslims. The party won a landslide majority in the 2007 UP state assembly elections.

The rise of Hindu ethno-nationalism from the mid-1980s, which sought to establish India as a Hindu state, was also related to the growing tensions among castes. These conflicts did not originate in Hindu–Muslim antagonisms. In fact, the making of Islam and Muslims in the 1980s into a viable threat to India and to its Hindu majority, as well as the sudden political success of this notion, had little to do with the changing nature of Islam or of Muslim politics at the time. Rather, it was related to the class and status anxieties of the minority of upper castes among Hindus over the growing assertion of the lower and backward caste majority, which threatened to upset the Hindu moral order (Shani 2007).

Growing caste tensions from the 1980s arose particularly around the increase in reservation quotas for the backward castes in educational institutions and government jobs. Backward caste lists sometimes included converts from SCs to non-Hindu religions and several states used this category to provide some concessions to sections of their Muslim population. State government attempts to include Muslims and converts from the SCs in their backward classes lists became more prevalent in the mid-1990s (Wright 1997; Dudley Jenkins 2001). These developments were partly a response to more politicized interest groups within a liberal citizenship paradigm. In 1994 the All-India Backward Muslim Morcha was set up with the aim of "getting recognition from the Indian state for over 100 million Dalit Muslims as Scheduled Castes so that they can enjoy the same privileges as the scheduled caste Hindus enjoy" (Sikand 2001: 280). The common conceptualization of the Muslim "problem" and Muslim citizenship, construed in terms of a majority–minority issue, did not easily stick. Rather, the Muslim minority could now be seen as a member in a large group of Hindu caste minorities. Indeed, from the viewpoint of emerging state policies, particularly from the 1980s, the minority included not only Muslims, but also the SCs, STs and OBCs – the poor majority, leaving only a small number of upper castes in the Hindu "majority."

At the same time, the liberal citizenship paradigm that was largely enhanced by processes of economic liberalization in India from the mid-1980s also worked to delimit the poor majority. The liberal conception of citizenship emphasized the equal rights of every citizen, but did little to ensure that socially and economically disadvantaged groups would have the capacity to act on and enjoy their rights. Economic reforms, which entailed privatization and deregulation, meant that the beneficiaries of preferential policies, mainly the lower and backward castes, would be less able to benefit from redistributive policy measures.

Both the ethno-Hindu-nationalist and the liberal citizenship conceptions posed a challenge to the integrity of India. From the mid-1980s, a Hindu ethno-nationalist vision for the nation led to widespread communal violence and deepening sectarianism. Economic liberalism deepened the gap between the "have" and the "have-not" citizens of India. This rift threatened to create a growing alienation of the poor majority from the nation. The Gandhian conception of citizenship, which understood the problem of untouchability from a religious viewpoint, facilitated the growing Hindu notion of the nation at that time. Indeed, some Hindu nationalists often identified themselves as adherents of "Gandhian socialism" (Fox 1989: 238–240). Yet, it was also the non-statist Gandhian citizenship conception that helped to counter the perils of both ethno-Hinduism and liberalism to the integrity of the nation. From the 1980s, a new form of people's power politics, informed by Gandhian notions of citizenship, as well as by Gandhian methods of resistance, gave a new bent to liberalism, which created a finer balance in the Indian citizenship regime, in the sense that it created scope for a share in the state resources for the poor. Burgeoning struggles by civil society and non-governmental organizations and social movements drove the emergence of a new discourse and politics of rights and governance based on the pursuit of social and economic rights.

The shifting balance and tension between the four predominant conceptions of citizenship has been part of the dynamic whereby India's citizenship regime was never fully monopolized by any one of the citizenship discourses, at least not for long. An extreme republican vision would have required a powerful central state capable of enforcing large-scale redistribution and state intervention for the attainment of the common good. This vision materialized for a short time at the cost of suspending a democratic order by repressive measures during the emergency. Complete economic liberalism and a minimalist state have tended to be viewed as unrealistic by governments in the face of such widespread poverty. Indeed, the slogan of "India Shining," in reference to its growing economy, was insufficient to keep the Hindu nationalist BJP in power in the 2004 elections. An ethno-nationalist vision for India, as expressed in Gujarat in the 1990s–2000s, led to widespread violence. Gandhian non-statism would mean no national collective at all. If any of these conceptions had been predominant for a longer period, India as a unitary state and a democracy might well have failed.

In the making of citizenship, the Indian state fragmented the majority of the poor, lower and backward castes, among them Muslims, into many minorities. Muslims were persistently discriminated against, and a "Muslim problem" was frequently hailed as a threat to national integrity. The denial of Muslims' citizenship transpired through a continual interplay and shifting balance between four competing dominant conceptions of citizenship. Each of these citizenship conceptions perceived of Muslims in terms of a homogenized religious minority that was not related to caste, thus narrowing Muslims' scope for membership claims and mobility through state preferential policies that the lower and backward castes were entitled to. Nevertheless, between the four alternative frameworks for membership, Muslims could chart a path for some share in the nation state. At the same time, each of these citizenship conceptions related to caste as integral to the definition of being a Hindu, thus containing them within a Hindu majority. This dual process served to inhibit critical caste–class unrests, which were perceived to be a grave threat to the nation.

Notes

1 For a discussion on some doubtful cases against so-called "operative activists" of the Student Islamic Movement of India see the investigative report by Ajit Sahi, *Tehelka*, 5, 32, August 16, 2008.
2 These groups are also referred to in this chapter as lower and backward castes. The constitution of India granted the scheduled castes (SCs) and scheduled tribes (STs)

reserved quotas of 14 percent and 7 percent respectively in the Lok Sabha (parliament) and the states' legislative assemblies, government jobs and educational institutions. Reservations in educational institutions and government jobs were allotted to the Other Backward Castes/Classes (OBCs) through state policies.
3 These findings relate to Assembly constituencies before the new delimitation notification came into effect on February 19, 2008.
4 In my analysis of the construction of the Indian citizenship regime I depart from the work of Shafir and Peled, which offers a theoretical framework of a multiple citizenship discourse to account for Israel's social and political structure and the evolution of its modern history.
5 This position was supported by some other members of the Constituent Assembly, like, for example, Shri Jaspat Roy Kapoor, Prof. Shiban Lal Saksena, and Pandit Thakur Das Bhargava.

Bibliography

Ahmad, I. (1980) "The Problem of Muslim Educational Backwardness in Contemporary India: An Inferential Analysis," *Journal of Muslim Minority Affairs*, 2, 2: 55–71.

Amin, S. (2004) "On Representing the Musalman," *Sarai Reader*, Crisis/Media: 92–97.

Chagla, M. C. (1962), "Muslims Stand Apart," *The Times*, 26 January. Online. Available http://archive.timesonline.co.uk/tol/viewArticle.arc (accessed September 12, 2008). Also produced in A. G. Noorani (ed.) (2003), *The Muslims of India: A Documentary Recorded*, New Delhi: Oxford University Press, p. 25.

Constituent Assembly Debates (CAD) (1999) Vol. IX, 30 July 1949–18 September 1949, New Delhi: Lok Sabha Secretariat, 1999 (third edn), August 11, 1949, p. 352.

Dalton, D. (1967) "The Gandhian View of Caste, and Caste after Gandhi," in Philip Mason (ed.), *India and Ceylon: Unity and Diversity*, London: Oxford University Press.

Dave (Justice), V.S. (1990) *Report of the Commission of Inquiry: into the incidents of violence and disturbances which took place at various places in the state of Gujarat since February, 1985 to 18th July, 1985*, Ahmedabad: Government of Gujarat.

Dudley Jenkins, L. (2001) "Becoming Backward: Preferential Policies and Religious Minorities in India," *Commonwealth and Comparative Politics*, 39, 1: 32–50.

Fox, R. G. (1989), *Gandhian Utopia: Experiments with Culture*, Boston: Beacon Press.

Galanter, M. (1991) *Competing Equalities: Law and the Backward Classes in India*, Delhi: Oxford University Press (first edn 1984).

Gandhi, M. K. *The Collected Works of Mahatma Gandhi* (CWMG), Vols 25, 56, 81, 82, 91, 96, 98. Online. Available www.gandhiserve.org/cwmg/cwmg.html.

Gandhi, M. K. (1954) *Sarvodaya: Its Principles and Programme*, Ahmedabad: Navajivan Publishing House.

Gould, W. (2004) *Hindu Nationalism and the Language of Politics in Late Colonial India*, Cambridge: Cambridge University Press, 2004.

Government of Gujarat (1983) *Report of the Socially and Educationally Backward Classes [second] Commission*.

Government of India (Gopal Singh Report) (1983) *Report of the High Power Panel on Minorities, SC, ST & Weaker Sections*.

Government of India (1976) The (forty-second amendment) Act, 1976.

Guha, R. (2007) *India After Gandhi*, London: Pan Books.

Harris, I. C. (1998) *Gandhians in Contemporary India: The Vision and the Visionaries*, Lampeter (Ceredigion), Wales: The Edwin Mellen Press.

Hasan, M. (1997) *Legacy of A Divided Nation: India's Muslims Since Independence*, Delhi: Oxford University Press.

Institute of Conflict Management, South Asia Terrorism Portal, Major Islamic Terrorist Attacks Outside Jammu & Kashmir and Northeast. Online. Available www.satp.org/satporgtp/countries/india/index.html (accessed July 30, 2009).

Khalidi, O. (2006) *Muslims in Indian Economy*, Gurgaon: Three Essays.

Mahajan, G. (ed.) (2000), *Democracy, Difference and Social Justice*, New Delhi: Oxford University Press.

Ministry of Home Affairs Government of India, *Annual Report 2008–09*. Online. Available www.mha.nic.in/uniquepage.asp?Id_Pk=288 (accessed July 30, 2009).

Ministry of Information and Broadcasting, Government of India (1951) *Indian Muslims' Views on Kashmir: Statements and Resolutions by Muslim Leaders and Muslim Organizations of India, July 21, 1951 – September 15, 1951*, Delhi: Publication Division.

—— (1967) *For A United India: Speeches of Sardar Patel 1947–1950*, New Delhi: Publication Division.

Nehru, J. (1948) *The Unity of India*, London: Lindsay Drummond.

—— (1985) *Letters to Chief Ministers 1947–1964*, Vol. 3, 1952–1954, New Delhi: Government of India, Jawaharlal Nehru Memorial Fund Teen Murti House.

Noorani, A. G. (ed.) (2003) *The Muslims of India: A Documentary Recorded*, New Delhi: Oxford University Press.

—— (2004) "The Muslim as Terrorist," *Frontline*, July 17–30. Online. Available http://www.hindu.com/thehindu/fline/fl2115/stories/20040730002608100.htm (accessed July 29, 2009).

Omvedt, G. (1973) "Gandhi and the Pacification of the Indian National Revolution," *Bulletin of Concerned Asian Scholars*, 2–8.

Pandey, G. (1999) "Can A Muslim Be an Indian," *Comparative Studies in Society and History*, 41, 4: 608–629.

Parekh, B. (1991) "The Marxist Discourse on Gandhi," in Dwijendra Tripathi (ed.) *Business and Politics in India: A Historical Perspective*, Delhi: Manohar.

Planning Commission Government of India (1957), *Review of The First Five Year Plan*, Delhi: Manager of Publications.

Planning Commission Government of India, Fifth Plan, chapter 5.166, Fourth Plan, chapter 21. Online. Available http://planningcommission.nic.in/plans/planrel/fiveyr/welcome.html (Accessed September 19, 2008).

Prime Minister's High Level Committee (Sachar Report) (2006), *Social Economic and Educational Status of the Muslim Community of India*, Delhi: Cabinet Secretariat Government of India.

Roy, S. (2007) *Beyond Belief: India and the Politics of Postcolonial Nationalism*, Durham and London: Duke University Press.

Sachar Committee papers (2006), File nos 32, Vol. I; 86, Nehru Memorial Museum and Library (NMML).

Sahi, A. (2008) *Tehelka*, 5, 32, August 16.

Shafir, G. and Peled Y. (1998) "Citizenship and Stratification in an Ethnic Democracy," *Ethnic and Racial Studies* 21, 3: 408–427.

—— (2002) *Being Israeli: The Dynamics of Multiple Citizenship*, Cambridge: Cambridge University Press.

Shani, Ornit (2007) *Communalism, Caste and Hindu Nationalism: The Violence in Gujarat*, Cambridge: Cambridge University Press.

Sikand, Y. (2001) "A New Indian Muslim Agenda: The Dalit Muslims and the All-India Backward Muslim *Morcha*," *Journal of Muslim Minority Affairs*, 21, 2: 287–296.

Singh Gopal Papers, File 19, 18/12/1980, "The Muslim Problem," New Delhi: Nehru Memorial Museum and Library (NMML).

Singh, U. K. (2007) *The State, Democracy and Anti-Terror Laws in India*, New Delhi: Sage Publications.

Sirnate, V. (2007) "The RSS and Citizenship: The Construction of the Muslim Minority Identity in India," in Mushirul Hasan (ed.) *Living With Secularism: The Destiny of India's Muslim*, New Delhi: Manohar.

Tarlo, E. (2003) *Unsettling Memories: Narratives of the Emergency in Delhi*, London: Hurst & Company.

Varadarajan, S. (2002) "Chronicle of a Tragedy Foretold," in S. Varadarajan (ed.), *Gujarat: The Making of A Tragedy*, New Delhi: Penguin Books India.

Wright, T. (1997) "A New Demand for Muslim Reservations in India," *Asian Survey*, 37, 9: 852–858.

Yashar, D. J. (2005) *Contesting Citizenship in Latin America: The Rise of Indigenous Movements and the Postliberal Challenge*, Cambridge: Cambridge University Press.

Zakaria, R. (2004) *Indian Muslims. Where have they gone wrong?*, Mumbai: Popular Prakashan.

Zamindar Fazila-Yacoobali, V. (2007), *The Long Partition and the Making of Modern South Asia: Refugees, Boundaries, Histories*, New York: Columbia University Press.

9 Women as the bearers of the nation

Between liberal and ethnic citizenship

Gila Stopler

Introduction

The situation of women in Israel is a complex one. While in many respects women enjoy advanced liberal citizenship rights, in other respects, especially in the domain of personal status law, they suffer from serious restrictions on their rights and from discrimination. It is customary to attribute these flaws in women's citizenship rights in Israel to the political influence exercised by powerful religious political parties (Halperin-Kaddari 2004: ch. 11). However, in this chapter I wish to suggest a different, more foundational, explanation for this state of affairs; an explanation, which, despite its apparent plausibility, is, to a large extent, hidden from the public eye and seldom discussed. I will claim that these flaws in the generally liberal regime of women's citizenship rights in Israel are the result of two factors: First, the fact that the state of Israel, which defines itself as a Jewish and democratic state, is the home of two national communities – the Jewish community and the Palestinian Arab community; and second, the fact that the Jewish community is in a continuous conflict with the Arab world and perceives itself as being in the midst of a struggle for self determination and for continued existence.

I will argue that from the perspective of the Jewish community the aforementioned facts create a foundational imperative that Israel maintain its character as a Jewish state through a preservation of a Jewish majority in Israel, an imperative which results in legal restrictions on the right to marry and on the right to have an abortion, both of which, as I will show, are strongly related to communal preservation. While explaining these legal restrictions in this manner may be unconventional and controversial, it is an explanation worth considering both because it highlights the uneasy relationship between democratic aspirations and ethnic aspirations, from the perspective of women's rights, and because identifying the true reasons behind these restrictions on rights is an important step in the struggle against them. In what follows I will briefly describe the relationship between law, citizenship and ethnicity in Israel and explain its factual and historical origins. I will then discuss women's citizenship rights in Israel, analyzing the way in which women are affected by the relationship between law, citizenship and ethnicity. I will show how women's special role as mothers and as those responsible for the preservation of the Jewish ethnic community can account for the flaws in the generally advanced liberal rights regime that women enjoy in Israel, and will discuss the legal arrangements maintaining these flaws. Subsequently, I will offer some reflections on the question of how these flaws can continue to exist, almost unchallenged, despite the considerable advance in Israeli women's rights regime in recent years.

Law, citizenship and ethnicity in Israel

The Israeli declaration of establishment states that the state of Israel will be a Jewish and democratic state.[1] Although the declaration of establishment itself does not have the force of law and its power is merely interpretive, the two fundamental features of Israel as a Jewish and democratic state, first set out in the declaration, are seen by many as the substantive basic norm of the Israeli state. This view has gained prominence after Israel's character as a Jewish and democratic state has been given constitutional status in the two basic laws on human rights – the Basic Law: Human dignity and liberty and the Basic Law: Freedom of Occupation.[2] The purpose clauses of these basic laws state that the Basic Laws' purpose is to give constitutional status to the rights specified in them in order to give constitutional status to the values of the state of Israel as a Jewish and democratic state.

These two basic features of Israel – a Jewish state and a democratic state – manifest the inherent and permanent tension that exists in Israeli constitutional and public law, as well as in Israeli society as a whole, between the universalistic aspiration to become a democratic liberal state that respects and promotes human rights, and the particularistic aspiration to become and to remain a Jewish state – the state of a specific ethnic community in which the community preserves itself and realizes its right to self determination. The possible implications of the Jewish character of the state are contested. While some regard it as a justification for making religious Halakhic law the law of the land, others see it as mandating respect only to some aspects of the Jewish religion or even to none, while emphasizing Jewish nationality and focusing on national symbols, language, shared history and the like (Gavison 1998).

Nevertheless, a minimum feature of the Jewish state on which there seems to be a general agreement among Israeli Jews is the need to ensure the continued existence of a solid Jewish majority in Israel. This is regarded not only as a cultural imperative but also, and even more importantly, as an existential imperative, which stems from the fear that the loss of a Jewish majority will result not only in the cultural annihilation of the Jewish community in Israel, but in its physical annihilation as well.[3] Thus, while the exact meaning and scope of the "Jewish" component of the state is bitterly contested among Jews, the core commitment to the continued "Jewishness" of the state is rarely challenged, and any such challenge invokes deeply set existential fears and goes straight to the heart of what Saban terms the taboo area (Saban 2002: 307).

Not surprisingly, the situation described above has significant implications for the contours of citizenship in Israel. Three models of citizenship are relevant to the discussion of citizenship in Israel; the liberal model, the republican model and the ethnic model. The liberal model emphasizes personal liberty and protects the freedom of the individual to pursue her conception of the good and to author her life free from any government interference. Thus, in the liberal model of citizenship individual rights are what Dworkin calls trumps, which cannot be sacrificed for the benefit of the community. Critiques of the liberal model argue that because liberalism is neutral with respect to its citizens' conceptions of the good and treats them all as abstract subjects entitled to universal and equal rights, it fails to develop within citizens a sense of identity and a sense of belonging to a community of value, and therefore leaves them strangers to each other (Shafir and Peled 2002: 4). Conversely, the republican model of citizenship views citizens as members of a moral community who acquire civic virtue by participating in the life of their political community, by identifying with its purposes, and by actively pursuing a shared common good. Civic virtue is measured through the active participation of citizens in the fulfillment of societal duties, such as army service. The higher a citizen's civic virtue is, the larger is her entitlement to a share of the community's resources (Shafir and Peled 2002: 5).

While the republican model of citizenship allows all citizens to belong by participating in the moral community and acquiring civic virtue, the third model of citizenship – the ethnic model – links citizenship inextricably to membership in a certain national ethnic group that is based on a common descent and on common cultural markers such as language, religion and history. The ethnic model of citizenship perceives nations as being radically different from one another and negates the possibility of cultural assimilation (Shafir and Peled 2002: 6). In this model the state and the ethno national group converge and the state is committed to advancing only the interests and wellbeing of the members of the ethno national group, treating non-members as second-class citizens (Smooha 1998: 199–200). Smooha defines countries espousing such a model, including Israel, as "ethnic democracies." An ethnic democracy, according to Smooha, is located in the democratic section of the democracy–non-democracy continuum and operates on the basis of two contradictory principles – the democratic principle which requires equal rights and equal treatment of all citizens and the ethnic principle which aspires to create a homogenous nation-state and privileges the ethnic majority (Smooha 1998: 199–200).

Thus, Smooha explains, Israel is an ethnic democracy that grants its Palestinian Arab citizens individual civil and political rights and even some collective rights, such as separate education and an official status for Arabic, but as a state Israel identifies with the Jewish majority residing in it and aspires to create a Jewish state of and for the Jews. Consequently, Israel promotes the Hebrew language, Jewish culture, the Jewish majority and the economic status and political interests of the Jews, while the Palestinian Arab citizens are treated as second-class citizens, feared as a threat, excluded from the national power structure and placed under various forms of control (Smooha 1998: 205–206, 216–227).[4]

This chapter seeks to highlight a less explored consequence of Israel's character as an ethnic democracy; the way in which the relationship between democracy and ethnicity affects the legal rights of women in Israel. While the liberal and collective rights of the Palestinian Arab citizens of Israel are restricted because they are not part of the ethnic group for whom the state is constituted, I will show that Jewish women's liberal rights are restricted because they are an indispensable part of the ethnic group for which the state is constituted and because it is seen as their primary duty to help the group survive by keeping and enhancing its numerical strength. Thus, Israel's character as an ethnic democracy exacts a price not only from the ethnic "others" but also from those of the "right" ethnicity, especially women.

Women's citizenship rights in Israel

The feminist critique of citizenship holds that women are perceived as entitled to citizenship rights not because of their humanity but because of their role as mothers. Thus, women's individual liberal rights are contingent on their fulfillment of their republican or ethno national duty as mothers (Yuval-Davis and Anthias 1989). Building on this critique, I will show that the legal rights of all women in Israel are subordinated to the imperatives of preserving the Jewish majority in Israel and sustaining the Jewish people.[5] Increasing the birth rate of Jewish community in Israel was always seen as the best way to achieve these imperatives.[6] In April 1967, following a report by the Commission for Natality Problems (the Beky Report),[7] the Israeli government released its first official decision concerning Israel's demographic policy. At the heart of the decision stood the need to promote Jewish natality in order to ensure the survival of the Jewish people.[8] This focus was reiterated in the government's second official decision regarding Israel's demographic policy, from 1986.[9] The decisions established a Center of Demography (COD) and entrusted it with implementation of the government's demographic policy.

In what follows I will describe the ways in which the legal regime of women's citizenship in Israel is crafted by the need to promote Jewish natality and to sustain the Jewish majority. In this respect it is important to note that although the conflict that the Jewish community (through its embodiment – the Jewish and democratic state) is engaged in is an ethnic conflict, the boundaries of the Jewish ethnic collective in Israel are determined almost exclusively by orthodox religious law. Consequently, religious law and doctrine play a direct and indirect role in determining women's citizenship rights and legal status in Israel. Thus, the perpetuation of the religious-national nexus is not merely the result of pressures applied by strong religious political parties, but is no less the result of the wish to use state law to demarcate and preserve the boundaries of the ethno religious Jewish community in order to ensure its continued physical and cultural existence.[10]

Through a discussion of the laws pertaining to women's rights in Israel and their evolvement, I will show that within a general legal framework of a democratic state that grants women quite extensive and continuously expanding liberal citizenship rights there exist areas – namely, abortion control and marriage and divorce – in which the imperative of maintaining the Jewish majority prevails and the legal framework of liberal rights retreats and is replaced by illiberal legal restrictions on rights. The ethnic motivation of these legal restrictions is obscured by their universal application and by the generally liberal character of the Israeli rights regime. I will start by giving a theoretical background on the importance the control over natality has to ethnic, religious and cultural groups. I will then describe the legal restrictions on abortions and on interreligious marriage in Israel, and finally, I will analyze the Israeli Women's Equal Rights Act, highlighting these two flaws in the legal protection of women's rights in Israel against its highly liberal setting.

Controlling natality

Women have the biological function, and to a large extent the cultural function, of ensuring the continuity of ethnic and national groups. As hostility between ethnic, national and cultural groups deepens, the reproductive role of women is emphasized and with it the monitoring of the woman's body and actions (Yuval Davis 1997: 22–23, 29–31). Every state and every society has a strong interest in natality rates. Natality rates can determine the future of the community; will it grow enough or too much, will it grow smaller or perhaps even disappear altogether. Throughout history states' population policy was pronatalistic and was based on the assumption that a constant increase in population size was necessary to ensure national strength, economic growth and protection from outside aggression (Finkle and McIntosh 1994: 3).

Pronatalistic population policy is also consonant with religious ideologies – such as Christianity, Islam and Judaism – which hold that procreation is a sacred duty, and with ethnic and nationalistic ideologies, which view the size of the ethnic/national community as the key to its strength. Thus, for example, the Catholic Vatican vigorously opposes abortions, and even any form of contraception, because of its belief that the holy purpose of the sexual act, which can only take place between married spouses, is procreation (Keely 1994: 222). According to Islam woman's role is bringing children into the world, and it encourages procreation as well as early motherhood (Mazrui 1994: 121–122). Similarly, in Judaism the duty to procreate is of the highest order and the use of contraception and abortion is highly restricted (Portugese 1998: 45–47). Controlling natality is equally important for ethnic and national communities, and especially in times of national or ethnic conflict. One of the main ways in which women contribute to the community in ethnic and national conflicts is as biological reproducers of members of the struggling community (Yuval-Davis and Anthias 1989: 7).[11] Women's reproductive role is central to ethnic and national communities because the "common origin" of the community members, whether true or imagined, is the central and sometimes the exclusive criterion for belonging (Yuval Davis 1997: 26–27). Consequently, control over women's fertility is, in addition to control over immigration, the central means ethnic and national groups, as well as states, have for controlling a community's demographic composition.[12]

Restrictions on abortions

One strategy through which the Israeli Center of Demography (COD) attempted to promote Jewish natality was focused on attempts to decrease abortions. At the time of the Beky Report Israeli law criminalized all abortions, making both the woman and the performing doctor criminal offenders (Beky Report: 20).[13] However, the law was not being enforced and illegal abortions were being carried out freely. The committee concluded that abortions constituted a serious demographic concern and that a drastic decrease in abortions could significantly raise birthrates (Beky Report: 19–20). Consequently, it recommended the enactment and strict enforcement of a new law that would criminalize all abortions unless they are approved by a special committee, which would only approve a minimal number of abortions and only after an attempt was made to persuade the woman to carry the pregnancy to term (Beky Report: 44). Thus, Israeli law, which was amended in 1977 according to these recommendations, criminalizes all abortions, except for those that have been approved by a Termination of Pregnancy Committee, which can only approve abortions that meet the specific criteria stipulated by law, and only after the woman has met with a social worker whose task it is to persuade her not to file the request, and to carry the pregnancy to term. While the Termination of Pregnancy Committee approves almost all the requests brought before it, many of the women seeking abortions never file a request, either because they realize that they do not meet the criteria stipulated by law, or because they have been persuaded by the social worker to carry the pregnancy through.[14] Consequently, the number of illegal abortions carried out in Israel each year matches the number of legal abortions carried out (Stopler 2008: 488–491).

A full discussion of the denial of abortion with all its implications to women's rights is beyond the scope of this chapter. Suffice it to say that the usurpation of a woman's control over her body, the demand that she expose the most intimate details of her life before a committee of strangers and entrust her wellbeing, her health and her entire future in their hands, and her coercion, in some instances, to carry the pregnancy to term, all constitute severe infringements of women's fundamental right over their bodies, as well as their fundamental rights to liberty, dignity, privacy and equality.[15] The most common consideration justifying restrictions on abortions around the world is the right to life of the fetus. However, importantly, the Israeli law on abortion is not motivated by a concern for the fetus' right to life, but by demographic considerations. This is evident from the fact that in addition to authorizing the committee to approve abortions due to health risks for the mother and the fetus, the law authorizes the committee to approve abortions whenever the pregnancy is out of wedlock. The reason that an out-of-wedlock pregnancy constitutes a good cause for abortion is that according to strict orthodox interpretations of Jewish religious law, under certain circumstances children who are born out of wedlock can constitute a threat to the continued existence of the Jewish collective (Amir and Shoshi 2007: 796).[16] Thus, this provision prioritizes the continued existence of the Jewish collective over the life of the fetus, just as the law restricting abortions prioritizes the continued existence of the Jewish collective over women's rights.

Restrictions on intermarriage

The attempts by communities to control women's reproductive capacity are not restricted to attempts to control their fertility rates, but also extend to restrictions on whom they can marry, whose purpose it is to maintain the purity of the community and its boundaries. Thus, for example in South Africa during Apartheid women were not allowed to become sexually involved with men from racial groups other than their own (Yuval-Davis and Anthias 1989: 9), and in the US it was not until 1967 that the Supreme Court held that the anti-miscegenation state laws that criminalized interracial marriage were unconstitutional.[17] Israeli law also includes a statutory limitation on mixed marriages, albeit of a less coercive nature. Thus, Israeli law does not include a criminal prohibition against interreligious marriages, but by recognizing only religious marriages conducted by a religious tribunal of a recognized religious community the law in effect prevents people of different religions from marrying in Israel.[18]

Unlike other liberal democratic countries Israel does not have any procedure for civil marriages. The current system of personal laws is essentially a continuation of the Ottoman *millet* system, which was based on the principle of community self-rule, giving each religious community full control over the personal status of its members, regardless of whether they wish to abide by the religious rules and even regardless of whether they consider themselves members of the community. Thus, religious prohibitions that are intended to protect the boundaries of the various religious communities by prohibiting interfaith marriages, have been turned into compulsory state laws, that apply to all, regardless of their religious convictions.

One of the main reasons for the decision of the Israeli legislature to adopt this statutory scheme was its concern that allowing civil marriages might lead to a decrease in the Jewish majority through social mixing and conversion. When introducing the Rabbinical Courts Jurisdiction (Marriage and Divorce) Act in 1953 the Deputy Minister for Religious Affairs explained that one of the purposes of granting legal recognition exclusively to religious marriages was to exclude the possibility of mixed marriages that might result in the conversion of Jews to other faiths (Triger 2005: 204, Fogiel-Bijaoui 2003).[19] Similarly, when it became known that the Muslim Sharia courts in Israel were willing to marry Muslim men to Jewish women, the Ministry of Religious Affairs instructed the Sharia courts to refrain from conducting such marriages (Shifman 2001).[20] One could argue that this prohibition does not stem from the fear of losing potential members of the Jewish people because the children of a Jewish woman are considered Jewish even when the man is of a different faith. However, the assumption behind the prohibition is that after marrying a man of a different faith the Jewish woman would convert to the man's faith, and consequently, their children will no longer be Jewish. These restrictions on intermarriage also serve the purpose of preventing marriages between Israeli Jews and non-Jewish foreign workers and are in line with other restrictions on the number of non-Jews in Israel (Triger 2007: 747–753; Fogiel-Bijaoui 2003: 33).[21]

While allowing only religious marriages in Israel restricts the rights of both men and women, it has a particularly severe impact on women's equality rights. This is because the religious personal laws as applied by the religious courts of the various religious communities are highly patriarchal and give clear preference to men over women in most matters pertaining to the marriage relationship, especially the resolution of the marriage (Halperin-Kaddari 2005: ch. 11). Moreover, the subordination of women within the marriage has far reaching effects on their ability to achieve equality in all areas of life (Halperin-Kaddari 2005: 239–240). While partial attempts have been made to ameliorate this situation by means such as the establishment of civil family courts, which have parallel jurisdiction to religious courts in matters that do not pertain directly to marriage and divorce, these attempts do not weaken the hold that religion has on marriage and divorce itself. (Halperin-Kaddari 2005: 228–229, 233–235). Thus, in this matter the Israeli legislature has chosen to subordinate the individual rights of women to the preservation of the Jewish nation.

The revised Women's Equal Rights Act

As early as 1951 the state of Israel passed the Women's Equal Rights Act (the original WERA) guaranteeing equality to women. In her research on the original WERA Nitza Berkovitch has shown that at the basis of WERA's legislation stood the perception that women deserve equality because of their role as mothers. Thus, she quotes Ben Gurion explaining the motivation for the law as follows:

> I will talk about my mother, but refer to all mothers. Mother is the most precious person to everybody… my mother died when I was ten … but still I know that she was the symbol of purity, love, devotion, and nobility. And there is nothing more desecrating and more offensive than thinking that my dear mother is not equal to me … I cannot accept that my mother, our mothers, my sister who is also a mother, and my daughter, who will also be a mother one day, will be inferior to anyone else. This is the simple, human reason for this law.
>
> (*DH*, vol. 9, p. 2131, quoted in,Berkovitch 1997: 611–612)

While the original WERA purported to guarantee equality to all women in any legal action it had one clear exception – the first flaw – the subordination of women to the discriminatory religious laws of marriage and divorce of their respective religious community (sec. 5). This subordination cannot be explained merely by the need to ensure women's continued role as mothers. Quite to the contrary, restricting women's options in marriage to spouses of their own religion actually decreases their options to become mothers. However, by preventing Jewish women from marrying non-Jewish spouses such restrictions significantly increase the chances that Jewish women's children will be born and remain Jewish, and thus will promote Jewish natality and the Jewish majority in Israel. The original WERA, which was passed at a time in which abortions were still strictly forbidden, did not refer to the issue of abortion or to woman's right to control her own body.

In 2000 as a result of vigorous feminist lobbying the Knesset revised the WERA to include a progressive and extensive list of rights for women. Among other things, the revised WERA adopts the legal doctrine of disparate impact, stating that any legislation adversely affecting women relatively to men will be considered discriminatory without a need to show discriminatory intent (sec. 1A); it includes an explicit sanction of affirmative action and requires all public bodies to actively ensure women's equal representation in all positions and at all levels (sec. 1B and 6C); it guarantees women the equal right to serve in any military and security position (sec. 6D); it guarantees women's right to equality in all social and economic rights, stating that woman and man have an equal right to exist in conditions of human dignity, including the right to equality in employment, education, health, housing, environmental conditions and social welfare (sec. 6); it guarantees women protection against violence, sexual harassment, sexual exploitation and sexual slavery (sec. 6B); and it declares that every woman has a full right over her body (sec. 6A).

Thus, the revised WERA contains an extensive protection for women's equality in civil and political rights, as well as their equality in economic and social rights, and imposes on the state both negative and positive duties toward women. Moreover, it goes well beyond the classic liberal feminist notion of equality as sameness and incorporates both the tenets of difference feminism, which prescribe that different treatment may be required in order to achieve substantive equality, as well as the tenets of radical feminism, which holds that affording women protection against violence, sexual exploitation and sexual harassment is essential in order to guarantee their equality.[22]

Within this impressively progressive legal framework for women's equality in Israel two provisions stand out. One is the first flaw – the unrevised section 5 of the original WERA which subordinates women's equality to the discriminatory religious laws of marriage and divorce of their respective religious communities. The second flaw is a new addition to the revised WERA, which was needed due to the fact that the revised WERA purports to guarantee a woman's full control over her body. The same sec. 6A that guarantees women full control over their body contains an enigmatic exception stating that this section is not intended to annul any prohibitions set by law. First and foremost among these prohibitions, which are not specified in the WERA, is the criminal law prohibition on abortion. Thus, under the guise of a progressive liberal law the revised WERA reveals itself as a unique blend of women's progressive liberal rights and women's ethnic duties which is aimed at ensuring the continued existence of a Jewish majority in a democratic Israel.

How can these flaws persist?

Until now I have argued that the citizenship regime that applies to women in Israel is a mixed one. Alongside a liberal citizenship regime guaranteeing women extensive and progressive legal protection of their individual rights, there exist legal restrictions on rights that at first glance seem to stem from a republican view of citizenship, which measures women's civic virtue through their role as mothers and hence views restrictions on their attempts to reject this role (for example through abortions) as justified. However, I have tried to show that what may seem to be republican duties are perhaps better understood as duties stemming from the requirements of ethnic citizenship – the preservation of the Jewish majority in Israel. An interesting question is what enables these flaws in women's liberal citizenship rights to continue to exist and obscures their ethnic motivation?

I would like to offer three possible responses to this question. The first answer is that although according to its own official policy Israel is concerned only with promoting Jewish natality, the aforementioned restrictions are universal, applying to all Israeli citizens with no distinction on the basis of race, religion or ethnicity. While differential application of these legal restrictions would have exposed the state to accusations that it is constituting a regime of ethnic citizenship, the universality of the restrictions allows them to be perceived as manifestations of a republican form of citizenship that emphasizes the civic virtue of motherhood, rather than manifestations of the differential treatment of members of different ethnic groups. This shields these legal restrictions from accusations of ethnic, racial and religious discrimination, thereby decreasing their incompatibility with Israel's democratic nature. Thus, while restricting abortion rights of Jewish women alone would constitute clear discrimination on the basis of ethnicity, and would be unacceptable in terms of human rights, restricting the abortion rights of all women can pass as a regrettable, but not unusual, use of the supervisory power of the state over women's bodies.

Similarly, the universal prohibition on interreligious marriage through the universal application of religious laws in matters of marriage and divorce is even more consonant with the democratic nature of the state, because it is encouraged by the communities themselves, and is presented as a way of sharing power with minority communities and granting them group rights. Furthermore, the narrative attributing the application of religious personal laws in Israel to political pressures by the religious political parties is so dominant that it too serves to obscure the existence of the Jewish majority imperative, and to explain religious personal laws as a politically necessary aberration rather than as an inherent feature of an ethnic democracy engaged in both an internal and external conflict and set on preserving the dominance of its ethnic majority.

The second answer to the question of how these flaws can persist unchallenged, is that the restrictive bite of these legal restrictions is mitigated by the fact that in practice they both can be bypassed relatively easily by most of the population. Thus, the restriction on interreligious marriage can be circumvented by marrying abroad, while the restrictions on abortions can be evaded by having illegal abortions. Both these ways around the restrictions can be obtained at a cost which is quite considerable but still affordable to most of the population. It seems quite clear that had the state established a criminal ban on intermarriage and strictly enforced the criminal prohibition on illegal abortions both of these restrictions would have been very difficult to maintain within the Israeli regime of liberal individual rights.

The ability to bypass the restrictions serves another important purpose – it facilitates the postponement of the inevitable public debate over the measures that the Jewish Israeli society is willing to take in order to ensure the continued existence of a Jewish majority in Israel. As already mentioned, according to Saban there is a taboo on questioning the continued existence of Israel as a Jewish state (Saban 2002: 307). Similarly, Triger argues that there is a taboo within the Jewish community in Israel surrounding interfaith marriage between Jews and non Jews. This taboo is facilitated by the fact that interfaith marriage is not explicitly prohibited, but merely unavailable (Triger 2007: 737). As to the issue of abortions, it has been remarked more than once that the silence surrounding this issue in Israel is quite extraordinary, considering the restrictive nature of Israeli abortion legislation on the one hand, and the visibility and the agitation surrounding abortion in other countries on the other (Amir and Shoshi 2007: 808). The continuation of these taboos would have been impossible had the state applied and enforced strict restrictions in these areas. The unacknowledged clash between the Jewish nature of the state and its democratic nature would have then been fully exposed, forcing the Jewish community to face up to hard questions regarding the nature of the state, which it would rather not face.

Finally, a third answer that can also explain the relative feminist and public inaction with respect to both restrictions on abortions and on interfaith marriages, is the belief of many members of the Jewish community, including many feminists, that some restrictions on individual rights may be justified in order to avoid the existential threat that would be posed by the loss of the Jewish majority in Israel. In the US for example, which is built on a highly individualistic ethos and faces no existential threat, most women's rights activists would find the notion that the state may have a legitimate demographic interest in controlling abortions untenable. Conversely, the Jewish community in Israel is a community with strong collective roots (both socialist and religious), which feels that it faces a continuous existential threat. These facts may affect the willingness of feminist activists to struggle for free abortions and civil marriages, as well as their ability to garner public support for such a struggle (Yishay 1997: chs 7–8).

Thus, it seems that by obscuring the ethnic motivation for these legal restrictions, thereby minimizing their conflict with Israel's democratic nature; by leaving open the possibility of going around the restrictions; and due to the existence of the Jewish collective ethos and of collective existential fears, the legal restrictions on abortions and intermarriage – the two flaws in the Israeli women's rights regime that are designed to maintain the Jewish majority in Israel – can continue to exist within an otherwise progressive legal regime of liberal citizenship rights for women in Israel.

Conclusion

After declaring the establishment of a Jewish state named Israel, the Israeli Declaration of Establishment goes on to make an explicit guarantee of full equality on the basis of race, religion and sex, as well as to guarantee freedom of religion, conscience, language, education and culture. For political reasons, none of the rights and freedoms enumerated in the Declaration of Establishment were explicitly included in Israel's Basic Laws on human rights, which were enacted over 40 years later. Despite the fact that the Declaration of Establishment does not enjoy the force of law, the first two clauses of the Basic Laws on human rights, which set the constitutional framework within which the Basic Laws should be understood, refer the reader to the principles set out in the Declaration of Establishment and to the values of Israel as a Jewish and democratic state. Consequently, the reference in the Basic Laws to the Declaration has become an interpretive channel through which legal scholars have been trying to widen the scope of the rights protected in the Basic Laws (Barak 1994: 305).

The Women's Equal Rights Act is not a basic law, though the court has ruled in the past that it is a "majestic law" that sets out the fundamental principle of full equality between men and women.[23] In order to emphasize its alleged majesty, signify its importance, and make it reminiscent of a Basic Law, the legislature has amended the first section of the revised WERA so that similarly to the Basic Laws it now includes a reference to the Israeli Declaration of Establishment. Thus, the first section of the revised WERA reads: "The purpose of this law is to set out the principles guaranteeing full equality between woman and man, in the spirit of the principles set out in the declaration on the establishment of the State of Israel." Ironically, while the presence of this provision in the WERA is intended to enhance and expand women's rights, its existence points to the opposite. In fact, the existence of this provision lends support, perhaps inadvertently, to the central claim of this chapter: that the two flaws in Israel's women's rights regime, that were enacted into the WERA, do not necessarily reflect a contingent political necessity, but rather may be seen as part and parcel of the defining feature of Israel, as set out in its Declaration of Establishment and reiterated in its Basic Laws; its incontestable nature as a Jewish and democratic state, which must be ensured through the preservation of a Jewish majority, even at the cost of restricting women's rights.

Notes

1 The Declaration of the Establishment of the State of Israel, May 14, 1948, Published in the Official Gazette, No. 1 of the 5th, Iyar, 5708 (May 14, 1948).
2 Basic Law Human Dignity and Liberty; Sefer Ha-Chukkim No. 1391 of the 20th Adar Bet, 5752 (March 25, 1992); Basic Law Freedom of Occupation; Sefer Ha-Chukkim No. 1454 of the 27th Adar, 5754 (March 10, 1994) p. 90.

3 This fear stems from the fact that from its inception the state of Israel has been in a continuous state of emergency and often in a state of war. The state of emergency declared in 1948 has not been removed until this very day, and there is an ongoing situation of war and hostilities with Israel's Arab neighbors, as well as a situation of permanent tension between the Jewish and Palestinian citizens of Israel. Consequently it has been suggested that Israeli democracy is a "garrison democracy" (Yishay 1993: 223).

4 Smooha's characterization of Israel as an ethnic democracy has been criticized by scholars who claim that the existence of an ethnic democracy is inherently impossible because a state that identifies only with the majority ethnic group cannot be considered a democracy. Consequently those critics claim that Israel should be understood as an ethnocracy (cf. Ghanem, Rouhana and Yiftachel 1998).

5 I will claim that while the main purpose of these legal restrictions on rights is to control the conduct of Jewish women, they apply to all women, for reasons that I will explain below.

6 This is because while increasing the number of Jews in Israel through the emigration of Jews from abroad can help strengthen the Jewish community in Israel, it can neither help to solve the larger problem of sustaining the overall Jewish population of the world, nor is it a long-term solution for ensuring the continued growth of the Jewish community in Israel.

7 See under Report on the Commission for Natality Problems.

8 Israeli Government decision number 428, 9.4.67 reads as follows: "Suggestions regarding the demographic policy... 2. The Government recognizes the need to act systematically in order to implement a demographic policy targeted at creating an atmosphere that will encourage natality, *considering its importance to the future of the Jewish people*... 3. For that purpose: a. Constant advertising campaigns will be held, economical and social barriers will be removed and incentives will be given, in the fields of education, housing, insurance and so on, within the scope of the state's ability, *in order to encourage families to increase their number of children*. b. *artificial abortions will be curbed* as their high rate is cause for concern, in both national-demographic terms, and in terms of women's health." (Italics added by author, G.S.)

9 Israeli Government decision number 1596, 18.5.86 reads as follows: "1596. The demographic trends among the Jewish people Decision:

a   The government is concerned by the demographic trends in Israel and the Diaspora and is particularly worried about the slow-down of population growth in Israel, the decreasing Aliyah, and the rate of emigration as well as by the increase in assimilation and in mixed marriages in the Diaspora.

b   The government decides to establish a comprehensive, coordinated, long-term demographic policy, that will strive to achieve a proper level of *Jewish population growth* and in order to achieve this goal it encourages cooperation with organizations representing the Jewish people and the Diaspora Jews.

The policy will be based on direction, coordination and the implementation of measures that can affect population growth such as: *encouraging the creation of families and their desire for children*, strengthening families and removing barriers in their way, *preventing unnecessary abortions – through proper information and guidance*; welfare assistance for families who have difficulties in raising their children, encouraging Aliyah; and taking steps to stop the emigration and to encourage Israelis living abroad to return to Israel." (Italics added by author, G.S.)

10 Family law in particular is regarded as having a crucial role in the preservation of the community and the demarcation of its borders, and it has even been argued that the function of family law vis-à-vis the community is parallel to the function of citizenship law vis-à-vis the sovereign state (Shachar 2001: 45–47).

11 According to Davis and Anthias there are five major ways in which women participate in ethnic and national processes: "(a) as biological reproducers of members of
ethnic collectivities; (b) as reproducers of the boundaries of ethnic/national groups;
(c) as participating centrally in the ideological reproduction of the collectivity and as
transmitters of its culture; (d) as signifiers of ethnic/national differences – as a focus
and symbol in ideological discourses used in construction, reproduction and transformation of ethnic/national categories; (e) as participants in national, economic,
political and military struggles."

12 On historical examples of the effects of nationalism and ethnic conflict on state reproductive policies see Albanese 2006.

13 Penal Law Ordinance, 1939.

14 The importance of the meeting with the social worker stems from the fact that if the
woman files a request and meets the criteria stipulated by law for allowing abortions,
such as that the pregnancy is out of wedlock, the committee will most likely approve
the abortion. The social worker's job is both to alert women to the fact that they do
not meet the criteria and should therefore not file a request, and even more importantly to persuade those women that do meet the criteria not to file the request and to
carry the pregnancy to term. It should be noted that the committee does not require a
woman who claims that the pregnancy is out of wedlock to prove her claim, and thus
potentially almost any woman can obtain an abortion by lying to the committee.

15 On the importance of the right to abortion and on the various rights that it implicates
see Balkin 2005; Thomson 1971.

16 According to Jewish religious law there is a risk that a child born out of wedlock will
be a Mamzer or Safek Mamzer, who is not allowed to marry another Jew (unless he/
she too is a Mamzer). The fact that a person is a Mamzer or Safek Mamzer places
him/her as well as all his/her future generations outside the Jewish collective and has
long-term effects on the community.

17 *Loving* v. *Virginia* 388 U.S. 1 (1967).

18 King's Order in Council, 1922, sec. 51; Rabbinical Courts Jurisdiction (Marriage and
Divorce) Act, 1953.

19 Zvi Triger, *There is a State for Love: Marriage and Divorce between Jews in Israel*,
in Trials of Love (Orna Ben Naftali and Hanna Nave eds., Ramot, 2005) 173–226, at
204.

20 It is interesting to note that although according to Islam the Sharia courts can marry
Muslim men to non-Muslim women, they cannot marry Muslim women to non-
Muslim men, most probably because of the assumption that the woman will eventu-
ally convert to the man's religion, and thus become non-Muslim.

21 Recently further restrictions were added that make it more difficult for Israeli Jews to
marry non-Jews. These restrictions target marriages between Israeli Jews and non-
Israeli non-Jews. While in the past an Israeli Jew marrying a non-Israeli non-Jew
could acquire Israeli citizenship for her spouse automatically through the law of
return, recently it was decided that non-Israeli non-Jewish spouses would have to go
through a five-year process in order to acquire permanent status in Israel, during
which the application may be denied for various reasons. See H.C.3648/97 *Stamka* v.
Ministry of Interior.

22 Other progressive Israeli laws that embody the tenets of difference feminism and of
radical feminism are the Equal Pay for Women and Men Act which was revised in
1996 to include a guarantee of equal pay for comparable worth and the 1998 Prevention of Sexual Harassment Act.

23 E.g., H.C. 1000/92 *Bavli* v. *The Rabinical Court*.

References

Albanese, P. (2006) *Mothers of the Nation: Women, Families and Nationalism in Twentieth-Century Europe*, Toronto: University of Toronto Press.

Amir, D. and Shoshi, N. (2007) "The Israeli Abortion Law," in Barak Erez, D. *et al.* (eds) *Readings in Law, Gender and Feminism*, Jerusalem: Nevo Publishing (Hebrew).

Balkin, J.M. (ed.) (2005) *What Roe v. Wade Should Have Said*, New York: New York University Press.

Barak, A. (1994) *Interpretation of Law: Constitutional Interpretation*, Jerusalem: Nevo Publishing (Hebrew).

Berkovitch, N. (1997) "Motherhood as a National Mission: The Construction of Womanhood in the Legal Discourse in Israel," *Women's Studies International Forum* 20: 605–619.

Finkle, J.L. and McIntosh, A.C. (1994) "The New Politics of Population," *Population and Development Review,* Vol. 20, Supplement: *The New Politics of Population: Conflict and Consensus in Family Planning*, 3–34.

Fogiel-Bijaoui, S. (2003) "Why Won't There be Civil Marriage any Time Soon in Israel?" *Nashim: A Journal of Jewish Women's Studies & Gender Issues* 6: 28–34.

Gavison, R. (1998) "Jewish and Democratic State – Challenges and Risks," in Mautner, M., Sagi, A. and Shamir, R. (eds) *Multiculturalism in a Democratic and Jewish State*, Tel Aviv: Ramot (Hebrew).

Ghanem, A., Rouhana, N. and Yiftachel, O. (1998) "Questioning 'Ethnic Democracy': A Response to Sammy Smooha," *Israel Studies* 3: 253–267.

Halperin-Kaddari, R. (2004) *Women in Israel – A State of Their Own*, Philadelphia: University of Pennsylvania Press.

Israeli Government decision number 428 (9.4.67).

Israeli Government decision number 1596 (18.5.86).

Keely, C.B. (1994) "Limits to Papal Power: Vatican Inaction after Humanae Vitae," *Population and Development Review,* Vol. 20, Supplement: *The New Politics of Population: Conflict and Consensus in Family Planning*, 220–240.

Mazrui, A.A. (1994) "Islamic Doctrine and the Policy of Induced Fertility Change: An African Perspective," *Population and Development Review,* Vol. 20, Supplement: *The New Politics of Population: Conflict and Consensus in Family Planning*, 121–134.

Portugese, J. (1998) *Fertility Policy in Israel – The Politics of Religion, Gender and Nation*, Westport, CT: Praeger Publishers.

Report of the Commission for Natality Problems (April 1966), Jerusalem (the Beky Report) (Hebrew).

Saban, I. (2002) "The Collective Rights of the Arab Palestinian Minority in Israel: The Is, the Isn't and the Taboo Area," *Iunei Mishpat* 26: 241–319.

Shachar, A. (2001) *Multicultural Jurisdictions – Cultural Differences and Women's Rights*, Cambridge: Cambridge University Press.

Shafir, G. and Peled, Y. (2002) *Being Israeli: The Dynamics of Multiple Citizenship*, Cambridge: Cambridge University Press.

Shifman, P. (2001) *By Religion or By Law,* Jerusalem: Association for Civil Rights in Israel. Online. (Hebrew) Available www.acri.org.il/story.aspx?id=290 (accessed June 22, 2009).

Smooha, S. (1998)"'Ethnic Democracy: Israel as an Archetype," *Israel Studies* 2: 198–241.

Stopler, G. (2008) "Israel's Natality Policy and the Rights of Women and Minorities," *Mishpat UMimshal – Law and Government in Israel* 11: 473–516 (Hebrew).

Thomson, J.J. (1971) "A Defense of Abortion," *Philosophy & Public Affairs* 1: 47

Triger, Z. (2005) "There is a State for Love: Marriage and Divorce between Jews in Israel," in Ben Naftali, O. and Nave, H. (eds) *Trials of Love*, Tel Aviv: Ramot (Hebrew).

Triger, Z. (2007) "Love and Prejudice: On the Paradox of the Phenomenon of Interfaith Marriages in Israel," in Barak Erez, D. *et al.* (eds) *Readings in Law, Gender and Feminism*, Jerusalem: Nevo Publishing (Hebrew).

Yishay, Y. (1993) "Public Ideas and Public Policy – Abortion Politics in Four Democracies," *Comparative Politics* 25: 207–228.

Yishay, Y. (1997) *Between the Flag and the Banner: Women in Israeli Politics*, Albany, NY: State University of New York Press.

Yuval Davis, N. (1997) *Gender and Nation*, London: Sage Publications.

Yuval Davis, N. and Anthias, F. (eds) (1989), *Woman–Nation–State*, New York: St. Martin's Press.

10 The Palestinian "visionary documents" in Israel

Background, implications and critique

Uri Ram

Introduction

The state of Israel was designated by the Zionist movement as a Jewish state and so it was constituted in 1948. It was only in the 1990s that the appellation "Jewish and Democratic State" became an official and a commonplace term. Yet the conditions of the combination of the "Jewish" and the "Democratic" dimensions have remained unspecified; or if they were specified, the combination itself became diffused. Can a state defined as "Jewish" be also "Democratic"? If it is "Democratic" how can it be "Jewish"? If there is a "simultaneity" between the two terms, what happens when they clash? Does the one overpower the other? Which one? In what cases? Who determines? Does Jewish and Democratic mean that Jews and Arabs enjoy the same rights? And if they do, do they have it only as individuals or also as communities? And do they have the same power? Do they share power? In what proportion? Once such questions are being posed, it becomes clear that the "Jewish and democratic" concept is riddled with contradictions and hollow. It is in this context the the texts known as The Visionary Documents were published in 2007 by a number of Palestinian Arab associations in Israel. The aim of this chapter is to decipher these texts in this context.

As long as Jews were dispersed among other nations, they were considered as belonging either to certain communities or to a certain religious faith. But as of late nineteenth century, the Zionist movement re-defined the Jews as a nation and organized Jewish immigration and settlement in Palestine. The state of Israel was established in 1948 and in it, non-Jewish residents are considered as either belonging to certain communities or to certain faiths. Thus the "demographic boundaries" of the nation and the "geographic boundaries" of the state do not overlap. Inside the state, some 20 percent of the population – the Palestinian Arabs – is perceived in fact as "foreign"; and outside of it, foreign citizens, who happen to be Jewish, are perceived in fact as part of the nation, even if they stay abroad and have no concern with Israel. (The Law of Return guarantees immediate citizenship to any Jew once he wishes it.) The Jewish nation is conceived of as an ethnic nation, a nation based on the *ius sanguinis* principle ("blood" affiliation), and no "Israeli nation" that is based on the principle of *ius soli*, i.e., common territorial residence or on common citizenship, is recognized by the state of Israel. This incongruence between geography and demography is the root cause of the tensions that Israeli democracy experiences.

As of recently, members of the Palestinian-Arab community in Israel have mounted a frontal challenge against the Jewish ethnic supremacy in the state. In discursive terms, this challenge is an historical milestone in the relationships between Jews and Arabs in Israel, and its analysis is the subject of this chapter. The great significance of the challenge is that it is the first time that the Arabs in Israel speak collectively the language of *recognition* – with a demand for the rights of a national group, rather then the language of *equality* – with a demand for more equitable allocation of resources on behalf of a discriminated group. This chapter aims to contextualize and interpret the documents that express this challenge, but also to offer a critique.

The paper first presents the Visionary Documents and their main claims. It then moves to analyze the documents in their context, and argues, first, that their formulation should be understood as a response of Palestinian-Arabs in Israel both to the Oslo peace process and to its collapse. Second, it is suggested that the formulation of the documents should also be understood on the background of changes in Israeli political culture in large, especially the relative decline of Zionist ideology, and the emergence of post-Zionist and neo-Zionist conflicting responses to it. Third, it is also suggested that the documents draw upon critical perspectives on Israeli democracy that had been elaborated on in the last two decades within the academic scene in Israel. Finally, in the conclusion, critical comments are offered on the approach of the Visionary Documents. These comments are offered from a perspective that transcends both the Zionist uni-national concept of Israel – as a Jewish state, and the Visionary Documents' bi-national concept of it – as a Jewish and Palestinian bi-national state. The comments highlight the absence of another kind of vision, a vision of Israel as a post-national state, or a non-national state, or a democratic republic of its citizens.

The "visionary documents" of the Palestinian-Arab citizens in Israel

The recent constitutional challenge posed by Palestinian Arabs in Israel is expressed in several published documents, of which this chapter relates mostly to the following three: "The Future Vision of the Palestinian Arabs in Israel" (published by *The National Committee for the Heads of the Arab Local Authorities in Israel,* 2007); "The Democratic Constitution" document (published by *Adalah, The Legal Center for Arab Minority Rights in Israel,* February 2007); and "The Haifa Declaration" (published by *Mada al-Carmel – Arab Center for Applied Social Research,* May 15, 2007).[1]

The documents mentioned touch upon issues of national identity, colonialist history, civil rights, equal citizenship and power sharing. The documents support the establishment of a Palestinian state in the occupied territories of 1967 (the

West Bank and the Gaza Strip) but their main concern is the status of the Palestinian Arabs within Israel, as defined by its 1948–1967 "green line" boundaries. The following three points encapsulate the essential claims and demands of these documents.

1   The Visionary Documents re-define the status of the Palestinian Arabs in Israel – not as a "minority" in a democratic state, but rather as a "homeland ninority" in an "ethnocratic state."

The documents define the Palestinian-Arab citizens of Israel as an integral part of the Arab nation and the Palestinian Nation, and more specifically they define the relevant group that resides in Israel as a "homeland minority" or as an "indigenous people." The regime in Israel is considered as colonialist and ethnocratic (the term will be explained shortly).

It is important to note that the Documents substitute the previously common appellation of a "minority" or a "national minority," with that of a "homeland nation" or an "indigenous people." This, of course, serves the Arab cause in the struggle over international moral support and legitimation, in that these new categories confer upon the Palestinians the aura of the original people of the land and its authentic owners, while they de-legitimize the state of Israel, as owned by foreign invading settlers, supported by imperial powers.

2   The Visionary Documents demand the restoration of rights, compensation for losses and equality in resource allocation by the state.

The Visionary Documents lay out a thorough indictment of the historical and contemporary wrongdoings and offenses that the state has perpetrated against the Palestinian Arabs. The list of wrongdoings is partially summarized in the following citation:

> The policies and practices of Israeli governments have caused severe injustice to the Palestinian Arab minority since 1948, some of which continues today, including this minority's physical detachment from its people and nation, the uprooting and destruction of villages, the demolition of homes, the imposition of military rule until 1966, the massacre of Kufr Quassem in 1956, the killing of young people in the first Land Day in 1976 and in mass protests of October 2000, the confiscation of properties from the Muslim Waqf, the expropriation of land, the non-recognition of Arab villages, the separation of families, policies of institutional discrimination in all fields of life, and the exclusion of the Arab minority based on the definition of the state as Jewish.[2]

The Documents demand recognition by Israel of its responsibilities for all this, as well as a delivery of compensation of property (especially land) and restitution of rights and equality in allocation of resources and power.

3   The Visionary Documents demand a far reaching transformation of the regime in Israel: its transformation from a "Jewish and Democratic State" into a bi-national state, Jewish and Arab, with institutionalized power-sharing and veto rights for the minority.

Finally, and most significantly, in order to reverse the situation described above, the Documents demand a radical transformation of the structure of the regime in Israel. They demand that Israel be transformed from a "Jewish state" into a bi-national Jewish and Arab state: a state of two nations. In this state, first, the Palestinian Arabs will become equal partners to power and decision-making, and, second, they will get some form of autonomy. (The document refers to "institutional self rule in the field of education, culture and religion" and at another point, towards "national institutions relating to all living aspects.") It is demanded in the documents that an autonomous representative body of the Palestinian Arabs is established, and/or that their parliamentary representatives will have veto power over Knesset decisions and enactments. (The Adalah document proposes a veto power by the minority on Knesset bills.)[3]

There is yet another set of demands that the documents present, and these relate to distributional inequalities, both on the socio-economic level and on the symbolic level. There are a great many issues here, but the distributional dimension is utterly subordinated in these documents to the recognitional level, which we summarized above, and thus has secondary priority. The demands for distributional justice are, in any case, not new and do not carry the same political edge as the demands for a regime change. Thus the novelty and importance of the visionary documents stem from their radical political vision (or re-vision).

Finally, a point of great significance that ought to be highlighted here is that the Documents do not express in direct and positive terms a recognition of the state of Israel. The state is mentioned in two capacities: one, as the culprit responsible for the offenses done to Palestinian Arabs, and, two, as an addressee for the demands of the documents. But these practical references to the state are never accompanied by a note of consent or complacency with the fact that the state of Israel had been established and does exist as a legitimate political structure (and is recognized by the United Nations). This evasiveness regarding the recognition of Israel contributes towards the suspicion with which Israeli public opinion relates to what it perceives as the hidden agenda of documents.

The visionary documents and the post-Oslo turn in Arab politics in Israel

The first step towards the understanding of the VD to be taken here, is to explain their formation on the background of the changing scene of Arab identity and politics in Israel.

The coalescence of a number of parallel groups that worked throughout the 2000s and issued a number of parallel documents almost simultaneously in 2007 must be seen as a result of the combination of both the tide of expectations and the ebb of disappointments that had been connected to the Oslo "Peace Process" and to its eventual crumbling. In the brief moment of the Rabin government between 1993 and 1995, Israel recognized for the first time the Palestinian nation and the PLO as its representative, and the Oslo accord seemed – at the time – to be aiming towards a Palestinian state within the general framework of the "two states solution." The spirit of peace generated a moment of unprecedented rapprochement between the Arabs in Israel and the state. Yet a shadow also loomed.

The expected withdrawal of Israel from the occupied territories was motivated, to a great extent, as things still are today, by the growing concern in Israel with what is called the "demographic bomb," i.e., the perceived threat that the continuation of rule over the Palestinian territories will soon turn Jews to a minority between the Mediterranean sea and the Jordan river. The left and center in Israel realized that a Jewish state, and certainly a "Jewish and democratic" state, can only persist within the "green line" borders of the state of Israel (the 1949 armistice lines). And so the "peace process" had a double meaning. Explicitly, Israel said to the Palestinians in the territories: "we give up your territories, you give us recognition and peace." Implicitly, it also transmitted to the Palestinians inside Israel that now there are going to be two states – one Jewish, one Palestinian – and that they have to make a choice: either to join the Palestinian state and move there or stay in Israel but recognize that they are a minority in a Jewish national state. So the potential repercussions of a "two states solution" on the status the Palestinian citizens in Israel were ambiguous. On the one hand, the reduction of hostilities could have eased their integration in Israel; but, on the other hand, the creation of a Palestinian state could have eased Israel's claim for Jewish superiority in Israel.

But in any event, the long-term consequences of peace did not have the chance to be examined. All hopes for a rapprochement have been dashed since Rabin's assassination in November 1995, and the cycle of violence has been renewed and is continuing with a vengeance.[4] After Rabin came Benyamin Netanyahu, whose populist campaigns had been based on exclusionary ethnic Jewish messages. After Netanyahu – and this turned out to be even worse – came Ehud Barak. Barak slid into power on the wings of his image as a substitute for Rabin, a kind of reincarnation of the leader of the "Peace Camp," and he gained wide support from the Arabs in Israel. Yet, as soon as he came to office he turned his back upon them and condoned their political de-legitimating.[5] In October 2000, under his premiership, relations between Jews and Arabs in Israel reached their lowest node in the recent times, when security forces killed 13 demonstrators (Or Commission Report 2003). Trust between the state and its Arab citizens has not been re-established since. Simultaneously, Barak played a key role in the disastrous failure of the last Camp David summit round (2000), a failure that heralded the onset of the second Palestinian Intifada (in September 2000). Thus as the first decade of the 2000s unfolded, the Palestinians in Israel found themselves bereft on both fronts; without a Palestinian state and also without the solace of equal integration in Israel. This is the historical juncture at which the new radicalism had been fanned.

Arab politics in Israel has radically transformed throughout time (Reches 1998; Ghanem 2001; Al-Haj 2004; Reiter 2009). In 1949 the Palestinian Arabs found themselves a defeated, dependent and denigrated minority in a Jewish state, totally cut off from the rest of the Palestinian people and the Arab world outside of Israel. They were granted Israeli citizenship but were simultaneously subjected to a military regime and became totally dependent upon the government and the ruling party, Mapai. Their patriarchal social structure was exploited to maintain clientelistic relations with the state. An exception from this was the Communist Party which, under the protecting wings of Moscow, became the major repository of Arab-Palestinian nationalism in Israel for many years. In accord with Moscow, the party became probably the first Arab political organ to recognize the existence of Israel in 1948 and to advocate "Jewish–Arab solidarity."

The military regime was removed in 1966. In 1967 the Six Day War broke out and the political reality of the country changed overnight. The domination over the occupied territories brought together the two separate communities of the Palestinian Arabs for the first time since 1948: the community in Israel and the community in the West Bank and Gaza that included large number of refugees from 1948. If their long presence in Israel brought the Palestinians in Israel a degree of social and cultural "Israelization," the meeting with the community in the West Bank and the Gaza Strip brought about their "Palestinization" in terms of identity and ideology (Smooha 1989; 1992).

In the mid-1980s, the Communist Party reached the zenith of its popularity in the Arab population and gained more then 50 percent of Arab votes in 1984. Yet the decline and eventual fall of the Soviet Union (1989) and the general demise of the Left were soon to hurt the party's status. In conjunction with this, the steep rise in the international exposure of the PLO and the consequences of the Islamist revolution in Iran (1979) invigorated the rise of Palestinian-Arab nationalist identification in the Arab community in Israel and stimulated also the emergence (in the 1990s) of the first significant movement of political Islamism in this community (on Arab electoral politics in Israel see Reches 2006).

As a result of all this, and together with the continuous and deepening estrangement of the state towards the Arab citizens, a further "radicalization" of Arab nationalist politics in Israel took place.

This political radicalization was in turn facilitated by social processes that took place in the Arab sector in Israel that are related to the globalization of Israeli society at large (see Ram 2007). This relates in particular to the emergence of a highly educated middle class, that includes intellectuals, academics, lawyers and other professionals. This stratum has spawned a widening network of Arab civil society in Israel, which is relatively independent of the Israeli state. It is largely organized in the form of NGOs (non-governmental organizations) that captured the former centrality of political parties in the representation of issues. The global reach of NGOs furnishes Arab actors inside Israel with financial means and, even more importantly, with an international political umbrella that Israel cannot easily dismiss (except at the price of losing face in western liberal circles; something it certainly is trying to avoid (see Hanafi and Tabar 2005)).

Thus we find that the itinerary of Arab politics inside Israel in the six decades since the establishment of the state includes the following three main steps: first, an initial parochial clientalistic dependency on the state; second, the formulation of national identity within the communist orbit under the auspices of Moscow; and finally, third, the emergence in the recent two decades of an outright radical secular nationalism (marked by the establishment of Azmi Bishara's Balad party in 1995) and, to a lesser extent, Muslim nationalism.

The Visionary Documents discussed here are a recent outcome of the political itinerary described above. They represent Arab nationalism in the time of globalization, when politics evinces a bifurcation between civic universalism and communal particularism, with an effort towards new synthesis of the ends under the banner of multiculturalism. The documents bring to fruition the development of the radical nationalism of the secular branch of the Palestinians in Israel within the context of a universal discourse of multi-culturalism and indigenous rights. It is the fruit of the highly educated stratum of the Arab population in Israel, a stratum which is the vanguard of what is called "the stand-tall generation" of Arabs in Israel. From today's standpoint, this generation is both more explicitly Palestinian and more implicitly Israeli – like the rest of Israel – blending cultural-nationalism with civic-libertarianism (Rabinowitz and Abu-Baker 2002).

The visionary documents and the post-Zionist and neo-Zionist turn in Israel

The surfacing of a new Palestinian national discourse in Israel, as expressed in the VD, manifests changes not only in the identity and politics of this sector itself but also in that of the surrounding Jewish-Israeli society. In this respect, one can find some affinity between the bifurcation of Israeli identity and politics into post-Zionism and neo-Zionism in the larger sector, and the emergence of a likewise parallel bifurcation within the minor Palestinian sector, as expressed in the VD. What we see in both cases is a discourse which is simultaneously more "civic" and universal, on the one hand, and more, "communal" and particularistic (nationalist), on the other.

The constitutional challenge of the VD may be thought of, to some extent, as a "second wave of post-Zionism." Whereas the first wave of post-Zionism was associated with the constitutional revolution of the 1990s, the second wave is associated with an implicit demand for a "second constitutional revolution." The Arab contenders wish that such a second constitutional revolution will effect a radicalization of the first one, yet it may happen that because of a number of factors – among them the radicalization of the Arab cause inside Israel as manifested by the Visionary Documents themselves – the result will be just the opposite: a "constitutional restoration" that will recharge the "Jewishness" of the state. The nationalistic, let alone racist, profile of the government that was elected in 2009, as well as the recent demand, made by both Ehud Barak and Benyamin Netanyahu, that the Palestinians (and the Arab world at large) recognize the state of Israel as "the state of the Jewish people," indicate such a direction.

The "constitutional revolution" (CR) was a judicial trend heralded by Chief Justice Aharon Barak in 1992 expressed in the enactment by the Knesset of two Basic Laws: Basic Law: Freedom of Occupation, and Basic Law: Human Dignity and Liberty. These laws anchored in Israel the liberal principles of individual rights and of private property in an unprecedented manner, accompanying – and also enabling – a transition from a collectivist society and centralized state into a civil society based on the competitive market. These laws also strengthened the status of the judicial branch as against the two other branches of government by providing, or so Barak claimed, for judicial review of primary legislation. In this regard, the Supreme Court, at least in its make-up during the 1990s, had become the linchpin of liberal individual civil rights, and therefore became a target for Jewish ethno-nationalist and religious groups seeking the curtailment of judicial powers, arguing (perhaps rightly) that the court did not represent the will of the majority. Two recent ministers of justice, Daniel Friedman (in office 2007–2009) and Yaakov Neman (in office since 2009), are prone to curtailing the CR and the exceptional status gained by the Supreme Court. This is yet another indicator of the "restitutive" direction that Israel's judicial culture has turned into as of recently, or what Navot and Peled call "constitutional counter-revolution" (Navot and Peled 2009).

On a yet another level, the CR functioned to strengthen the position of the secular Ashkenazi elite, at a time when its political power had suffered a severe decline in the representative political organs (Hirschl 1997, 2009). Overall, the CR was thus a dimension of what we termed elsewhere the globalization of Israel, and what others termed the transition to a liberal regime of incorporation or citizenship (Ram 2007).

Nevertheless, as much as the CR was effective, even militantly, at the level of individual rights, it remained mute on the level of collective rights, be it those of organized laborers or of various communities. In a famous axiom, Israel was declared by the Supreme Court to be "a Jewish and democratic state." The Court exercises a delicate balance between the "Jewish" and the "democratic" dimensions of Israel, in a desperate effort to save the feasibility of this formula.

Yet the concept of the "Jewish and Democratic state" could not have come to pass without contestation. The broad liberal center cherishes the radical transition to capitalism and the relative moderation of nationalism. The nationalist and religious right wing considers this process to be "too democratic," whereas left-wing critics consider it to be "too Jewish."

By and large, then, the CR did not radically change the status of the Arab citizens of Israel and, furthermore, the Supreme Court – exactly because it portrayed itself as a champion of liberal rights – was deployed as a legitimizing rubber stamp for the regime of occupation in the Palestinian territories (Kretzmer 2002).

The Visionary Documents articulate, for the first time at such a level of generality, the Arab sector's critique of the de facto constitution of Israel and its de jure identity as "Jewish and democratic." The present Arab constitutional challenge was ushered in 15 years after the onset of the first CR, and, as mentioned above, it in fact constituted an explicit call for a radical change in the nature of the regime, or a "second CR."

The great achievement of first-wave post-Zionism was its radicalization of the first CR by its call for the extension of the liberal concept up to the level of state identity. This is the deep meaning and ultimate significance of the post-Zionist, counter-hegemonic concept of "a state of all its citizens," a concept countering the dominant concept of "the Jewish and democratic state" (Ram 2005). The visionary documents may be conceived as ushering in, at least conceptually, a second-wave post-Zionism, which further politicizes this concept and mobilizes citizens under its banner. One can say that the center of gravity of post-Zionism began to shift now from the intellectual "bubble" of Tel Aviv into the Arab towns and villages of the Galilee, from aloof university intellectuals to public activists, from the Jewish sector to the Arab sector, and from the cultural arena to the political arena. With all these shifts, it is to be expected that post-Zionism will also shift its appellation. It will probably be termed, from now on, the struggle for a "free state" or the campaign for constitutional reform. But most significantly, while the radical point of the first CR was the individualization and universalization of rights, the point of the present call for a second CR is the nationalization and particularization of rights, i.e., an emphasis on the collective rights of the contending nations inside the state.

The Arab constitutional challenge is indeed groundbreaking. It is the first time in the history of Israel that spokespeople for the Arab population – and actors whose legitimacy cannot be easily dismissed by the state – not only protest against discrimination in various aspects of the allocation of resources, or state oppression, but rather demand an abolition of the Jewish identity of Israel and the sharing of power with its dominant majority. In other words, it is the first time that the Arab sector does not speak the language of an under-privileged minority but rather the language of a homeland nation that contests the hegemony of the invading majority nation, and demands a change in the structure of the regime itself.

The challenge to the Jewish definition of the state is not a small matter, especially when it comes from Arab contenders. In the past, movements that tried to contest the Jewishness of the state were declared a security threat, outlawed and disbanded. The possibility that such a scenario will repeat itself once more cannot be excluded from consideration. It may happen, therefore, that the actual outcome of the constitutional challenge, at least in the short term, would be the opposite of what it meant to achieve; that is to say, that it will provoke a Jewish nationalist backlash and a sharp retrenchment of the ethnic Jewish dimension of the state, which will feel threatened from within in addition to the threats inflicted on it from abroad. One already hears the talk in Israel about a "defensive democracy," i.e., the need of a democracy to practice harsh measures, sometimes by transgressing democratic stipulations, in order to secure the very existence of the state. The experience of the Jewish treatment of the Arab population under its control, whether in the military rule in the first two decades of the state, or, since 1967, in the military rule over the occupied territories, does not leave much room for doubt about how far things may get.

This was very clearly indicated by the head of Israel's General Security Service (Shabak), who in a direct response to the publication of the "Visionary Documents," declared openly that his organization will pursue any group or movement that will demand a change in the Jewish nature of the state – even if such demands are made through legal and peaceful means. In the otherwise persistent efforts that Israel invests in avoiding self-incrimination in the arena of global public opinion, this was a remarkable move. Under the recent right-wing government that entered office in 2009 (with Benyamin Netanyahu as Prime Minister) there is a noticeable increase in the public expressions of explicit anti-Arab racism in Israel that reaches the highest echelons of the state.[6] With this, it can be argued nevertheless, that even if the backlash scenario does take place, it will be very consequential to the presently held pretence of the "Jewish and democratic state." A Jewish retrenchment scenario will openly pull the veil from the "Jewish and democratic" pretence – and will serve as a platform for a further and wider demand for a change, a demand that in such circumstances is expected to gain wider international support, even in states that are generally supportive of Israel.

Whatever happens next, one may already observe that the new constitutional discourse, which has been opened by the "Visionary Documents," is one more vector in the post-modern and post-national set of pressures that dissolve the dominant modern-national phase of the country. Whereas the first CR expressed the interests of the new bourgeoisie and the transition from etatism to capitalism, it may be observed that the demands for a second CR that emerge within the Arab sector express the transition from a cohesive nation-state into a competitive market society and (at least potentially) from hegemonic nationalism to multi-culturalism – trends that presently characterize Israeli society as a whole. Yet, as mentioned above, again and again, no linear development is expected here, and the "backlash" or "restorative" scenario is no less realistic (if not more so) than the vision of a successful second CR.

By and large, the transition to neo-liberalism has cracked the nationalist, collectivist and homogeneous dimensions of the Israeli regime and has thus created a new space for opportunities, in which both neo-Zionist and post-Zionist identities and ideologies could surface.

Post-Zionism exposed the inherent tension between the Jewish domination over the state and the latter's democratic pretensions. Whereas since the beginning of the current decade, post-Zionism was declared by observers to have exhausted itself with no tangible achievements, it turns out that in fact a second wave of post-Zionism is now unfolding, albeit with noticeable changes from the first wave, yet with an even more invigorated impetus.

During the 1990s, post-Zionism emerged in association with the individualist culture and the privatized economy that took hold in the country, which had undergone neo-liberal restructuring. The transition from national to global capitalism involved state contraction, economic marketization and the commoditization of culture. The Oslo "Peace Process" was part and parcel of this overall scheme. It was intended to pacify hostilities, to make the region safer for investors and to open hitherto closed markets to Israeli exporters. Another component of this shift was what was termed the CR of civil rights, which was discussed above.

First-wave post-Zionism was the accompanying left-wing intellectual and political culture of this wide shift. It was expressed audaciously in critical sociology, the new history and other branches of Israel studies, and was circulated in the wider public discourse through the media. Yet as the 1990s waned, as Jewish settlement in the occupied Palestinian territories continued unimpeded, and the "Peace Process" faltered, post-Zionism had subsided. The decline of PZ was aggravated since 2000 by the second Palestinian Intifada and since 2001 by the worldwide change in the political atmosphere in the wake of 9/11 (see Ram 2005).

But the inherent contradiction at the core of the Israeli polity exposed by post-Zionism – the incongruence between geography and demography, or the inconsistency of the "Jewish and democratic state" – did not disappear. On the contrary, the combined failure of "Oslo" and the continuous structural discrimination and systematic exclusion of the Palestinian citizens in Israel led to the surfacing of a second wave of post-Zionism, this time in the shape of a public demand by the Arab-Israeli citizens for a radical constitutional reform. The publication of the Arab Visionary Documents in 2007 ought to be understood, then, as a result of both the democratization of Israeli political culture, that raised expectations among Arabs, and of the dashing of such expectations, that brought about a neo-nationalist backlash. In the face of this particular juncture of the growing tensions in Israel between post-Zionism and neo-Zionism, Palestinian-Arab intellectuals have also embraced, in the Visionary Documents, the languages of new universalism and of old particularism.

The visionary documents and the controversy over democracy in Israel

We have discussed so far the political-cultural sources of the visionary documents, both in the Palestinian-Arab sector and in the Jewish-Israeli sector in Israel. Another resource on which the Documents draw is a controversy that has taken place in the last two decades among Israeli social scientists over the nature of Israeli democracy in general and the status of the Palestinian citizens within it in particular. One may discern three main approaches to the question of democracy that have emerged in this controversy: *a liberal position, an ethno-centered position,*[7] and *a social position.* The liberal position emphasizes the formal structure of the regime; the ethno-centered position emphasizes the informal national composition of Israel; and the social position emphasizes the political economy and its socio-political effects. One can also discern two versions of each of these positions.

The *liberal position* on Israeli democracy includes the following two versions. First is the official and the commonly accepted version of the liberal position, which considers Israel is a "Jewish and democratic state." In this view,

Israel resembles almost any other standard democratic Western state, in which there are equal universal citizenship rights (such as one person one vote, etc.) and wherein there are majority and minority population groups (among famous subscribers to this position are retired Chief Justice Aharon Barak and law professor Amnon Rubinstein; Yakobson and Rubinstein 2003).

The second liberal position offers a moderate critique of the first. In this view, Israel is indeed a liberal democracy, but a blemished liberal democracy, because in practice it does discriminate against its Arab citizens. This is conceived of as a matter of policy, not of structure, and therefore as a contingent matter and not as an essential feature of the regime as such. The conclusion is that an improved policy can improve the status of the Arab minority and the allocation of resources to it (among the advocates of this view are political scientists such as Benjamin Neuberger).

Noticeably, the liberal position acknowledges and accedes explicitly to the "Jewishness" of the state, yet this characteristic is taken to be based on a basic democratic principle – the will of the majority. It is acknowledged that the minority suffers an inferiority, but this is conceived of as a normal state of affairs in democratic states, where there is always a bias in favor of the majority group. And yet, even so, the situation of the minority can be improved and such improvement does not require a regime change but only a change of policies.

The *ethno-centered position* on democracy in Israel, on the other hand, regards the presence of the two national groups in the state as fundamental to its structure. The approach fully acknowledges the consequences of the struggle between these groups, though with two divergent conclusions drawn from this. These are the two ethno-centered positions.

The first ethno-centered position is known as the "ethnic democracy" model (espoused by Sammy Smooha; Smooha 2002). According to this model, Israel is an exemplary case of a new type of democracy – an "ethnic democracy" – in which one ethnic group owns a kind of a "gold share" in the state, which deposits in its hands some core areas of decision making (security, immigration, etc.). Members of other groups enjoy almost full individual citizenship rights, but not the same measure of collective rights as the dominant group. It is frankly admitted that such a democracy is of a "low quality," but yet it is maintained that it is a legitimate and common model, and that, most importantly, this model is an imperative for the continued existence and security of the Jewish people in Israel. Critics of this model contend that while it is more realistic then the liberal model, it falters in its normative acquiescence with the fundamental inter-group inequality of ethnic-democracies.

If the ethnic-democracy model can be said to be realistic and conservative, then the realistic and radical ethno-centered response to it is delivered in the form of the "ethnocracy model" (espoused by Oren Yiftachel; Yiftachel 2006). Not incidentally, the term "democracy" does not appear in the label of this model. According to it, Israel is a state under the domination of only one "ethnos," the Jewish ethnos, and the principal rationale of the regime is the "Judaization" of all material and symbolic resources of the country. According to this model, Israel does not simply "fail" to fairly address the concerns of its Arab citizens (as in the "soft" liberal version), but rather, the inferior status of the Arabs is the expected consequence of the basic logic of the state. Israel therefore is not democratic but rather ethnocratic, and its democratization must mean the expiration of the superiority and special status of the Jewish nation in the state. The Arab Visionary Documents fully acquiesce with the ethnocratic model of Israel.

While these models are somewhat essentialistic and static, the last approach – the *social position* – is historical and dynamic.

The first version of the social analysis of Israeli democracy is the "triadic citizenship model" offered by political scientists Gershon Shafir and Yoav Peled (Shafir and Peled 2002). According to this model there is in Israel a compound social regime of incorporation that includes three distinct discourses of citizenship: a republican Zionist discourse, an ethnic Jewish discourse and a civic liberal discourse. The relative weight of each component depends on changing circumstances and power relations among the groups in society. The relative democratization that has taken place in Israel since the 1990s is related to its rapid transition to capitalism since 1985. The effect of the latter process is the faltering of the "republican" Zionist discourse and thus the surfacing, in a more contentious manner, of the two adverse discourses; the ethnic and the liberal. The liberal discourse reinforces the universalist civic component in Israeli citizenship, and hence, the space of opportunity for Arab citizens to demand a change in their status; the ethnic discourse revitalizes the particularistic-Jewish component of it, and hence, the ethno-national nature of the Arab demands.

The second version of the social model is the "bifurcation model" offered by the present author (Ram 2005, 2007). This version focuses upon the recent transformation of Israel into a neo-liberal society under the impact of capitalist globalization. According to this model, in the last two decades, Israel has moved from its modernization dynamics, which was produced by a homogeneous and centralized national elite, into a dynamic of globalization, in which it is being bifurcated between the two contrasting poles of post-nationalism and neo-nationalism while oscillating between them. This has potential implications for the relations between the state and society, different state agencies and distinct groups. Thus, in the wake of the exhaustion of nation-building and the modernization stage – underpinned by the collectivist orientation of the Labor movement – Israel has passed into a market-building and globalization stage underpinned by neo-liberal economic orientation, which is accompanied by a multi-cultural inter-group orientation. In this new post-Fordist reality, Israel is bifurcating between a capitalist, liberal and de-colonization vector, on the one hand, and a nationalist, communalist and pro-colonization vector on the other hand.

Both versions of the social model mentioned above maintain that Israel's globalizing elites and wide middle classes have developed in the last two decades an interest in civil and market society, and have relegated nationalism to secondary preference. This may result in a relative relief of the ethnocentric nature of the state. On the other hand, it is exactly against this de-ethnicization (or de-Judaization) and the accompanying retreat of the welfare state that the lower classes are being politically mobilized, whereas Jewish identity – religious and ethnic – is deployed as their call to arms (see Peled 1998; Levy 2006; Filc 2007). Thus, we witness in Israel a growing tension between liberalization, on the one hand and ethnization, on the other (figuratively "McWorld" versus "Jihad"; Ram 2007).

The Arab constitutional challenge emerges in the intersection between liberalization, which encourages the surfacing of demands for a variety of universal rights; and ethnicization, which encourages the call for reinvigoration of particular communal identities. The Arab Visionary Documents may be thought of as partaking in this fundamental ideological schism from the location of the Arab minority within the larger society. That is, these are documents that speak a universal language of rights in order to foster particularistic communal identity. Let me now conclude this account and offer a critical comment upon the Documents.

Concluding comments: beyond uni-nationalism and bi-nationalism

The new wave of Arab struggle for a constitutional reform in Israel is of supreme importance on three grounds.

First, it gives new and vigorous voice to the Palestinian citizens of Israel and upholds the promise of the "stand-tall generation" to stand firmly upon its rights.

Second, the Documents aim to pass the discourse between the majority and the minority groups in Israel into a new phase, where the issue is not that of "distribution," but that of "recognition," and thus of a change in the nature of Israel and of power-sharing among the two groups.

And third, this new wave of demands will compel a "reality check" upon the state of Israel and the Jewish sector at large. Exposed to the new challenge, Israel will be forced to dispose of the untenable stance of being both Jewish and democratic, and to make an open and clear choice – either Jewish or democratic. Israeli public opinion is thus expected to bifurcate between those who will prioritize a "Jewish state" (Zionists and neo-Zionists)[8] and those who will prioritize a democratic state (post-Zionists).

Yet, despite their great significance, the Visionary Documents fail to signify a transcendence of the ethno-national principles that define the state of Israel, which they overtly defy, but rather, they signify an implicit entrenchment of these very principles. Even while they call for a transition from a uni-national to a bi-national state, they ossify communal identities rather then encouraging their gradual dissolution within a democratic state of its citizens.[9]

Thus, the gravest problem with the Visionary Documents is that they themselves are anchored fundamentally in an ethno-nationalist perspective, despite allusions to universalism and multi-culturalism. Their underlying logic is that of ethno-national restitution, not of democratic resolution. Ironically, the flaw of these documents is that they present to the state of Israel a mirror-image of its own ethno-nationalist principles, rather then aiming to transcend these principles.

And so, as the state is ethno-nationalist, so do the documents define the Palestinian Arabs on similar grounds; as the state does not recognize their national rights, so the documents do not recognize the right of Israel to exist (they do it performatively of course, as they recognize the fact of the existence of Israel but do not evince any consent to this);[10] as the state does not wish to integrate the Arab citizens in the tissue of its civic life, so do the documents speak the language of separatism and aim to create separate and autonomous communities with some kind of parity in separation. They demand their fair share, but do not express an interest in the whole. And finally, as the state regards itself as uni-national, so do the documents offer their own uni-national perspective, only "doubled," so to speak, through a bi-national guise. The political entity that the Arab Visionary Documents envisage does not accommodate a public of seven million citizens, but rather two belligerent communities.

This is a thorough failure that results from 60 years of expropriation and exclusion. The Visionary Documents are an expression of the Palestinian rage with the past and the present, but they do not hold a genuine hope for a better future. If the state does not become inclusive and universalist, honoring its own citizenry and citizens, it will find itself more and more sliding in the direction of a clash between its national communities. The present Visionary Documents represent this inimical scenario. They are one representation of the democratic dead-end but not a recipe for its successful resolution. The documents fail to engage in the vision of a non-national state, or a post-national state, or a democratic state of its citizens (see Koffman 1999). That this civic option is not so fashionable in these days of multi-culturalism does not make it less recommendable. The inhabitants of the region had suffered all too long and all too much from the consequences of ethno-national "visions." It's time they discover the vision of universal democratic citizenship.

Notes

1 Two other important documents in this "series" are a judicial position document that was produced by the Moussawa Center (NGO) in conjunction with a United Nations agency and an initiative by the Ibn Khaldun Center to create a separate elective representative body for the Palestinian citizens of Israel. See National Committee for the Heads of the Arab Local Authorities 2007; and Mada-al-Carmel, 2007. A different version of the article was published in *Constellations* 16(3) 2009.

2 Adalah, The Legal Center for Arab Minority Right in Israel, February 2007, page 5.

3 The veto power will be deposed in a special parliamentary committee, half of its members composed of Knesset Members from Arab parties; a special majority of the Knesset (two-thirds) will be able to overpower the committee. Alternatively any bill will have to be approved by 75 percent of Knesset members from Arab parties.

4 Incidentally, one cannot "predict" what would have happened had Rabin not been assassinated. After all, he did not remove, or even promise to remove even one Jewish settler from the occupied territories – a required condition for any peace settlement. In addition, at that time Rabin was trailing Netanyahu in the polls.

5 In Israeli parliamentary politics, controversial decisions, especially those concerned with national security, that are based on the support of the Arab parties are contested by the right wing as illegitimate.

6 Among these recent expressions (in 2009) is a procedure started by the minister of interior to repeal the citizenship of a number of Arab citizens and a proposed Knesset law to penalize with arrest anybody who will commemorate the Nakba on Israel's Independence Day, and more. A recent poll conducted by the Association for Civil Rights in Israel finds that 75 percent of the respondents will not live together with an Arab in the same building; 55 percent support the encouragement of Arab emigration outside Israel; 78 percent think that Arab parties should not be included in the government, and so forth (Meirav 2007); see also Navot and Peled 2009.

7 In the context of the current issue the term "ethno" refers to ethnos in the sense of defining a national category; so the relevant ethnos are Jews and Palestinian-Arabs. In a different context the term "ethnicity" is used in Israel to denote an inter-Jewish division between Ashkenazim (Westerners) and Mizrahim (Orientals); in this latter case the Hebrew word is "eda" (and in plural "edot"), to which the closest translation is community.

8 The difference is that Zionists uphold the "Jewish and democratic" stance, while neo-Zionists uphold upright the "Jewish" dimension of the state without regard for the democratic dimension (see Ram, "Post-Zionist Studies of Israel").

9 Obviously there are different assessments of the Visionary Documents. For a critique see Smooha 2009; for an advocacy see Jamal 2009.

10 A recent poll conducted by Prof. Sammy Smooha from Haifa University finds that in 2009 only 53.7 percent of Arab citizens of Israel recognize the right of Israel to exist as an independent state, compared to 81.1 percent who recognized that in 2003 (Fadi 2009).

Bibliography

Adalah, The Legal Center for Arab Minority Rights in Israel. 2007. *The Democratic Constitution.* February 2007. www.adalah.org/eng/democratic_constitution-e.pdf.

Al-Haj, Majid. 2004. "The Status of the Palestinians in Israel: a Double Periphery in an Ethno-National State" in A. Dowty, ed. *Critical Issues in Israeli Society*, Westport, CT: Praeger, pp. 109–126.

Fadi, Eyadat. 2009. "Poll: 40% of Israeli Arabs believe Holocaust never happened," *Haaretz*, May 17, 2009. www.haaretz.co.il/hasen/spages/1086115.html.

Filc, Dani. 2007. *Populism and Hegemony in Israel.* Tel Aviv: Resling (Hebrew).

Ghanem, Asad. 2001. *The Palestinian Arab Minority in Israel: A Political Study.* New York: SUNY Press.

Hanafi, Sari and Linda Tabar. 2005. *The Emergence of a Palestinian Globalized Elite: Donors, International Organizations and Local NGO's.* Jerusalem: Institute of Jerusalem Studies; Muwatin – The Palestinian Institute for the Study of Democracy.

Hirschl, Ran. 1997. "The 'Constitutional Revolution' and the Emergence of a New Economic Order in Israel." *Israel Studies* 2 (1): 136–155.

Hischl, Ran. 2009. "The Socio-Political Origins of Israel's Juristocracy." *Constellations* (guest editor U. Ram) 16 (3): 476–492.

Jamal, Amal. 2009. "The Contradictions of State-Minority Relations in Israel: The Search for Clarifications." *Constellations* (guest editor U. Ram) 16 (3): 493–508.

Koffman, Ilana. 1999. "The Option of an Israeli State" in Sara Ozacky-Lazar, Ghanem, Asad and Ilan Pappe (eds.). 1999. *Seven Roads: Theoretical Options for the Future of the Arabs in Israel.* Givaat Haviva: The Institute for Peace Research, pp. 201–243.

Kretzmer, David. 2002. *The Occupation of Justice: The Supreme Court of Israel and the Occupied Territories.* New York: SUNY Press.

Levy, Yagil. 2006. "The War of the Peripheries: A Social Mapping of IDF Casualties in the Al-Aqsa Intifada." *Social Identities*, 12 (3): 309–324.

Mada-al-Carmel. 2007. *The Haifa Declaration*, May 15. Haifa.www.mada-research.org/archive/haifaenglish.pdf.

Meirav, David. 2007."Racism in Israel". *NRG-Ma'ariv*, December 8. www.nrg.co.il/online/1/ART1/668/722.html.

National Committee for the Heads of the Arab Local Authorities in Israel. 2007. *The Future Vision of the Palestinian Arabs in Israel*. www.mossawacenter.org/files/files/File/Reports/2006/Future%20Vision%20(English).pdf.

Navot, Doron and Yoav Peled. 2009. "Towards a Constitutional Counter-Revolution in Israel?" *Constellations* (guest editor U. Ram) 16 (3): 429–444.

Or Commission Report, 2003. "The Official Summation of the Or Commission Report," *Haaretz*. September 2nd. www.haaretz.com/hasen/pages/ShArt.jhtml?itemNo=335594.

Peled, Yoav. 1998. "Towards a Redefinition of Jewish Nationalism in Israel? The Enigma of Shas." *Ethnic and Racial Studies*, 21 (4): 703–727.

Rabinowitz, Dan and Khawla Abu-Baker. 2002. *The Stand-Tall Generation*. Jerusalem: Keter (Hebrew).

Ram, Uri. 2005. "Post-Zionist Studies of Israel – The First Decade." *Israel Studies Forum*, 20 (2): 22–45.

Ram, Uri. 2007. *The Globalization of Israel: McWorld in Tel Aviv, Jihad in Jerusalem* New York: Routledge.

Reches, Eli (ed.) 1998. *Arabs in Israeli Politics: A Dilemma of Identity*. Tel Aviv: Tel Aviv University, Moshe Dayan Center (Hebrew).

Reches, Eli. 2006. "The Arab Minority in Israel and the Seventeenth Knesset Elections: The Beginning of a New Era?" in A. Arian and M. Shamir (eds.) *The Elections in Israel 2003*, New Brunswick, NJ: Transactions Books, pp. 156–185.

Reiter, Yitzhak. 2009. *National Minority, Regional Majority: Palestinian Arabs Versus Jews in Israel*. New York: University of Syracuse Press.

Shafir, Gershon and Yoav Peled. 2002. *Being Israeli: The Dynamics of Multiple Citizenship*. Cambridge: Cambridge University Press.

Smooha, Sammi. 1989. *Arabs and Jews in Israel. Vol. 1: Conflicting and Shared Attitudes in a Divided Society*. Boulder, CO and London: Westview Press.

Smooha, Sammi. 1992. *Arabs and Jews in Israel. Vol. 2: Change and Continuity in Mutual Intolerance*. Boulder. CO and London: Westview Press.

Smooha, Sammy. 2002. "The Model of Ethnic Democracy: Israel as a Jewish and Democratic State." *Nations and Nationalism*, 8 (4): 475–504.

Smooha, Sammy. 2009. "The Israeli Palestinian-Arab Vision of Transforming Israel into a Binational Democracy." *Constellations* (guest editor U. Ram) 16 (3): 509–522.

Yakobson, Alexander and Amnon Rubinstein. 2003. *Israel and the Family of Nations: Jewish Nation-State and Human Rights*. Tel Aviv: Schocken.

Yiftachel, Oren. 2006. *Ethnocracy – Land and Identity Politics in Israel/Palestine*. Philadelphia: University of Pennsylvania Press.

Part IV

Social and economic citizenship in wartime

11 Democracy's disappearing duties

The Washington Consensus and the limits of citizen participation

Timothy A. Canova

Conceptions of citizenship that focus on duties as well as rights are grounded in classical civic republicanism and seventeenth-century theories of social contract (Plato 2007: 51e-52d; Hobbes 1996; Locke 1988; Rousseau 1968). These ideas find modern form in communitarian social and political thought (Barber 2003: 298–303; Etzioni 1998; Macedo 2005; Putnam 2000; Sandel 1996: 319–324; Walzer 1983: 68).

According to these "reciprocal" views of citizenship, government is instituted with the consent of the governed to secure for citizens their fundamental rights of life, liberty, and property. In return, citizens accept certain duties and give up certain freedoms they would otherwise have enjoyed in a state of nature. Civic obligations are seen as an evolutionary imperative, designed to place curbs and prohibitions on man's most destructive instincts of aggression and egoistic self-satisfaction (Freud: 1961). Duties must be reciprocal to rights to ensure the state has the capacity to defend the most fundamental freedoms and protect each from all.

Although the needs of the state and the vulnerability of the individual are always present, they become more acute during wartime when civic obligation becomes a matter of practical necessity. Military and civilian service, payment of taxes, and limits on personal consumption and wealth have all been considered as duties inherent in citizenship in a democracy at war. Perhaps this reciprocal view of citizenship was best articulated by President Theodore Roosevelt when he said, "Unless democracy is based on the principle of service by everybody who claims the enjoyment of any right, it is not true democracy at all" (Roosevelt, T. 1956: 62–64).

In contrast, dominant today is a politics of asymmetrical citizenship that enables an agenda of privatized authority, deregulated markets, and liberalized capital flows – the so-called Washington Consensus. This asymmetrical approach has privileged rights over duties, and thereby distorted the American way of waging war while undermining the foundations of soft power and conditions of socio-economic stability so important to maintaining peace.

The so-called Greatest Generation that came of age in World War II and the early Cold War practiced the politics of reciprocal citizenship (Brokaw 1998). Civic obligations were widespread, meaningful, and essential to victory in the war and to eventual success in the Cold War. With so many Americans serving in harm's way, imposing civic duties on the home front seemed only fair and just. Moreover, the duties of citizens were mutually reinforcing. Military and civilian service made it easier to impose limits on bankers and wealth-holders. Meanwhile, the restraints and obligations imposed on private finance helped the Treasury to fund the massive war effort.

In more recent years, American citizenship has come to mean mostly rights and not many actual duties (Brinkley 1995: 10). There are likely many factors, material and cultural, that have contributed to such an "asymmetrical" view of citizenship. Nationality is often equated with intolerance while liberal theory celebrates the rise of a global or cosmopolitan citizenship (Schuck 2007; Appiah 2007). Yet we still live in a world in which citizenship is bounded by territory and divided into nation-states that are relatively strong or weak in relation to the loyalty, support, and sacrifice of citizens.

As the United States emerged as the world's premier military and economic superpower, the civic obligations of Americans were reduced. Military service and other sacrifices were no longer seen as necessary to maintain the nation's security. To the contrary, the right of the citizen to spend and consume freely came to be seen as more than a right, but rather as an actual duty – the citizen's contribution to the common defense by maintaining consumer demand and economic growth.

Greatest generation citizenship: shared sacrifice and wartime mobilization

When war broke out in Europe in September 1939, the U.S. had fewer than 190,000 men in its armed forces, its lowest level since the end of the Civil War (Jarecki 2008: 53). There were still only 270,000 Americans in uniform when France fell to Hitler in the spring of 1940 (O'Neill 2002: 254; Canova 2006). Within weeks, President Franklin Roosevelt articulated the case for universal service:

> Today, all private plans, all private lives, have been in a sense repealed by an overriding public danger. In the face of that public danger all those who can be of service to the Republic have no choice but to offer themselves for service in those capacities for which they may be fitted.
>
> (Roosevelt, F.D. 1940)

This was the reciprocal view of citizenship. When public danger threatens the freedom and security of all, it becomes the duty of all to serve and defend those endangered rights and freedoms. It was a view based on notions of justice, an implicit compact between citizens, that all shared in the benefits of living in a civilized democracy and all should therefore share in the burdens of maintaining that civilization.

Two decades earlier, in *Arver* v. *United States*, the Supreme Court had upheld wartime conscription with a reciprocal view of citizenship: "It may not be doubted that the very conception of a just government and its duty to the citizens includes the reciprocal obligation of the citizen to render military service in case of need, and the right to compel it" (Arver 1918: 378). The *Arver* Court traced the civic obligation of military service back to England prior to the Norman Conquest, Colonial America, and the states during the Revolutionary War. The Court quoted from the Pennsylvania Constitution of 1776:

> That every member of society hath a right to be protected in the enjoyment of life, liberty, and property, and therefore is bound to contribute his proportion toward the expense of that protection, and yield his personal service when necessary, or an equivalent thereto.
>
> (*Arver* 1918: 380)

The power to conscript was considered by *Arver* as essential to the power of Congress to declare war and raise and support armies under the Constitution. In 1940 the U.S. was not in a declared state of war, but there was a strong consensus that the moment constituted a national emergency. Roosevelt and others justified the peacetime draft as within the constitutional powers of the federal government and as necessary to deter foreign aggression and thereby keep the country out of any foreign wars in the future (Miller 1983: 457). Congress responded with the Selective Training and Service Act of 1940, the nation's first peacetime draft.

Some ten million American men would be drafted and another six million voluntarily enlisted during World War Two. Local draft boards preferred to call up single men younger than age 40, and unlike much of the Vietnam War, there were no student deferments (Selective Service System 2002a). Thirty percent of all draftees – more than five million men – were classified as 4-F and rejected for a wide range of physical and mental conditions (Canova 2006). As William O'Neill concluded, "Selective Service was generally regarded as fair, in part because conscription was not as rigorously applied in the United States as in most other belligerent nations" (O'Neill 2002: 162, 254, 323).

The Selective Service system recognized conscientious objectors – those who objected to combatant and sometimes even noncombatant training and service on moral or religious grounds (Selective Service System 2002b, 2002c). About 25,000 conscientious objectors served in the U.S. military in noncombatant roles during the war, including many unarmed medics who served in combat. Another 20,000 objectors served on the home front, building conservation projects in rural areas and taking care of the mentally ill in hospitals. Some of these objectors served by fighting forest fires, including the smoke jumpers in Oregon who parachuted down to fight fires started by thousands of timed incendiary balloons released in Japan. As one public television documentary concluded, "Thus ironically, the only direct attacks on the continental United States during World War Two were repulsed, in part, by conscientious objectors" (Smith 2003).

About 16,000 men refused to register for the draft, were convicted of draft resistance, and sentenced to a maximum of five years (Canova 2006). This was a remarkably low number of draft resisters given the total size of the U.S. draft population and the number of American men actually drafted, and was perhaps an indication of the ethic of shared sacrifice and reciprocal notions of citizenship.

The military draft was the centerpiece of the war effort, and conscription undermined arguments against all other civic obligations. The wealthy were taxed, business freedoms were constrained, consumer goods were rationed, prices were controlled, and credit was channeled away from luxury investments (Vatter 1985). Every social class from rich to poor was brought into the war effort and every citizen was expected to bear some portion of the war's burdens.

Conscription also necessitated a paradigm shift in economic policy. Federal spending was required to mobilize and equip the citizen army. In the first six months of the war, the federal government placed over $100 billion in war contracts, thereby ordering more goods than the economy had ever produced in a single year (Miller 1983: 486). The portion of the economy committed to war production more than doubled in 1942 from 15 to 33 percent (Friedman and Schwartz 1963: 556). Total wartime spending was more than $320 billion, twice as large as all previous federal spending combined (Blum et al.1977: 683).

The dramatic increase in federal spending translated directly into an enormous economic boom (Turgeon 1980: 47). The nation's gross national product (GNP), the sum of all goods and services produced in a single year, grew from $99.7 billion in 1940 to $211.9 billion in 1945. The mobilization of resources – human, industrial, technological, and financial – exceeded the efforts of all other belligerents combined. By any measure, World War II was the most impressive economic expansion in American history, with real (inflation-adjusted) economic growth rates exceeding 15 percent a year during the war's three peak years and averaging double digits throughout the war (CEA 1984: 220, 223).

Public finance and the sharing of burdens

The ethic of shared sacrifice was crucial to financing the U.S. effort in World War II. High-income households were expected to pay near-confiscatory tax rates on marginal incomes above a certain level; wealth-holders were to earn negative real returns on their holdings of government debt securities; and those earning high returns on active investments were often subject to a windfall profits tax. The tax structure was broadened and deepened. But although the marginal income tax rate was raised to 94 percent for the top tax bracket, tax revenues covered only about 41 percent of the total war effort (O'Neill 2002: 112–113). The rest came from government borrowing.

In 1944 alone, the federal deficit was $50 billion, twice the size of the 1941 federal debt (representing the sum of all previous federal deficits combined). To provide some historical comparison, today the federal deficit is about 13 percent of U.S. gross domestic product. In World War II, the deficit was more than twice as large as today, at more than 30 percent of GDP. Likewise, after a year of enormous financial bailouts the total federal debt in 2009 is about 90 percent of GDP. By the end of World War II, the national debt was more than 120 percent of GDP (CEA 2005: 304; Canova 1995: 1301 n.17).

According to today's economic orthodoxy, rising federal deficits should result in rising interest rates (BOG 1994: 25, 30). Yet, from 1941 to 1951, interest rates on U.S. government borrowing were "pegged" at low levels: during the war years at 0.375 percent for short-term 90-day Treasury bills and usually at about 2.5 percent for long-term (ten-year) Treasury bonds (Chandler 1969: 482–493; Friedman and Schwartz 1963: 562–563, 578–579). These interest rate pegs were maintained by the Federal Reserve which was required to purchase government securities in any amounts and at any price needed to keep the yields at the pegged levels.

As a practical matter, the Treasury Department and White House directed the central bank's conduct of monetary policy for more than a decade, an arrangement completely contrary to today's orthodoxy of central bank autonomy. Throughout this "pegged period," the Federal Reserve's subservient position was enforced not by statute, but by political convention and necessity (Canova 2006).

The financial burdens of these pegged interest rates fell on wealth-holders who saw the inflation-adjusted yields on their holdings of government securities fall to negative territory for a dozen years. Finance capital had to bend to the needs of industrial capital; old wealth had to accommodate the needs of the present. Without such financial burden sharing, and with sharply rising public debt levels, the U.S. wartime effort could well have buckled under the weight of high interest rates. Servicing the national debt would have cost the Treasury many billions of dollars siphoned from the war effort, and private industry may have found itself increasingly crowded out of capital and lending markets. The Federal Reserve's support of the interest rate pegs allowed the Treasury to borrow and spend without significant limitation for an entire decade, and without crippling private markets in the process.

There was ample precedent for such burden sharing in wartime finance. When Lincoln faced difficulties financing the North's mobilization for the Civil War, Congress passed legislation creating the greenback, a direct issuance of $450 million in currency by the Treasury Department (Canova 2009b; Hixson 1993: 131; Ritter 1997: 29–30).

Neither Germany nor Japan was able to reduce interest rates on government wartime borrowing to the low U.S. levels. Both fascist regimes had to contend with private financial interests that were unrestrained by the countervailing demands of public opinion (Homer 1963: 469, 476–477, 535; Schaller 1985: 5). This was a variant of asymmetrical citizenship: private corporate and financial interests enjoyed privileged access to power, without reciprocal obligations to fully support the wartime financial needs of the state, while harsh duties and fewer rights were afforded ordinary citizens in Germany and Japan.

The 1941–1951 suspension of the Federal Reserve's independence was made possible because of the politics of shared sacrifice and the practical demands of mobilization (Janeway 1951: 13). The Federal Reserve's own 1947 description of its wartime role is telling: "In time of war the *duty* of the Federal Reserve, as of everyone, is to support the country's war effort" (BOG 1947: 105) (emphasis added). Accordingly, the amount of government wartime spending was properly determined by Congress, and according to the Fed itself, it was the Treasury Department's responsibility to determine the character of the government's borrowing obligations, including the distribution of long-term versus short-term borrowing and the rate of interest Treasury would pay to investors. It was only after those policy decisions had been made by the politically accountable branches of government that it would become "the duty of the Federal Reserve to see to it that the banking system is in a position to absorb any public debt essential for war expenses that is not purchased by investors other than banks."

This highly regulated system of public finance raised important policy challenges. The Federal Reserve recognized that the "[p]revention of inflation had to become secondary" to the demands of mobilization. It could not rely on the blunt instrument of raising interest rates for the entire economy and would have to rely instead "on selective rather than general methods of control" (BOG 1947: 107, 100). The Federal Reserve used selective credit controls to channel credit away from private consumption and speculation, particularly by imposing interest rate ceilings and high margin requirements (such as minimum down payment requirements) on private borrowing for housing, autos, consumer durable goods, and corporate securities (Meltzer 2003: 602–605; Smithies 1964: 94–105).

These margin requirements resulted in the rationing of credit away from private sub-prime borrowers while ensuring that public borrowing would remain prime by facilitating the Federal Reserve's efforts to set yields and prices on Treasury securities. This paradigm was the polar opposite of today's Federal Reserve which uses only one policy instrument – short-term interest rates – to slow the economy without any selective credit controls to prevent speculative bubbles from developing. As was made apparent since the financial panic of 2008, the result was a rise in sub-prime borrowing, higher and therefore riskier interest rates, and unsustainable bubbles in housing and securities markets (Canova 2009a).

During this pegged period, the administration had to find other methods to keep consumer prices stable. The federal government turned to price controls, high taxes and massive bond sales to dampen consumer purchasing power (Barber 1996: 142–151; Janeway 1951). In 1942, Congress created the Office of Price Administration (OPA) under the direction of a Price Administrator appointed by the President and empowered under the Emergency Price Control Act to set up a comprehensive scheme for the setting of maximum prices and rents. Perhaps no other regulatory program during the war exacted as much sacrifice from so many Americans.

The OPA's power was tempered by its accountability to public opinion. Rising consumer prices could be punished at election time. In fact, the consumer price inflation peaked at 9.2 percent in 1942, the Democrats suffered at the polls, and the 1942 congressional elections left Roosevelt with the most conservative Congress in decades (Blum *et al.* 1977: 698).

Democracy eventually provided its "spontaneous dramatics," Congress held hearings, there were purges of top OPA officials, but in the end Congress kept the OPA strong and funded (Janeway 1951: 13). In *Yakus* v. *United States*, the Supreme Court upheld the OPA's power to impose price controls: the Congressional delegation of regulatory authority to the OPA did not violate the non-delegation doctrine since Congress provided an intelligible principle to guide the regulators by mandating that prices set be "generally fair and equitable" (Yakus 1944: 414, 420, 424).

Yakus was a decision based on the logic of reciprocal citizenship with the burdens imposed by price controls generally reciprocal to the benefits that Americans on the home front were receiving thanks to the sacrifices of so many others on the war fronts of Europe and Asia. Moreover, while the delegation was broad and somewhat vague, the Court's ruling implicitly recognized that the voters would get the last word, that ineffective OPA appointees would have a way of killing off incumbents at the polls. In judging the relative fairness of price control as well as rationing programs, citizens themselves had the final say precisely because OPA was accountable to elected officials through the administration's appointment of top administrators and Congressional budgetary oversight.

The *Yakus* Court contrasted the OPA with the industry councils that had imposed civic burdens under the National Recovery Administration (NRA), the centerpiece of the first New Deal which was so concerned with stopping a deflationary spiral in 1933 by setting minimum prices and minimum wages. But those industry councils were in private hands, completely unaccountable to voters. For such reasons, in 1935 a unanimous Supreme Court in *Schechter Poultry* v. *United States* (the so-called "Sick Chicken case") struck down the NRA as an unconstitutional delegation of lawmaking power. In his concurrence, Justice Cardozo characterized the delegation to private trade councils as a case of "delegation running riot" (*Schechter* 1935).

Private industries never captured control of the OPA as they had dominated the NRA trade councils. The OPA administrators who set prices were public bureaucrats, subject to appointment and removal. In contrast, the NRA trade councils were composed of and dominated by big industry representatives (Bernstein 1987: 194–198). The fox was running the NRA henhouse.

While the OPA had broad authority, it also had to get the job done. Annual CPI rates were brought down to 6.3 percent in 1943 and 2.6 percent for each of the next two years. From October 1942 to September 1945 at the war's end, the CPI rose only 8.7 percent, less than 3 percent a year for three years. Historians have concluded, "For all its unpopularity, especially among businessmen, politicians, and farm leaders, the OPA was one of the war's brilliant successes" (Blum *et al.* 1977: 685).

With the beginning of the Cold War and the strategy of containment, U.S. military spending rose three-fold, but private consumption was rising as well. Unlike in World War II, the sacrifices abroad were not matched by reciprocal burden sharing by Americans at home. This time the Federal Reserve would offer stiff resistance to the Treasury's wartime financing program.

President Truman and Congress fought over the OPA's authority, which was weakened, vetoed, lapsed, and then renewed. Not surprisingly, inflation returned to over 10 percent in 1946 and the Democrats took a beating in the 1946 Congressional elections, with the Republicans carrying both houses of Congress for the first time since 1928. Between the outbreak of the Korean War in June 1950 and the imposition of price and wage controls in January 1951, the cost of living rose at an annual rate of nearly 12 percent (Blum *et al.* 1977: 722, 730).

When price controls were finally imposed, they were not as effective as during World War II. In 1951, with inflation at 7.8 percent, and with the help of some key allies in Congress, the Federal Reserve prevailed in its campaign for independence. The result was the Treasury–Federal Reserve Accord of March 1951 which became known as the Fed's Magna Carta for freeing it from Treasury control (Friedman and Schwartz 1963). The pegged system of finance soon came to an end; monetary policy was re-activated and once again became the primary tool against inflation. Fiscal policy was necessarily pinched and the U.S. promptly went into a recession, its first of three recessions that would plague the eight years of Eisenhower's presidency (Turgeon 1996: 55, 72, 84; Vatter 1963).

For more than a decade, the pegged system of public finance accomplished great objectives. Based as it was on the financial sacrifice of wealth-holders, it had helped to finance the service and sacrifices of so many others: mass conscription for military and civilian service, the most massive military buildup and spending program in recorded history, nearly four years of total war, and great programs of post-war reconstruction at home and abroad. Although there are few periods in history as compelling, the decade of the pegged period has been all but airbrushed from the leading texts in economics and finance and the Federal Reserve's own official histories (BOG 1947: 105–110; Frank and Bernanke 2007: 280–286; Cecchetti 2005; CEA 1996: 280–284; Samuelson and Nordhaus 2005: 191–211; Rosen 2002: 425–426). Economics texts that do discuss the peg were usually published during that period itself or are written by heterodox economists (Samuelson 1948: 351–352; Galbraith and Darity 1994: 240–242). It is also noteworthy that the pegged period has been left out of military histories even though military theorists have long recognized the first rule of war is to mobilize resources, beginning with the mobilization of the state's finances to support the mobilization of armed forces (Sun-Tzu 1993: 103, 107).

The shared benefits: democracy renewed

Shared sacrifice translated into significant shared benefits. The scale of the mobilization was decisive in turning the tide of the war. Without the enormous buildup in Allied forces, the war would surely have gone on much longer. Behind the military armor pumped a fully mobilized economy, a vast infrastructure of industry, technology, and intelligence. The multi-billion dollar and highly secretive Manhattan Project brought together industry, science, and the academy to invent an atomic bomb before the Germans. Many thousands of citizens were trained for intelligence and support roles such as cryptographers and translators in many strategically important languages (Canova 2006: 8). From the Battle of Midway to D-Day, victory turned at critical moments on Allied capabilities in cracking enemy codes (Persico 2001; O'Neill 2002: 168–171). Had the U.S. delayed and the Germans mobilized earlier, the very outcome of the war itself could have been altered by German breakthroughs in missile and jet engine technologies (Shirer 1990; O'Neill 2002: 136–137, 225–226; Garlinski 1978: 112–137). Fortunately for the U.S., the Federal Reserve directed financial resources to the Treasury through its pegging policy while delaying private consumption through the use of selective credit controls.

The U.S. emerged from the war with enormous productive capacity and as the world's largest creditor and with huge trade surpluses, conditions which allowed it to play a much larger role on the global stage (Kennedy 1987: 327). By the end of the war, with the jobless rate at only 1.2 percent, full employment was a reality for perhaps the first and only time in American history, and the distribution of income became much more equitable as a result of the strong economy, low pegged yields on Treasury securities, and progressive taxation. In 1929, the wealthiest 5 percent of U.S. households had received 30 percent of income; by 1944, their share was down to 20.7 percent (Turgeon 1996: 5; Blum *et al.*1977: 685).

These conditions of full employment, high production, rising wages, and more equitable distributions of wealth and income would contribute to post-war prosperity. The wartime mobilization also carried over into the post-war occupations of Germany and Japan by providing boots on the ground for security followed by armies of civil administrators. In terms of scale and effectiveness, these occupations were much larger, more comprehensive, and far more successful than any occupations the U.S. has attempted since (Canova 2006: 9).

As the end of the war approached, Congress passed the Servicemen's Readjustment Act of 1944, the so-called G.I. Bill of Rights, to assist veterans with jobs, training, education, and health care. Mass conscription now translated into social policy on a grand scale. More than 16 million veterans received federally subsidized low-interest loans for home mortgages, and between 1945 and 1952 – the final years of the pegged period – veterans received $13.5 billion for education and training. The average length of service for U.S. soldiers during World War II was two years and eight months. In return, they received tuition-free university education, along with living stipends (O'Neill 2002: 142, 323). Rights and duties were indeed reciprocal, even though for many (particularly those killed or injured in action) the burdens either preceded or preempted the benefits.

Peter Drucker considered the G.I. Bill of Rights as perhaps the most important single event of the twentieth century, signaling an important shift to a technologically advanced knowledge society (Drucker 1993: 3). Without conscription, the G.I. Bill would have been merely a benefits plan for a relatively smaller segment of American society. Conscription spread those benefits to an enormous portion of the American population and thereby transformed the generation and society itself. The education boom provided the foundation for years of economic growth and scientific and technological advances, including the space program with all of its own technological spinoffs for the economy.

The pegged system of public finance meant sacrifice by wealth-holders, but the results were common benefits, public goods that benefitted all. Service in the armed forces, as well as the booming economy, became integrating forces for people of all races, ethnic groups, and genders. New immigrant groups mixed for the first time with English-speaking populations and soon entered a vastly expanded middle class. For more than half a million African-Americans, though largely relegated to second-class status, military service provided a big boost. By the war's end, African-Americans held 7.5 percent of all jobs in war industries, less than their share of the overall population, but a great improvement from their pre-war condition (O'Neill 2002: 3–4).

As O'Neill has pointed out, "For whites each year of military service was worth as much to their earning power as an additional year of education. But for blacks each year of service was worth up to three years of education." Although blacks and other minorities were often last in line for G.I. Bill benefits, and often unjustly excluded, many did receive the range of benefits.

Martin Luther King, Jr. would later recognize the utility and justice of tying service to benefits when he offered the G.I. Bill of Rights as a model for a program of economic and social development for Americans of all races (King 1986: 94–95, 157, 326, 367–368).

Foreign assistance: reciprocal benefits and burdens go global

In 1940, Britain was in dire need of American arms and supplies and fast running out of money, with less than $2 billion to pay for $5 billion of orders from U.S. factories. The U.S. Neutrality Act required belligerents to pay cash for arms, and loans were prohibited to nations like Britain that had not paid their debts from World War I (Miller 1983: 459–460). Roosevelt solved the problem with a "flash of genius": the U.S. would lend or lease the supplies and equipment to Britain in return for British overseas military bases that Britain could suddenly ill afford to defend. The president offered a "homey parable":

> Suppose my neighbor's home catches on fire, and I have a length of garden hose four or five hundred feet away. If he can take my garden hose and connect it up with his hydrant, I may help him put out the fire. Now what do I do? I don't say to him before that operation, 'Neighbor, my garden hose cost me fifteen dollars; you have to pay me fifteen dollars for it.' No! What is the transaction that goes on? I don't want fifteen dollars – I want my garden hose after the fire is over.

The Lend-Lease program was signed into law three months later. It eventually provided more than $50 billion worth of American supplies to Britain, the Soviet Union, France, China, and other Allied nations. This again was the citizenship of reciprocal rights and duties, although now the sacrifices and burdens were borne to help foreign allies related not by national citizenship but by membership in a community of nations and often by ties of ancestry, language, and culture.

The Lend-Lease program anticipated the Marshall Plan, the largest peacetime foreign aid program in American history under which the U.S. taxpayer gave away more than $13 billion in goods and services between 1947 and 1951 – the final years of the pegged period of public finance – to help rebuild war-torn countries, including its recent wartime enemies. This time the aid was not in the form of loans, but in grants. The Truman administration recognized America's role as a global citizen with obligations to help foster and sustain liberal democracies and institutions around the world, not just with military aid and coercive force, but through the use of "soft power" – a wide range of economic, political, and diplomatic policies to attract free alliances and ideological loyalty (Nye 2004). The wise management of soft power served to reduce the need for exercising direct military power while also ensuring more success when military power was actually employed.

The Marshall Plan made up about 13 percent of the total U.S. budget in 1948, the equivalent of more than $400 billion today, compared with present U.S. foreign aid budgets of about $20 billion a year. The impact was immediate. Economic growth increased by nearly 40 percent in recipient countries in only four years (Canova 2007: 382, 394). The benefits did not just flow to the recipient countries. Marshall Plan exports also provided significant stimulus to U.S. economic growth and labor markets.

Without the Marshall Plan, the course of the Cold War may have been far different and far more dangerous. Yet, there would likely have been no Marshall Plan if America's 16 million veterans and their families – about one-third of the U.S. population by 1950 – had not successfully readjusted to civilian life thanks to the benefits of the G.I. Bill (Bennett 1999: O'Neill 2002: 142). And there would not have been a G.I. Bill extending benefits so broadly without the pegged system of public finance that channeled credit away from private speculative purposes and into the Treasury for public expenditures on collective goods.

Democracy's disappearing duties

The Greatest Generation achieved enormous objectives by practicing the politics of reciprocal citizenship at home and abroad. During this period, according to Tony Judt, "[t]here was a great faith in the ability (and not just the duty) of government to solve large-scale problems by mobilizing and directing people and resources to collectively useful ends" (Judt 2005: 69). John Kennedy reflected this faith in collective efforts and civic obligations with his calls for shared sacrifice. In his inaugural address he called on Americans to "ask not what your country can do for you, but what you can do for your country." Earlier, while campaigning for the presidency, Kennedy articulated an inter-generational and reciprocal view of citizenship:

> I want to be sure we haven't lost something important in this country, that we haven't gone soft, that we don't have so many cars and iceboxes and television sets that we just look to our own private interests and not to the

welfare of the country. We who sit here today are the beneficiaries of millions of Americans who have fought and died and lived for this country to make it what it is.

(Kennedy 1988)

In his short presidency, Kennedy launched new programs for national civilian service, including the Volunteers in Service to America (VISTA) and the Peace Corps. He also recognized that the ability of the U.S. to engage in foreign assistance was enhanced by a favorable balance of trade and payments (Canova 2007: 409 n.337).

But the idea of reciprocal rights and duties was slowly undermined in the decades since and eventually replaced by an asymmetrical view of citizenship as consisting almost solely of rights with little appreciation of the need for civic duties. It is typical now at academic conferences on citizenship for paper after paper to deal only with rights of citizens in wartime, without even passing references to burden sharing and other civic obligations (Cole 2007: 2541–2548).

By the 1990s, the orthodox policy agenda, the so-called Washington Consensus, was based on this narrower conception of citizenship and represented the polar opposite of the economic and financial system that had prevailed during World War II and the early Cold War period. The agenda now consisted of privatizing central banks, deregulating financial institutions and markets, liberalizing currency and portfolio capital flows, and imposing austerity on public sectors at all levels. Instead of a Federal Reserve accountable to elected branches, and therefore ultimately to the voters, there would be an "autonomous" central bank largely directed by the forces of private finance. Instead of low interest rates for the Treasury and credit rationing away from socially frivolous purposes, there would be enormous growth in the size and influence of private financial actors and the creation of an unsustainable bubble economy.

One of the chief implications of an unfettered central bank was a constrained Treasury. Instead of national service – military or civilian – and a G.I. Bill of Rights to spread benefits broadly throughout society, the all-volunteer armed forces would be much smaller, in both absolute and relative terms, and would not bring the widespread social benefits that could maintain some sense of social justice and equity for American society. Instead of a productive export-oriented economy capable of providing massive foreign aid around the world, the economy would become distorted by endless consumption, the reliance on foreign capital for Treasury financing, and significant financial and political constraints on U.S. foreign aid capabilities. As recognized by economic historians, high levels of private consumption, a truncated public sector, and the transition from a manufacturing to a service economy – attributes of the so-called "American way of life" – "have had a deleterious effect upon the ability of the federal government to respond to contemporary economic decline" (Bernstein 1994: 377, 384).

The asymmetrical citizenship of the Washington Consensus

Barely a week after the September 11 terrorist attacks, public opinion polls showed that nearly 80 percent of Americans supported a national military draft (Jones 2001: 1). This was a higher level of support than at the time of the 1940 Conscription Act and on a par with the levels of support following the Japanese attack on Pearl Harbor (O'Neill 2002: 320–325). This sudden support for a national military draft reflected the shocking nature of the September 11 attacks, and there was overnight a visceral consensus on the obligations of citizenship in wartime, a view that all citizens should share in the burdens and sacrifices of war. This was a moment of opportunity for the Bush administration to mobilize the nation's resources and increase its military and soft power capabilities. But that would have meant a far different economic model than private financial interests would support, and the moment was lost. The quagmire in Iraq – itself a reflection of inadequate resources – dramatically shifted public opinion and soon 80 percent of Americans were opposed to any national military draft (Carlson 2003: 1).

After September 11, it was common to hear that everything had changed, that nothing would ever be the same. But nothing ever really changed on the home front. President Bush made no calls for shared sacrifice whether in the form of national military service or higher taxes, and waited more than three years to first call for energy conservation or any significant increase in fuel efficiency standards for vehicles sold in the United States (Leonhardt *et al.* 2005: A1). At the core of the Washington Consensus is an asymmetrical view of citizenship that glorifies rights and freedoms while denigrating civic obligations and service. The right to spend freely in the marketplace was now conflated with a supposed patriotic duty to spend freely.

Mr. Bush continued to push his tax-cutting agenda while urging Americans to keep shopping and to visit Disneyland no less. Nearly a decade later, the same private consumption patterns continue, with the same dependence on foreign imported oil and the same enormous trade and current account deficits. By September 2003, the Federal Reserve estimated that 46 percent of federal debt was held by foreign investors, including a significant amount by Persian Gulf monarchies and the People's Republic of China (Ferguson 2005: 268–269, 280–285). By the end of Mr. Bush's presidency, the distribution of wealth and income had become the most top-heavy in modern history, more top-heavy in fact than existed at the time of the 1929 stock market crash (Saez 2009). Instead of civic obligations that might entail genuine burdens or shared sacrifice, Americans continued the same spending and consumption patterns that had already made the U.S. into the world's largest debtor nation and highly dependent on massive foreign imports and capital inflows. Those spending and consumption patterns fueled the rise of an enormous bubble economy in stock and housing markets – bubbles that would eventually prove unsustainable.

At the very center of the Washington Consensus are the Federal Reserve and the influence of Wall Street and private financial interests. During the pegged period, private finance was neutralized by making the Federal Reserve more accountable to the White House and Treasury, an arrangement that was ultimately subject to Congressional oversight. Since then, the Federal Reserve's autonomy has become a euphemism for its capture by the same private financial interests the Federal Reserve is supposed to regulate. The fox is once again in the hen-house.

The members of the Federal Reserve Board of Governors enjoy 14-year terms, longer than any other federal officials, and do not rely on Congress for any budgetary appropriations. Perhaps more troubling is the structure of the Fed's Open Market Committee, which includes interested parties, namely the presidents of the twelve private regional Federal Reserve Banks. This arrangement clearly violates the rule laid down by the Supreme Court in the *Schechter Poultry* case against delegations to private groups. It is certainly a case of "delegation running riot" that would not pass constitutional scrutiny on the substantive merits. Yet, every legal challenge has been dismissed on procedural grounds by the U.S. Court of Appeals for the D.C. Circuit, the gatekeeper for the Supreme Court. The D.C. Circuit has either denied standing to private plaintiffs, or when members of Congress have brought suit, it has exercised its "equitable discretion" to dismiss the suit (*Melcher* 1987; *Committee for Monetary Reform* 1985; *Riegle* 1981; *Reuss* 1978).

Unelected federal judges are understandably reluctant to strike down the Federal Reserve on constitutional grounds. But there are significant costs of disposing of these cases on procedural grounds without a full discussion of the substantive constitutional issues. The Supreme Court's only contribution has been to deny *certiorari* and the legal academy has remained complicit in this silence about such a significant departure from the rule of law and basic norms of democratic accountability. It is not surprising that the public discourse itself has also been diminished by this historical amnesia.

In *The Revolt of the Masses*, José Ortega y Gasset compared modern western man to a spoiled child, concerned with only his own well-being, at the same time ignorant of the causes of that well-being, believing that the material and social organization of civilization has been placed at his disposal like the air, unable to see that behind the benefits of civilization are marvels of invention and construction which are maintained only by great effort and foresight (Ortega y Gasset 1932: 58–60). Our own generation has been distracted by all the wonders of civilization, apparently too busy to remember that our own prosperity was built on a foundation of massive public investment on a scale far grander than today. And so we witness deteriorating infrastructure, from collapsing bridges and levees to failing public schools and institutions.

Democratic citizenship should presume a range of civic obligations, including the duty to become informed and to vote. Yet, Americans are woefully uninformed about matters of war which are now fought with drones, guided missiles, and by relatively few Americans in all-volunteer military and private mercenary armies. This new American way of war presents a classic "free-rider" problem, with most Americans getting the free ride and incurring few direct burdens. The end of universal military service has also resulted in a dangerous gap in experience and culture between civilian society and the military service. Perhaps the primary casualty has been "the loss of candid and realistic discussion concerning matters of a military nature" (Mazur 2003: 608).

The idea that citizenship consists of reciprocal rights and duties has been a fundamental principle in democratic theory and in the survival of democracies throughout the ages. Yet for most Americans today, citizenship consists almost exclusively of rights, with few duties, particularly few obligations that may involve significant burdens or sacrifice. This aversion to civic duties has become even more pronounced now as the United States is engaged in wars in Iraq and Afghanistan.

There are a host of dangers in the world today, including threats of cyber-attacks on critical infrastructure and terrorist attacks with conventional weapons, dirty nukes or some other weapons of mass destruction. There are also major potential security threats that have been identified as stemming from climate change and natural disasters. Whether the dangers to civilization are natural or man-made, there is now a widespread and complacent perception that they can be faced without the participation of citizens, without service, sacrifice, or incurring civic obligations or burdens of almost any kind. Perhaps the most significant threat to the strength and even the survival of democracy is as it has always been, not primarily from foreign enemies, but from within, from the complacency of citizens themselves.

References

Appiah, K. (2007) "Global Citizenship," *Fordham Law Review*, 75: 2375–2391.

Arver v. United States, 245 U.S. 366, 378 (1918).

Barber, W. (1996) *Designs Within Disorder: Franklin D. Roosevelt, the Economists, and the Shaping of American Economic Policy, 1933–1945,* Cambridge: Cambridge University Press.

Barber, B. (2003) *Strong Democracy: Participatory Politics for a New Age*, Berkeley, CA: University of California Press.

Bennett, M. (1999) *When Dreams Came True: The GI Bill and the Making of Modern America*, Dulles, VA: Potomac Books.

Bernstein, M. (1987) *The Great Depression: Delayed Recovery and Economic Change in America, 1929–1939*, Cambridge: Cambridge University Press.

Bernstein, M. (1994) "American Economics and the American Economy," *The American Century: Doctrinal Legacies and Contemporary Policy Problems*, eds. M. Bernstein and D. Adler, Cambridge: Cambridge University Press.

Blum, J., Morgan, E., Rose, W., Schlesinger, A., Stampp, K., and Woodward, C. (1977) *The National Experience*, New York: Harcourt Brace Jovanovich, Inc.

Board of Governors (BOG 1947) *The Federal Reserve System: Purposes and Functions*, 2nd ed., Washington, D.C.: Board of Governors of the Federal Reserve System.

Board of Governors (BOG 1994) *The Federal Reserve System: Purposes and Functions*, 8th ed., Washington, D.C.: Board of Governors of the Federal Reserve System.

Brinkley, A. (1995) T*he End of Reform: New Deal Liberalism in Recession and War*, New York Vintage Books.

Brokaw, T. (1998) *The Greatest Generation*, New York: Random House.

Canova, T. (1995) "The Transformation of U.S. Banking and Finance: From Regulated Competition to Free-Market Receivership," *Brooklyn Law Review*, 60: 1295–1354.

Canova, T. (2006) "American Wartime Values in Historical Perspective: Full-Employment Mobilization or Business as Usual," *ILSA Journal of International & Comparative Law*, 13: 1–23.

Canova, T. (2007) "Closing the Border and Opening the Door: Mobility, Adjustment, and the Sequencing of Reform," *Georgetown Journal of Law & Public Policy*, 5: 341–414.

Canova, T. (2009a) "Financial Market Failure as a Crisis in the Rule of Law: From Market Fundamentalism to a New Keynesian Regulatory Model," *Harvard Law & Policy Review* 3: 370–396.

Canova, T. (2009b) "Lincoln's Populist Sovereignty: Public Finance Of, By, and For the People," *Chapman Law Review* 12: 561–590.

Carlson, D. (2003) "Public Support for Military Draft Law," *Gallup Poll News Service*, Nov. 18, 2003, at 1.

Cecchetti, S. (2005) *Money, Banking, and Financial Markets*, New York: McGraw-Hill (no mention of the fiscal and monetary expansion of the pegged period).

Chandler, L. (1969) *The Economics of Money and Banking*, 5th ed., New York: Harper & Row.

Cole, D. (2007) "Against Citizenship as a Predicate for Basic Rights," *Fordham Law Review* 75: 2541–2548.

Committee for Monetary Reform v. *Board of Governors of the Federal Reserve System*, 766 F.2d 538 (D.C. Cir. 1985).

Council of Economic Advisers (CEA 1984) *Economic Report of the President and Annual Report of the Council of Economic Advisers*, Washington, D.C.

Council of Economic Advisers (CEA 1996) *Economic Report of the President and Annual Report of the Council of Economic Advisers*, Washington, D.C. (providing GDP statistics no earlier than 1959).

Council of Econoimc Advisers (CEA 2005) *Economic Report of the President and Annual Report of the Council of Economic Advisers*, Washington, D.C.

Drucker, P. (1993) *Post-Capitalist Society*, New York: Harper.

Etzioni, A. (1998) *The New Golden Rule: Community and Morality in a Democratic Society*, New York, Basic Books.

Ferguson, N. (2005) *Colossus: The Rise and Fall of the American Empire*, New York: Penguin Books.

Frank, R. and Bernanke, B. (2007) *Principles of Macroeconomics*, 3d ed., New York: McGraw-Hill (providing Federal Reserve and monetary history that includes pre-pegged and post-pegged periods, but nothing on the pegged period itself).

Freud, S. (1961) *Civilization and Its Discontents*, transl. J. Strachey, New York: W.W. Norton & Co.

Friedman, M., and Schwartz, A. (1963) *A Monetary History of the United States, 1867–1960*, Princeton, NJ: Princeton University Press.

Galbraith, J. and Darity, W. (1994) *Macroeconomics*, Boston Houghton Mifflin.

Garlinski, J. (1978) *Hitler's Last Weapons*, New York: J. Friedmann.

Hixson, W. (1993) *Triumph of the Bankers: Money and Banking in the Eighteenth and Nineteenth Centuries*, Westport, CT: Praeger.

Hobbes, T. (1996), *Leviathan*, Cambridge: Cambridge University Press.

Homer, S. (1963) *A History of Interest Rates*, Piscataway, NJ: Rutgers University Press.

Janeway, E. (1951) *The Struggle for Survival*, New York: Weybright and Talley.

Jarecki, E. (2008) *The American Way of War: Guided Missiles, Guided Men, and a Republic in Peril*, New York: Free Press.

Jones, J. (2001) "Support Remains High Even if Military Action is Prolonged, Involves Casualties," *Gallup Poll News Service*, Oct. 4, 2001, at 1 (reporting results of Gallup poll survey conducted Sept. 21–22, 2001).

Judt, T. (2005) *Postwar: A History of Europe Since 1945*, New York: Penguin Books.

Kennedy, J. (1988) *John F. Kennedy: A Self-Portrait*, Harper/Caedmon Audio, Sept. 1988, Side 1.

Kennedy, P. (1987) *The Rise and Fall of the Great Powers*, New York: Random House.

King, M.L. (1986) *A Testament of Hope: The Essential Writings and Speeches of Martin Luther King Jr.*, ed. J. Washington, New York: HarperOne.

Leonhardt, D., Mouawad, J., and Sanger, D., "To Conserve Gas, President Calls for Less Driving," *N.Y. Times*, Sept. 27, 2005, at p. A1.

Locke, J. (1988) *Two Treatises of Government*, Cambridge: Cambridge University Press.

Macedo, S., ed. (2005) *Democracy at Risk: How Political Choices Undermine Citizen Participation, and What We Can Do About It*, Washington, D.C.: Brookings Institution Press.

Mazur, D. (2003) "Why Progressives Lost the War When They Lost the Draft," *Hofstra Law Review* 32: 553.

Melcher v. Federal Open Market Committee, 836 F.2d 561 (D.C. Cir. 1987).

Meltzer, A. (2003) *A History of the Federal Reserve, Vol. I, 1913–1951*, Chicago: University of Chicago Press.

Miller, N. (1983) *F.D.R.: An Intimate History*, New York: Meridian.

Nye, J. (2004) *Soft Power: The Means to Success in World Politics*, New York: Public Affairs.

O'Neill, W. (2002) *The Oxford Essential Guide to World War II*, New York: Berkley Books.

Ortega y Gasset, J. (1932) *The Revolt of the Masses*, New York: W.W. Norton & Co.

Persico, J. (2001) *Roosevelt's Secret War: FDR and World War II Espionage*, New York: Random House.

Plato (2007) *Crito*, trans. Woods and Pack, at: http://papers.ssrn.com/sol3/papers.cfm?abstract_id=1023145.

Putnam, R. (2001) *Bowling Alone: The Collapse and Revival of American Community*, New York: Simon & Schuster.

Reuss v. Balles, 584 F.2d 461 (D.C. Cir. 1978), *cert. denied*, 439 U.S. 987 (1978).

Riegle v. Federal Open Market Committee, 656 F.2d 873 (D.C. Cir. 1981).

Ritter, G. (1997) *Goldbugs and Greenbacks: The Antimonopoly Tradition and the Politics of Finance in America*, Cambridge: Cambridge University Press.

Roosevelt, Franklin D. (July 19, 1940) "Address by Franklin Delano Roosevelt to the Democratic National Convention," *Multimedia Archive*, Miller Center of Public Affairs, University of Virginia, at http://millercenter.org/scripps/archive/speeches/detail/3318.

Roosevelt, T. (1956) *The Free Citizen: A summons to service of the democratic ideal*, ed. H. Hagedorn, New York: Macmillan Company.

Rosen, H. (2002) *Public Finance*, 6th ed., New York: McGraw-Hill.

Rousseau, J. (1968) *The Social Contract*, New York: Penguin Putnam.

Saez, E. (Aug. 5, 2009) "Striking it Richer: The Evolution of Top Incomes in the United States" (Update with 2007 estimates), Berkeley, CA, available at: http://elsa.berkeley.edu/~saez/saez-UStopincomes-2007.pdf.

Samuelson, P. (1948) *Economics*, New York: McGraw-Hill.

Samuelson, P. and Nordhaus, W. (2005) *Macroeconomics*, 18th ed., New York: McGraw-Hill (historical overview of the Federal Reserve and monetary policy omitting any mention of pegged period).

Sandel, M. (1998) *Democracy's Discontent: America in Search of a Public Philosophy*, Cambridge, MA: Harvard University Press.

Schechter Poultry Corporation v. *United States* (1935) 295 U.S. 495.

Schuck, P. (2007) "The Meaning of American Citizenship in a Post-9/11 World," *Fordham Law Review*, 75: 2531–2540.

Selective Service System (2002) "How the Draft Has Changed Since Vietnam," *History and Records*, available at: www.sss.gov/viet.htm.

Selective Service System (2002) "Classifications," *About the Agency,* available at www.sss.gov/classif.htm.

Selective Service System (2002) "Conscientious Objection and Alternative Service," *Fast Facts*, available at www.sss.gov/FSconsobj.htm.

Schaller, M. (1985) *The American Occupation of Japan*, New York: Oxford University Press.

Shirer, W. (1990) *The Rise and Fall of the Third Reich*, New York: Touchstone.

Smith, M. (2003) *Perilous Fight: America's World War II in Color*, Public Broadcast System, at www.pbs.org/perilousfight/social/objectors/.

Smithies, A. (1964) "Uses of Selective Credit Controls," *United States Monetary Policy*, ed., N. Jacoby, 2nd ed., New York: Praeger.

Sun-Tzu (1993) *The Art of Warfare*, transl. R. Ames, New York: Ballantine.

Turgeon, L. (1980) *The Advanced Capitalist System: A Revisionist View*, Armonk, NY: M.E. Sharpe.

Turgeon, L. (1996) *Bastard Keynesianism: The Evolution of Economic Thinking and Policymaking Since World War II*, Westport, CT: Greenwood Press.

Vatter, H. (1963) *The U.S. Economy in the 1950s*, New York: W.W. Norton & Co.

Vatter, H. (1985) *The U.S. Economy in World War II*, New York: Columbia University Press.

Walzer, M. (1984) Spheres of Justice: A Defense of Pluralism and Equality, New York: Basic Books.

Yakus v. *United States* (1944) 321 U.S. 414, 64 S.Ct. 660, 88 L. Ed. 834, 1944 U.S. LEXIS 1311.

12 The reversal of citizenship

The Lebanon War and Intifada in the 1980s and the 2000s

Lev Luis Grinberg

There is a tendency to attribute the weakening of citizenship to the state of "global war against terror" declared by President Bush after September 11, 2001 (Peled 2007). This chapter will challenge the idea that a state of war is in itself sufficient to weaken citizenship and disregard civil rights. In order to do so it will compare two different decades in Israeli history, the 1980s and the 2000s, and their opposite effects, despite relatively similar "states of war."

The First Lebanon War (1982–1985) and the First Intifada (1987–1993) led to mass mobilization of Israeli citizens against the use of violence and to the establishment of several civil society organizations and human rights movements, finally leading to Israeli recognition of the PLO and peace talks in 1993. The Second Intifada (2000–2004) and the Second Lebanon War (2006) produced opposite effects: suspension of political negotiations, demobilization of civil society, human rights deterioration, and the conclusion that the military must be better prepared for future wars.[1] In short, the "state of war" in the 1980s empowered civil society and the political parties vis-à-vis the military, while similar events in the 2000s empowered the military vis-à-vis the political parties and civil society.

In both cases, the context was a state of war, accompanied by a sense of threat, but the political dynamic was exactly the opposite. This chapter will suggest that the change occurred during the 1990s due to globalization, neo-liberalization and the so-called "peace process." The structural implications of all three processes were similar: the citizens were weakened and the political mediation between them and the state became irrelevant to the decision-making process. I will argue that the proper context for understanding this "reversal of citizenship" is the concentration of autonomous power in the hands of a small elite controlling the Israeli economy – Treasury and Bank of Israel executives, and a small group of capitalist families – and the military elite. The latter, I will argue, gained its autonomous power thanks to a manpower restructuring of the IDF (Israel Defense Forces) (Shafir and Peled 2000, 2002; Ram 2008; Levy 2007; Peri 2006; Grinberg 2010).

These non-democratic processes during the 1990s and the correspondent weakening of civil society and political mediation occurred not only in Israel. A similar case is the power of North-American civil society to struggle against the war in Vietnam, compared to its current weakness against the war in Iraq. The paper will analyze the changes in Israel as a microcosm of global tendencies that weakened both subordinated social groups and the capacity of nation-state democratic institutions to regulate its markets and control its borders. The net result is a weakening of political actors and democratic institutions, threatening the legitimacy of the political system as a whole. Under such conditions, collective feelings of threat and insecurity effectively facilitate the legitimization of government by non-elected elites.

Civil, military and political societies

While civil society and state institutions are relatively autonomous, the most salient feature of politics is its lack of autonomy and dependency on state and society. Political actors constitute what Linz and Stepan (1996) termed "political society," having only mediating power. The power of the political society vis-à-vis state institutions depends on its ability to mobilize civil society support, while their power vis-à-vis civil society depends on state institutions and their ability to use state power. Political actors mediate between sides to a conflict, either within civil society, between dominant and subordinate groups, or between civil society and the state. When the two sides are powerful and their power is balanced, the need for mediation grows, opening up political space for representation. When one is significantly more powerful, however, the space for mediation and negotiation shrinks, as the powerful side tends to prefer ruling without dialogue and impose its will unilaterally.

Political space is a symbolic field of representation (Bourdieu 1992), so it may be opened up and closed, its dynamic determined by the autonomous powers that frame it, society and the state (Grinberg 2010). Given their dependency on changing external conditions and their mediating position, political actors can appear and disappear, and their most distinctive quality is their symbolic ability to perform credible roles and manipulate public opinion. Changing political contexts determine political actors' ability to fulfill their promises to their constituencies.

Democratic rules of the game institutionalize the dynamic opening and closing of political space. Historically, this became possible when the inclusive borders of the nation-state were consolidated, and a balance of power between competing forces prevented unilateral rule (Rustow 1970; Grinberg 2010). Capitalism was a crucial factor in the development of democracy precisely because it empowered subordinated classes vis-à-vis dominant capital (Rueschemeyer et al. 1992), and citizens vis-à-vis the nation-state, which sought to extract taxes from and conscript them (Tilly 1992).

Although the democratic rules of the game facilitate the dynamic opening of political space, given changes in social discourses, agendas, interests and identities, they cannot prevent its closure. The closure of political space can serve the interests of the military elites in a power struggle with civil society and political actors, but it can also serve the interests of dominant economic and political actors against new actors that challenge their power. When such conditions materialize a coalition of military, economic and political actors can close political space, either under the existing democratic rules of the game or by revoking them. The concept of political space helps to explain the dynamic expansion or shrinkage of civilian power vis-à-vis the state. In other words, it is a critical theory of politics that rejects essentialist interpretations of democracy.[2]

Violence is one of the most effective means to close political space to new agendas and ideas representative of marginalized interests and identities, because it produces collective feelings of threat, fear, and hate. Violence can be exercised against internal opposition, external enemies, or groups within national borders that are constructed as "outsiders." Obviously, military elites and dominant political actors control the means of violence and can use them to serve their interests. They can also manipulate fear. The question is, however, under what conditions the use of violence succeeds to mobilize support, and under what conditions it fails, so that the dominant elites have to face popular resistance.

As argued by Hanna Arendt (1969) and recently by Michael Mann (2005), violence can be effective only if a concrete group of people are ready to exercise it. Physical violence requires presence, while political power is symbolic and representative, and can therefore be exerted in the absence of the social group. Political power is imagined and constructed by political leaders who speak in the name of a group that comes to be only when someone claims to re-present it (Bourdieu 1992). The delegated power of the political actor can be used to manipulate his followers (Mills 1958). However, when soldiers are at war they must believe in what they do; they cannot ignore the fact that they are in danger, and must be ready to kill and be killed.

Military elites are political actors, because their decision to use violence determines whether the political space for negotiation is opened up or closed. However, their ability to use violence is framed by the political context, the political construction of the threat, and the ability to mobilize obedient fighting units. When the military only protects the state's citizens by controlling its external borders, it is considered apolitical; when it intervenes in internal power relations or takes power directly, it is seen as a political actor.[3] In both cases, however, the military behaves as a political actor, and is the most crucial factor in creating the two fundamental preconditions for opening up political space: it demarcates the state's external borders that define the shared identity of potentially equal citizens, and facilitates a balance of power when it does not use violence against the dominated population.

Military institutions are never monolithic, and there are significant differences among units and ranks. However, they have a collective interest to conceal their internal debates and to appear in public as a monolithic, professional institution. When public debates and struggles in civil society penetrate the military and it is no longer able to maintain this pretense, its political power as a corporation vis-à-vis the political and civil society is weakened.

In order to understand the fluctuation between broad support of belligerent government actions and popular opposition to them, I suggest analyzing three critical factors:

1   *The political context*, namely, the interest of the dominant political actors to use violence to legitimize their policies and their ability to construct a collective sense of threat;
2   *The degree of military autonomy*, or its internal cohesion and ability to mobilize its fighting units; and
3   *The power of civil society* to organize and confront the military and political elites.

I will analyze these three factors in the context of the First Lebanon War and First Intifada, in the 1980s, and the changes that took place during the 1990s that have weakened political mediation and facilitated the manipulation of fear through the use of violence by military elites after 2010.

Historical background: the formation of Israeli political society

In order to understand the political context of civil resistance to military violence in the 1980s it is important to review the historical background of the peculiar relations between the state apparatuses, political actors, social forces, and the military in Israeli society. Israel was dominated by the same political party (*Mapai*, or Labor)[4] from its establishment in 1948 until the rise to power of the main opposition party, Likud, in 1977. Over this period, Israeli society's ethno-cultural composition changed radically due to immigration waves. While in 1948 most Israeli Jews had originated mainly from Eastern and Central Europe (generically called *Ashkenazim*), most immigrants after 1948 came from Arab countries (*Mizrachim*). The latter were placed in geographically and economically peripheral positions and the ruling party became the party of the dominant veteran *Ashkenazi* middle classes, despite their "working class" discourse. This discrimination and the resulting ethnic-class tensions were capitalized on by the right-wing *Likud*, particularly after 1973 Yom Kippur War (Shapiro 1991; Chetrit 2004).

Well before statehood, *Mapai* had established powerful quasi-state bureaucratic apparatuses that controlled a weak civil society that depended on it for essential services, mainly employment, housing and healthcare. *Mapai* appointed its loyal members to leading positions in the *Histadrut* labor union federation and military organizations, and after 1948 in the IDF (Shapiro 1976, 1977; Horowitz and Kimmerling 1974; Peri 1983, 2006; Shalev 1992; Grinberg 1993; Ben Eliezer 1998). Combat units and military elites were composed mainly of *Ashkenazim* who identified with the Labor Movement, or, as it came to be called later on, "the left" (Smooha 1978; Levy 2007; Peri 1983).

The weakness of civil society before 1948 resulted from two structural conditions: (1) economic competition of Jewish immigrants with local Arabs over land and labor; and (2) the absence of democratic state institutions (Shapiro 1976; Kimmerling 1983; Shafir 1989; Shalev 1992). During the 1950s the massive wave of *Mizrachi* immigrants served to perpetuate this weakness of civil society. Later on, however, full employment (for Jews) and democratic state institutions strengthened the Jewish middle and working classes, empowering their organizations that threatened the dominant position of *Mapai* and the *Histadrut* (Grinberg 1993). The expansion of state domains in 1967 and the inclusion of Palestinian workers and captive markets under military occupation weakened peripheral Israeli workers competing with them – mainly the *Mizrachi* lower ethno-class – but empowered other workers in state-owned companies, skilled jobs, and the public service, belonging mainly to the *Ashkenazi* ethno-class (Grinberg 1991, 1993).

Since 1967, Israel/Palestine became a dual economy and a dual regime, with blurred economic and territorial borders, and the military playing a critical political role controlling the Palestinians under occupation. The IDF controls the external borders of the Occupied Territories (with Egypt and Jordan), the pre-1967 borders with the sovereign territories of the State of Israel, and since the 1993 Oslo Accords also internal borders between cities and villages within the occupied West Bank (Grinberg 2008). The military is thus structurally positioned as a political actor, because it defines the borders of the sovereign state of Israel and demarcates those of its Occupied Territories.[5]

The IDF uses violence against the occupied Palestinian population and protects Israelis throughout the lands under Israeli domination. Its power to rule the Palestinians depends on its apolitical, non-expansionist image as a force used only for defense purposes. In accordance with this image, prior to the First Lebanon War of 1982 Israel's wars had been called, in the Israeli political discourse, "no-choice wars." Importantly, this is a purely political construction rather than an "objective" historical fact (Golani 2002). With the rise of the Likud to power in 1977, however, the defensive image of wars and the apolitical image of the IDF changed radically.

The Likud's political platform combined three apparently unrelated agendas: (1) Ethnic-class protest against the discrimination against *Mizrachi* Jews, claiming the national unity of all Jews; (2) a liberal-economic critique of the Labor's interventionist welfare policies and of the power of unionized workers; and (3) a religio-nationalist claim to the entire territories occupied by the IDF (so-called Greater Israel). The Likud was strengthened by the 1967 war which materialized its claim to rule all of Greater Israel, as well as by the 1973 war, widely interpreted as a failure of Labor's leadership. It took four more years of internal disintegration of the Labor Party, in the context of an economic crisis and US pressure to withdraw from the Sinai Peninsula, for the Likud to win the elections and form a coalition government for the first time.

Civil vs. military society: the 1980s

Shortly after the 1977 elections a group of reservists, mainly officers in combat units, wrote a letter to newly installed Prime Minister Menachem Begin warning him not to expand the Jewish settlements in the Occupied Territories, because they would not serve in an army that implemented expansionist policies (Reshef

1996). The Officers' Letter as it came to be called was the first warning that the military might face difficulties if it were to realize the Likud's Greater Israel vision. The context was the lack of trust in the new government's policies by *Ashkenazi* middle-class soldiers who supported the opposition parties. Indeed, a peace movement based on young Labor Party supporters serving in reserves – Peace Now – soon held mass demonstrations, first in support of the peace with Egypt, and later in protest against the invasion of Lebanon (ibid.).

The Likud's rise to power provoked two types of mobilization against it: one against its economic policies, mainly by the working classes, and the other against its expansionist policies, mainly by the middle class. The well-organized working class also mobilized the weak peripheral *Mizrachi* ethno-classes in protest against the economic liberalization policies that resulted, in the long run, in hyper-inflation.[6] On May Day of 1980, this mobilization culminated in the largest workers' demonstration ever seen in Israel. In this paper, however, I focus on the second type of protest – against military oppression, aggression and war – which culminated in the so-called 400,000 Demonstration[7] against the September 1982 massacre in the Sabra and Shatila Refugee Camps in West Beirut.

As previously mentioned the civil movement against Likud policies in the Occupied Territories began immediately after Begin was elected in 1977. However, following the peace negotiations with Egypt that began that same year and culminated in the 1979 peace agreement, Peace Now went to the streets to encourage Begin to compromise with Egypt. Only smaller, more radical groups protested the expansion of settlements and oppression of Palestinians at that time.[8] It was only after the completion of Israel's withdrawal from Sinai and the invasion of Lebanon that Peace Now and larger mainstream middle-class groups began to openly oppose the Likud's military aggression.

The Israeli Air Force began bombing PLO targets in Lebanon on June 4, 1982, in retaliation for a terrorist attack by an extremist Palestinian organiza-tion.[9] After 48 hours of IDF bombings and Katyusha rocket attacks by the PLO, the IDF invaded Lebanon in an operation initially called Peace for the Galilee. The government declared that it had only one objective – to stop the Katyusha attacks – and that the IDF would penetrate only 40 kilometers inland, to cover the rockets' range. However, within 72 hours the IDF attacked the Beirut–Damascus road, 100 kilometers from the Israeli border, and laid siege to Beirut.

The internal events following the invasion of Lebanon are very revealing of the dynamics among Israeli civil, political, and military societies. Initially, Oper-ation Peace for the Galilee was supported by all Zionist political parties, includ-ing the opposition Labor Party.[10] Only small radical leftist groups took to the streets. After three weeks of besieging Beirut, however, Peace Now organized its first demonstration, to be followed by a second one after a month, in which an estimated 100,000 demonstrated against occupying the Lebanese capital. It was only the massacre in Sabra and Shatila and the unprecedented popular reaction against it that forced the Labor Party to join the opposition to the war, initially mobilized by civil society organizations.

At the same time, substantial opposition rallied within military society, reinforcing the civil society mobilization. The most significant act was Colonel Eli Geva's public refusal to command his troops should the IDF enter Beirut. At the same time, Yesh Gvul ("There's a Limit"), a new conscientious objectors' movement based on reservists, declared its members would refuse to serve in Lebanon (Helman 1999).

Although public refusal to serve was the most visible and radical form of protest, there were other forms of opposition to the war within military circles, as well as more silent and implicit forms of refusal. A dynamic of mutual facilitation developed: civil society protest in the streets penetrated military ranks, while debates within the military encouraged civil protest. The military lost its monolithic image and became politicized, its internal debates becoming part of public discourse. However, it must be made clear that this was due to the combatants' political opposition to the government's expansionist policies.

In short, the Likud's rise to power shattered the apolitical image of the military and the war, whereas wars initiated by Labor governments could be more easily legitimized as "no-choice wars."

Public criticism of the occupation of Lebanon played a key role in civil society organization and struggle against the repression of the Intifada in 1987–1993. However, a more complex explanation must also take into account the economic and socio-cultural transformations of the 1980s. The economic crisis of 1983–1984 led to new elections in 1984, and to the formation of a National Unity Government (NUG). This government faced two difficult challenges: halting inflation and withdrawing from Lebanon, and accomplished both within a year. Shimon Peres's 1985 Economic Stabilization Plan halted inflation and started a long-term process of neo-liberalizing the Israeli economy, empowering the middle classes vis-à-vis the state and military. It also nurtured a new liberal and individualist culture among the middle classes, eroding the nationalist-collectivist mobilization that had characterized Labor Zionism (Shalev 1992; Shafir and Peled 2002; Ram 2008; Levy 2007).

The military oppression of Palestinian civil demonstrations that began in December 1987 was criticized within Israel by a strong and mobilized civil society. The organizations that took the lead in safeguarding Palestinian civil rights included the Association for Civil Rights and *B'Tselem* ("In His Image"). It was the new liberal civil rights discourse which underlay their persistent appeals to the High Court of Justice against military brutality, as well as the renewed activities of the conscientious objection movement (Ezrachi 1997).

Although the Labor Party was now part of the government, with Yitzhak Rabin as Minister of Security, the civil society opposition was very effective in influencing the actions of the IDF. The most direct evidence of its impact was the statement by IDF Chief of Staff General Dan Shomron that "there is no military solution" to the Intifada (Levy 2003: 175). This did not mean that the military had no solution, but that it had no soldiers willing to exert the violence necessary. The political role of the IDF became obvious: if it had public support it could continue controlling the Palestinians, but if soldiers interpreted their

actions as political oppression, rather than "self defense," the military was powerless, opening the political space up for negotiations.

Public pressure restrained military oppression of Palestinians, and in 1990 the
Labor Party concluded it could no longer participate in the second NUG government formed in 1988. It seceded from the NUG and turned to the opposition and
in 1992 won the elections with a platform proposing mutual recognition and
peaceful negotiations with the Palestinians. Power relations between Palestinian
society and the IDF became balanced thanks to the mobilization of Israeli civil
society, facilitating the opening up of political space for mediation by the Labor
and other moderate political parties. An era of negotiations had begun.

Globalization and peace: the 1990s

After winning the elections and securing the PLO's recognition, new Labor
Chairman Rabin alluded to the role played by civil society opposition in opening
up political space to negotiations with the Palestinians: "Arafat will not be both-
ered by the Israeli High Court and the Israeli Civil Rights Association," meaning
the PLO would be more effective than the IDF in controlling the Palestinians
(*Yediot Ahronot*, September 7, 1993). A new period of political negotiations and
mediation began, with military leaders deeply involved in the political process.
Deputy Chief of Staff Amnon Lipkin-Shahak headed the negotiations team, and
since then nothing occurred without the IDF's agreement.[11] As argued elsewhere, the Israelis already imagined themselves in peace, and imagined a Palestinian state, but tended to ignore the continued expansion of Jewish settlements
and the paving of bypass roads that divided and disarticulated the areas designated for the future Palestinian state (Grinberg 2001).

One of the most crucial results of the mutual recognition in September 1993
was the integration of the Israeli economy in the global market. This had been
one of the most important motivations for peace since the late 1980s. Indeed,
following the signing of the Oslo Accords in 1993 foreign capital began to flow
into Israel and markets all over the world opened to Israeli products and investments (Shafir and Peled 2002; Ram 2008). The globalization of the Israeli
economy was accompanied by the privatization of *Histadrut* institutions, the
weakening of organized labor, and the erosion of the welfare state.

Histadrut-owned economic enterprises had been weakened since the 1985
economic plan because it had drastically cut capital subsidies (Grinberg 1991;
Shalev 1992). However, it was only after 1994 that most *Histadrut*-owned companies became privatized (Grinberg and Shafir 2000). In particular, its healthcare
service (Israel's largest by far) was privatized, weakening its organizational
power.

The weakening of worker organizations was another crucial element of the
economic reform policies. It included non-renewal of collective agreements, the
introduction of individual wage agreements, hiring manpower companies and
outsourcing. One of the most visible forms of weakening worker organizations
was the substitution of Palestinian workers by immigrant workers (mainly from

the East Asia, Eastern Europe, and Latin America), who were almost totally dependent on their employers, unprotected by legislation or state control (Rosenhek 1999; Mundlak 2007; Kemp and Raijman 2008). This policy package weakened most workers, apart from small pockets of privileged workers in state-owned companies, mostly utilities and the ports.

The economic outcome of globalization was widening class gaps. However, due to the weakening of organized labor, the social and political manifestations of these gaps did *not* take the form of class mobilization and protest. Rather, the result was ethnic-class tensions between those peripheral groups disadvantaged by the economic policies – the *Mizrachim*, new immigrants from the former Soviet Union, ultra-orthodox *Ashkenazi* Jews – and Palestinian citizens, on the one hand, and the secular *Ashkenazi* upper classes on the other, as well as among the peripheral groups themselves. The result was a growing sense of disintegrating collective national identity, mainly because the "external" Palestinian enemy was apparently ready to end hostilities and sign a peace agreement (Grinberg 2010, Ch. 7).

The only state institution which realigned its relationship with some of the peripheral groups was the military. Given the weakening motivation of the *Ashkenazi* secular middle classes to serve in the military and volunteer to combat units, the military began to replace them with peripheral social groups (Levy 2003). While neo-liberalization fatally weakened low-wage workers belonging to peripheral ethno-classes, the restructuring of the military weakened the secular middle classes vis-à-vis the military, because their mobilization was no longer required. The combined weakening of both the middle and lower classes is the social context that facilitated the re-escalation of violence in the 2000s.

The re-escalation of violence: the 2000s

While the structural transformations of the 1990s are critical for understanding the power relations between state institutions and civil society, we must always keep in mind the political context of renewed violence and the political construction of its meaning. Benjamin Netanyahu was elected in 1996 shortly after Rabin's assassination. His economic policies, coupled with internal ethnic-class tensions between his coalition partners, led to the disintegration of his coalition. Labor Party leader Ehud Barak succeeded him as Prime Minister in 1999, only to call new elections within a mere 18 months. The most important political fact, however, is that the Second Intifada and violent oppression by the military started in the period of Labor government, a period of allegedly renewed peace negotiations and Israeli readiness to compromise.

Barak's government declared itself ready to sign a peace agreement within a year, and succeeded in creating the illusion that the Palestinians were declining generous offers. Whether this was a mere manipulation is irrelevant from a sociological point of view, because the crucial fact is that the Jewish public bought it. The Palestinians' ostensible unwillingness to make peace was widely accepted at the moment the Intifada broke out, and became a new national myth uniting most Israelis behind the military.[12] As military officers recognized, the Labor government, and in particular the failed Camp David negotiations, significantly contributed to their ability to crush the Intifada and escalate the violence.

The Israeli reaction to the initial Palestinian demonstrations was extremely disproportionate, provoking more violent protests. This vicious circle ultimately took violence to unprecedented levels, including shooting from tanks and helicopters at civil targets, and suicide bombing attacks in Israeli cities. This time internal debates in the military did not leak to the media, and it was only four years later that senior officers began to give interviews and to condemn the escalation of violence by the IDF (Eldar 2004; Harel and Issacharoff 2004; Drucker and Shelah 2005). During the Second Intifada soldiers did not protest their orders; on the contrary, they disobeyed orders designed to contain the violence and acted to prevent a cease fire. There were no massive demonstrations against the military during the first 18 months of oppression,[13] and almost no interventions by the High Court of Justice against the military. Popular support of oppression was expressed by the slogan "Let the military win," and by the electoral successes of Likud Chairman Ariel Sharon in 2001 and 2003 elections (Peled 2004).

The military's interpretation of the Second Intifada was diametrically opposed to that of the first. Whereas in the first officers argued there was no military solution, in the second they argued there was no *political* solution, only military. This position was expressed through their criticism of politicians who attempted to reach a cease-fire agreement while the violence continued, arguing that negotiations weakened the military. In addition, they argued that the objective was to *prevent* political compromise, because this would signal to the Palestinians that the use of violence could achieve positive results. The only option for the Palestinians, in the view of IDF command, was to surrender, and the goal of the military was to "etch into the Palestinian mind" the realization that they could not achieve their goals by using violence. The means of shaping the Palestinians' consciousness was, obviously, using more and more violence against them (Grinberg 2010: Part IV).

The key point is that in the absence of a powerful civil society within Israel, the second Palestinian uprising could no longer facilitate the opening up of political space for negotiations. The recruitment of peripheral social groups weakened by neo-liberal policies to combat units neutralized the opposition of the middle classes and their capacity to negotiate their rights (Levy 2003). In addition, the violent clashes with Palestinians also reunited a Jewish Israeli society that had become disintegrated in the period of imagined peace by economic reforms and the consequent hostility between ethno-classes. Moreover, the political consensus over the need to fight and oppress the Palestinians reconstructed the legitimacy of the Israeli regime which had been severely damaged during the neo-liberalization of the 1990s and the ethnic-class tensions it provoked. The weaknesses of civil society also weakened the political parties vis-à-vis the military elite, who succeeded in mobilizing national support for the use of violence against the reconstructed enemy. When civil society is weak there is no avenue for the political articulation of claims, agendas, and identities, and citizens become dependent on state institutions.

The 2000s are thus characterized by debilitated civil and political societies, and by the empowerment of the military institutions, discourses and "solutions." Israel ceased escalating the violence after Arafat's death in 2004 and in preparation for its 2005 unilateral withdrawal from Gaza. However, violent military attacks and the economic strangulation of Gaza were renewed in 2006, reaching new peaks in July–August of that year (during the Second Lebanon War) and in December 2008–January 2009 (Operation Cast Lead in Gaza). Regrettably, the most significant element in all these events, for our purposes, is the almost complete absence of political criticism of the use of violence, with all Zionist parties supporting the military unreservedly.

Conclusion

This paper argues that the weakness of political parties and the lack of political space for representing alternative perspectives reflect the weakening of Israeli civil society and the empowerment of military and economic elites in the 1990s. This is evidenced by the fundamental difference between the public reactions to military violence in the 1980s and the 2000s. The reversal of civilian mobilization was the result of two interrelated changes: (1) the structural power transformation in the 1990s; and (2) the reconstruction of political society designed to legitimize the new structures and ruling elites in the 2000s.

The structural changes that weakened civil society and the state's redistributive role closed the political space for representation and mediation. The imbalance between the autonomous power of economic and military elites, on the one hand, and of the citizen body on the other, debilitated political society, making political actors increasingly dependent on the economic and military elites. Given the weakness of political mediation, civil society organizations and state welfare institutions, a new form of apolitical organizations emerged – NGOs – as a substitute for the political dynamic between civil society, political parties and the state.

The second change is related to the political reconstruction of the Israeli–Palestinian conflict as a "total war" where democratic, i.e. negotiated compromises are simply impossible. The unilateral policies of the stronger party designed to impose its will on the weaker side are acts of violence that provoke violent reactions and escalation. The use of violence increased citizens' dependence on the security forces, because it increased their insecurity (Tilly 1985). This "state of war" legitimized the concentration of power by economic and military elites that took place during the 1990s, and also weakened the citizens as social actors with legitimate demands.

In the new global era the State of Israel regained its traditional role in the confrontation between the "democratic West" and the "anti-democratic Rest." During the global war against terror democracy is no longer a matter of civil and human rights, citizenship and civil society mobilization, political representation and mediation. Democracy has become a slogan that reflects the political affiliation to the only super-power that has the military might to fight against "global terrorism."

The total support of the IDF by the Israeli public and the consensus over foreign policies among all Zionist parties is the most salient fact in Israeli politics today. Fortunately, however, politics is a dynamic process, and there are already signs of change, at least in the US. The elections in the US (2008) and in Israel (2009) seem to represent two opposite directions of development: the US is apparently withdrawing from its previous expansionist policies, while the Israeli polity continues to support violence as the central vehicle of national policy. The question is whether US and world politics will change sufficiently to affect Israeli politics. In other words, will the democratic game of the dynamic opening up of political space by the mobilization of civil society be renewed?

Notes

1 See the report by the Commission of Inquiry into the Events of Military Engagement in Lebanon, 2006 ("Winograd Report"; Winograd 2008).
2 For a detailed discussion of my conceptualization of political space see Grinberg (2010) Chapter 2.
3 For the various forms of military-political intervention, see Stepan (2001, Chapter 4).
4 The party was founded in 1930 as *Mapai* (acronym for *Mifleget Poalei Eretz Israel* – The Land of Israel Workers Party), and in 1968 it merged with two smaller parties and renamed *Mifleget Ha'avoda*, or Labor Party.
5 The military has played a political role since 1948, among other things because Israel's Palestinian citizens were subjected to a military administration.
6 The Likud governments reacted to these protests by replacing the Minister of Finances three times in 1977–1984, and designing a populist economic plan to help it win the 1981 elections, that provoked hyper-inflation during 1983–1984 and ultimately the fall of the government (Grinberg 1991).
7 Although almost certainly an exaggeration, this number lingered in the collective political memory due to the demonstration's unprecedented (and hitherto unequalled) size.
8 For the sake of transparency I must report here that I was active in those radical groups, Campus and the Committee for Solidarity with Bir Zeit, that formed the Committee against the War in Lebanon and the soldiers' movement Yesh Gvul in June 1982.
9 The attempt to assassinate the Israeli ambassador in London (who was severely wounded) was organized by an Abu Nidal's extremist organization that had split from the PLO.
10 Only four Knesset Members voted against the war and two abstained.
11 During the period of secret negotiations, prior to mutual recognition, the military elite had been kept away. Once public negotiations started, the military took the lead (Savir 1998).
12 See Grinberg (2010) for more detailed description and analysis of the political construction of the "Israel has no partner" myth; see also Meital (2006).
13 There were two middle-sized demonstrations (10,000–20,000) on February 9 and 16, 2002, during the unilateral cease fire declared by Arafat.

References

Arendt, H. (1969) *On Violence*, New York: Harcourt, Brace and World.
Bourdieu, P. (1992) *Language and Symbolic Power*, Cambridge, MA: Harvard University Press.

Ben Eliezer, U. (1998) *The Making of Israeli Militarism*, Bloomington, IN: Indiana University Press.

Chetrit, S. S. (2004) *The Mizrahi Struggle in Israel, Between Oppression and Liberation, Identification and Alternative*, 1948–2003, Tel Aviv: Am Oved (Hebrew).

Drucker, R. and O. Shelah (2005) *Boomerang*, Jerusalem: Keter (Hebrew).

Eldar, A. (2004) "His True Face," *Ha'aretz*, June 11 (Hebrew).

Ezrachi, Y. (1997) *Rubber Bullets: Power and Conscience in Modern Israel*, New York: Farrar, Straus and Giroux.

Golani, M. (2002) *Wars Don't Just Happen*, Israel: Modan Publishing House: Ben Shemen (Hebrew).

Grinberg, L. L. (1991) *Split Corporatism in Israel*, Albany, NY: SUNY Press.

Grinberg, L. L. (1993) *The Histadrut Above All*, Jerusalem: Nevo (Hebrew).

Grinberg, L. L. (2001) "The Israeli-Palestinian peace in the mirror of the left," in Adi Ophir, ed., *Real-Time: The Al-Aqsa Intifada and the Israeli Left*. Jerusalem: Keter Publishers (Hebrew).

Grinberg, L. L. (2008) "Israel's Dual Regime Since 1967," *MIT-EJMES*, 3: 59–80.

Grinberg, L.L. (2010) *Politics and Violence in Israel/Palestine, Democracy vs. Military Rule*, London and New York: Routledge.

Grinberg, L.L.and G. Shafir (2000) "Economic Liberalization and the Breakup of the Histadrut's Domain," in G. Shafir and Y. Peled, eds., *The New Israel: Peacemaking and Liberalization*, Boulder, CO: Westview Press, pp. 103–127.

Harel, A. and A. Issacharoff (2004) *The Seventh War*, Tel Aviv: Yediot Aharonot (Hebrew).

Helman, S. (1999) "Negotiating Obligations, Creating Rights: Conscientious Objection and the Redefinition of Citizenship in Israel," *Citizenship Studies*, 3, 45–69.

Horowitz, D. and B. Kimmerling (1974) "Some Social Implications of Military Service and the Reserves System in Israel," *European Journal of Sociology*, 15(2), 252–276.

Kemp, A. and R. Raijman (2008) *Migrants and Workers: The Political Economy of Labor Migration in Israel*, Jerusalem and Tel Aviv: The Van Leer Jerusalem Institute and Hakibbutz Hameuchad Publishing House (Hebrew).

Kimmerling, B. (1983*) Zionism and Territory: The Socio-territorial Dimension of Zionist Politics*, Berkeley: Institute of International Studies, University of California.

Levy, Y. (2003) *Israel's Other Army*, Tel Aviv: Yediot Ahronot (Hebrew).

Levy, Y. (2007) *Israel's Materialist Militarism*, Madison, MD: Rowman & Littlefield/ Lexington Books.

Linz, J. and A. Stepan (1996) *Problems of Democratic Transitions and Consolidation*, Baltimore: Johns Hopkins University Press.

Mann, M. (2005) *The Dark Side of Democracy: Explaining Ethnic Cleansing*, New York, NY: Cambridge University Press.

Meital, Y. (2006) *Peace in Tatters: Israel, Palestine and the Middle East*, Bolder, CO: Lynne Rienner Publishers.

Michael, K. (2003) *Truth or Legend? Why has the Israeli-Palestinian Military Security Cooperation Failed? A Personal Retrospective Outlook on a Hope without a Prospect*, Jerusalem: Lady Davis Institute, Hebrew University (Hebrew).

Mills, C.W. (1958) "The Structure of Power in American Society," *British Journal of Sociology*, 9(1), 29–41.

Moore, Barrington Jr. (1966) *Social Origins of Dictatorship and Democracy*, Harmondsworth: Penguin Books.

Mundlak, Guy (2007) *Fading Corporatism: Israel's Labor Law and Industrial Relations in Transition*, Ithaca, NY: ILR Press/Cornell University Press.

Peled, Yoav (2004) "Profits or Glory? The Arik Sharon's Elul 28," *New Left Review*, 29, 47–70. (Hebrew).

Peled, Yoav (2007) "Towards a Post-Citizenship Society? A Report from the Front," *Citizenship Studies*, 11(1), 95–104.

Peri, Y. (1983) *Between Ballots and Bullets*, Cambridge: Cambridge University Press.

Peri, Y. (2006) *Generals in the Cabinet Room: How the Military Shapes Policy*, Washington: USIP Press.

Ram, U. (2008) *The Globalization of Israel: Mcworld in Tel Aviv, Jihad in Jerusalem*, New York: Routledge.

Reshef, T. (1996) *Peace Now*, Jerusalem: Keter (Hebrew).

Rosenhek, Z. (1999) "Migrant Workers in the Israeli Welfare State: Trends of Exclusion and Inclusion," *Bitahon Sotziali* [Social Security], 56: 97–112 (Hebrew).

Rueschemeyer, D., E.H. Stephens and J.D. Stephens (1992) *Capitalist Development and Democracy*, Chicago: University of Chicago Press.

Rustow, D.A. (1970) "Transitions to Democracy: Toward a Dynamic Model," *Comparative Politics*, 2: 337–363.

Savir, U. (1998) *The Process*, Tel Aviv: Yediot Ahronot (Hebrew).

Schiff, Z. and E. Ya'ari (1984) *Israel's Lebanon War*, New York: Simon and Schuster.

Schiff, Z. and E.Ya'ari (1990) *Intifada: The Palestinian Uprising – Israel's Third Front*, New York: Simon and Schuster.

Shafir, G. (1989) *Land and Labor in the Making of Israeli Nationalism*, Cambridge: Cambridge University Press.

Shafir, G. and Y. Peled (2000). *The new Israel: Peacemaking and Liberalization*, Boulder, CO.: Westview Press.

Shafir, G. and Y. Peled (2002) *Being Israeli: The Dynamics of Multiple Citizenship*, New York: Cambridge University Press.

Shalev, A. (1991) *The Intifada: Causes and Effects*, Jerusalem: Jerusalem Post Press.

Shalev, M. (1992) *Labor and the Political Economy in Israel*, Oxford University Press.

Shapiro, Y. (1976) *The Formative Years of the Israeli Labour Party: The Organization of Power, 1919–1930*, London: Sage Publications.

Shapiro, Y. (1977) *Israeli Democracy*, Ramat Gan: Masada (Hebrew).

Shapiro, Y. (1991) *The Road To Power: The Herut Party in Israel*, Albany, NY: State University of New York Press.

Smooha, S. (1978) *Israel: Pluralism and Conflict*, Berkeley: UC Press; London: Routledge and Paul Kegan.

Stepan, A. (2001) *Arguing Comparative Politics*, New York: Oxford University Press.

Tilly, C. (1985) "War Making and State Making as Organized Crime," in P. Evans, D. Rueschemeyer and and T. Skocpol, eds., *Bringing the State Back in*, New York: Cambridge University Press.

Tilly, C. (1992) *Coercion, Capital and European States, AD 990–1992*, Cambridge: Basil Blackwell.

Winograd, E. (2008) "Final Report of the Commission of Inquiry into the Events of Military Engagement in Lebanon 2006," Jerusalem: Government of Israel (Hebrew).

Index

For Product Safety Concerns and Information please contact our EU
representative GPSR@taylorandfrancis.com
Taylor & Francis Verlag GmbH, Kaufingerstraße 24, 80331 München, Germany

www.ingramcontent.com/pod-product-compliance
Lightning Source LLC
Chambersburg PA
CBHW070812270326
41927CB00010B/2386